Illuminate
Publishing

WJEC/Eduqas
GCSE
Media Studies

Hayley Sheard

Published in 2018 by Illuminate Publishing Ltd,
PO Box 1160, Cheltenham, Gloucestershire GL50 9RW

Orders: Please visit www.illuminatepublishing.com
or email sales@illuminatepublishing.com

British Library Cataloguing in Publication Data
A catalogue record for this book is available from the British Library

ISBN 978-1-911208-48-8

Printed in Standartu Spaustuvė, Lithuania

08.18

The publisher's policy is to use papers that are natural, renewable and recyclable products made from wood grown in sustainable forests. The logging and manufacturing processes are expected to conform to the environmental regulations of the country of origin.

This material has been endorsed by WJEC/Eduqas and offers high-quality support for the delivery of WJEC/Eduqas qualifications. While this material has been through a WJEC/Eduqas quality assurance process, all responsibility for the content remains with the publisher.

WJEC/Eduqas examination questions are reproduced by permission from WJEC/Eduqas.

Editor: Roanne Charles, abc Editorial
Design and layout: Kamae Design
Cover design: Nigel Harriss

Author's Acknowledgements
Enormous thanks to Eve and Rick at Illuminate Publishing for being so patient, understanding and supportive throughout the process.

Many thanks to Roanne at abc Editorial for the massive amount of help and encouragement. Thanks also to Darrell Chart-Boyles for the detailed comments and feedback.

Huge thanks to Jo Johnson at WJEC Eduqas and to Christine Bell for sharing their invaluable professional wisdom and experience, and offering much appreciated support and advice.

Grateful thanks to the teachers and students who allowed their work to be used in this book:

Christine Bell and the following students from Heaton Manor School: Liam Brusby, Ahmedy Khatoon and Elliot Rae;

Lucey Banner and George Hutchinson from Seaford Head School.

Contents

4 Assessment of Component 1: Exploring the Media — 110

5 Component 2: Understanding Media Forms and Products — 112

Introduction

How to Use this Book

This student book is designed to provide you with detailed information and guidance about the new Eduqas GCSE Media Studies specification. It introduces you to the theoretical framework of media, which is essential for developing your understanding of the subject.

The book also outlines the key media forms and products that you will study, and includes a range of examples to broaden your knowledge of the media.

You will find advice and guidance to help you to prepare for the written examinations at the end of the course and for the practical, non-exam assessment.

This book provides plenty of opportunities for you to apply your knowledge, understanding and skills by completing the questions and activities suggested throughout the different sections.

Key Features and Structure of the Book

The book is structured around important aspects of the specification and the individual components that will be assessed. Each chapter includes the following features:

- **Example analyses** of a range of media forms and products, including products set by Eduqas as well as wider examples, to extend your knowledge and understanding of each form. Identified within these examples are the main codes and conventions of the various media forms that you will need to analyse when you study the set products and prepare for the unseen resources in the examination.

- **Key Terms:** Definitions of the terminology that is specific to Media Studies. You will need to use this terminology to demonstrate your knowledge and understanding of the theoretical framework in each component.

- **Top Tips:** Brief advice to help you gain the most from your studies and prepare for the assessments.

- **Quickfire** questions to reinforce your learning. You can use these to test your knowledge and understanding in each chapter. You will also find the Quickfire questions helpful to revisit as you revise for the written examinations.

- **Activities:** Exercises that encourage you to apply the knowledge and understanding you have gained to an analytical task or set of questions. This will help you to develop the skills you will need to demonstrate in the written examinations, for example applying a theory to a product.

- **Stretch and Challenge:** Tasks to extend your knowledge and understanding by undertaking some further research or independent work. These exercises will help you to develop a broader and deeper grasp of the subject.

The book is organised into chapters based on the course specification, shown opposite.

Key Term

Top Tip

Quickfire

Activity

Stretch and Challenge

Chapters 1 and 2

These chapters introduce you to GCSE Media Studies.

Chapter 1 outlines the theoretical framework of media, which is the basis for exploring all elements of the specification. The framework consists of:

- Media language
- Representation
- Media industries
- Audiences.

These areas are explained using specific media terminology and supported by concrete examples.

Chapter 1 also introduces you to the theoretical perspectives and contexts of media that you will need to study in relation to the set products.

Chapter 2 provides an overview of the specification, giving a summary of the forms, products and areas of the framework that you will study in each component.

Chapters 3 and 4

These chapters explore Component 1, Exploring the Media, in detail.

Chapter 3 examines the broad range of forms and products that are studied in Sections A and B of Component 1. There is some reference to the set products, but also analysis of further examples to deepen your understanding of each form and develop your analytical skills.

Chapter 4 explains how Component 1 will be assessed.

Chapters 5 and 6

The focus of these chapters is Component 2, Understanding Media Forms and Products. Here you will study Television in Section A, and Music (music videos and online media) in Section B.

Chapter 5 explores each form in depth, including an overview of the industry and an outline of the genre conventions for the different options offered in the specification. Analysis of examples from the set and wider products is included, linked to contexts and theoretical perspectives.

The assessment of Component 2 is explained in Chapter 6.

Chapters 7 and 8

These chapters focus on the non-exam assessment, offering guidance on the production process, from responding to the set brief and undertaking research to planning the finished product. There are tips to help you to create a successful production and examples from past GCSE student projects to demonstrate the required levels of skill in each form.

Chapter 8 explains the Statement of Aims that must be submitted with the production and offers advice on how to complete it.

Chapter 9

This chapter will help you to prepare for the written examinations.

There is an explanation of how the structure of each component will appear in the exam, with some example questions and suggestions for points that could be included in a response.

The chapter offers tips and advice on how to approach the exams, including time management, interpreting questions and structuring extended responses.

Chapter 10

The theories and theoretical perspectives that you need to study in relation to media products are summarised in Chapter 10.

Glossary

This provides a reference of the media-specific terminology used in the book.

What is Expected from You

This student book gives a detailed overview of the specification, the theoretical framework and the forms and products that you will study. It is important that you develop good study habits and take responsibility for your learning.

- Throughout the GCSE course you will explore the set products and will need to make your own detailed notes on these. Your notes will be extremely useful when you revise for the examinations.

- Additionally, you will need to study at least two further examples of products from each form in Component 1, Section A. Looking at wider examples will develop your knowledge and understanding of the form and will help you to practise your skills in preparation for the unseen analysis in the exam.

- Review your notes regularly and revise the key terms and theoretical perspectives. This will help you to consolidate and reinforce the work you complete in class.

- Undertake some additional research into the topics and products that you study. You could, for example, find out a little more about the historical context of a product you have analysed or research the media organisation that produced it.

- Prepare for the non-exam assessment, where you will work independently and apply your knowledge and understanding to a practical production. You could keep a notebook of ideas for new media products or draft some designs in the form you intend to complete.
  In advance of the actual production, you could undertake some practice tasks, for example by using the sample briefs outlined in Chapter 7.

- The Eduqas website, www.eduqas.co.uk, has many materials to support your learning. The specification is an important document that outlines all of the areas for study. There are also additional resources that your teacher might recommend.

- In order to prepare for the exams you should practise writing responses under timed conditions. The Sample Assessment Materials, also available on the Eduqas website, will provide you with some example questions.

Top Tip

Use the glossary (pages 248–257) in your revision – make sure you understand each term and use terminology in your examination responses.

Top Tip

The additional examples analysed in Chapter 3 will give an indication of the types of product that you could study.

Top Tip

Use the Quickfire questions and Activities in this book to reinforce your learning.

Top Tip

Use the Stretch and Challenge tasks in this book to extend your knowledge and understanding of the subject.

The WJEC GCSE Media Studies Specification

This book is designed for learners following the Eduqas GCSE Media Studies specification in England and Northern Ireland. Centres in Wales will study the WJEC GCSE Media Studies specification, which has significant differences in content and structure from the Eduqas qualification.

The structure of the WJEC specification is summarised below:

Unit	Assessment	Forms and products
1. Exploring the Media: 30% of qualification	Written examination: 1 hour 30 minutes; 60 marks	**Advertising, video games, newspapers and music** All products chosen by the teacher following criteria set out in the specification
2. Understanding Television and Film: 30% of qualification	Written examination: 1 hour 30 minutes; 60 marks	**Television**: one television programme chosen from four options set by WJEC **Film**: one film chosen by the teacher following criteria set out in the specification
3. Creating Media: 40% of qualification	Non-exam assessment: 80 marks	Choice of briefs in the following forms: Television, Magazines, Film, Music, Advertising

Main differences in the WJEC specification

- The structure of the units and assessments is different; as detailed in the tables here.
- Some of the forms are explored in different ways. Magazines and radio, for example, are studied only in relation to the music topic; film is studied in greater depth.
- Most of the products for study will be chosen by the teacher. The television product will be selected from a choice of options set by WJEC.
- The specification includes a Welsh dimension and the television topic involves the study of a product that is made or set in Wales. Set products include options in the Welsh language.
- The non-exam assessment includes research, planning and reflective analysis tasks that are assessed in addition to the production.

Similarities

There are similarities, however, and this book will be relevant to the WJEC specification in the following ways:

- The theoretical framework underpins both specifications and the key concepts of media language, representations, media industries and audiences are the basis for exploring and creating the media. Chapter 1 of this book introduces learners to these concepts and defines much of the subject-specific terminology that should be applied when studying the media. The sections in Chapters 3 and 5 that outline the codes and conventions of print and audio-visual products will help learners to develop the analytical skills that they need.

- The same forms are studied in both specifications and the introduction to each form or industry in Chapters 3 and 5 will provide learners with background information that might apply to the chosen products. Some of the Eduqas set products might be appropriate to study for the WJEC specification.

The table below outlines the WJEC qualification in more detail and includes examples of the ways in which this book is relevant.

WJEC specification	Area of the framework / key concepts	Products	Assessment	Relevant sections of this book
Unit 1 Section A: Advertising and Video Games	Representation (gender)	Print products representing men and women: contemporary advertisements and video game covers; at least one historical (pre-1990) print advertisement	**One** stepped question based on unseen print-based resource material related to advertising, video games **or** newspapers	Chapter 3: advertising section and analysis of examples **Possible overlap with Eduqas set product** Quality Street advertisement, 1956 (Chapter 1)
Unit 1 Section A: Newspapers	Representation (events)	One national or local newspaper representing at least one event		Chapter 3: newspapers section and analysis of examples **Possible overlap with Eduqas set products** the *Sun*, the *Guardian*
Unit 1 Section B: Music	Media language, representation, media industries and audiences	• Two contemporary music magazines and one of their websites • One contemporary music video and one music video pre-1990 • Two contemporary music radio programmes • Examples of social media in relation to one artist	**One** stepped question and **two** single questions	Chapter 5: music industry information; analysis of examples of music videos, websites and social/participatory media **Possible overlap with Eduqas set products** 'Bad Blood', 'Roar', 'Uptown Funk', 'Freedom', 'Rio'
Unit 2 Section A: Wales on Television	Media language, representation, media industries and audiences	One television programme chosen from four options set by WJEC	**One** stepped question based on the set 'Wales on Television' product.	Chapter 5: television industry information; analysis of examples of television sequences
Unit 2 Section B: Contemporary Hollywood Film		One Hollywood franchise film: marketing, such as posters, trailers and websites	**One** stepped question and **two** single questions.	Chapter 3: film marketing section and analysis of examples of film posters; film industry section

WJEC specification	Area of the framework / key concepts	Products	Assessment	Relevant sections of this book
Unit 3: Creating Media	Media language, representation and audiences	Production in **one** of: • Television: audio-visual **or** online media • Magazines: print **or** online media • Film: audio-visual **or** print media • Music: audio-visual **or** print media • Advertising: audio-visual **or** print media	Non-exam assessment: research and planning; production; reflective analysis	Chapter 7: process of researching, planning and creating media products (audio-visual, print or online) in the following forms: Television, Magazines, Film Marketing or Music Marketing

The Media Studies Theoretical Framework

Key Terms

Products
Individual examples of media output, such as an advert and a newspaper.

Forms
The different types of media, for example television and advertising.

Codes and conventions
The expected elements that will be included in products from particular media forms and genres.

Social groups
A way of categorising people, for example by gender (females form a social group).

Platforms
Different technological ways in which media products are made available to audiences (a website, for example, is an online platform).

Target
Aiming a product at a particular group of people; a target audience.

Respond
How media audiences receive and react to a media product.

Encode
Media producers include messages when creating products. These might be encoded through specific language or images.

Decode
Audiences interpret encoded messages. They might or might not decode the messages in the way the producers intended.

Genre
A category of media product defined by a set of codes and conventions, for example news or comedy.

OVERVIEW

The GCSE Media Studies specification is based on a framework for exploring and creating media **products**. This provides a foundation for your studies in all components and will help you to explore the subject in a critical way. The theoretical framework is divided into four inter-related areas:

- **Media language**: How the media communicate meanings through their **forms** and **codes and conventions**
- **Representation**: How the media portray events, issues, individuals and **social groups**
- **Media industries**: How the media industries' processes of production, distribution and circulation affect media forms and **platforms**
- **Audiences**: How media forms **target**, reach and address audiences, how audiences interpret and **respond** to them, and how audience members become producers themselves.

Media Language

Every media product you study will use media language to communicate meanings to audiences. Media producers **encode** particular messages and viewpoints that they want to convey, and audiences **decode** and interpret these meanings. The particular elements of media language that a media product uses will vary depending on the form and type of product. A music video, for example, will use moving images, whereas a DVD cover will use still images. Each media form and **genre** has different codes and conventions.

You will learn about the particular elements of media language that are used in each form, including: visual codes, technical codes and language codes. This will form a 'toolkit' that you can apply to your analysis of any media product.

Analysing Media Products

When you analyse a media product, it is important to consider the meanings communicated. It is helpful to start by thinking about the different elements of media language in a product, for example a headline in a newspaper or an image on a magazine cover. In Media Studies, we analyse products using a system called **semiotics**. We need to consider each element of media language, or **sign**, that is used and consider the following:

- The denotation of a sign: this is its literal meaning. For example, a picture of an oak tree **denotes** a tree.

- The connotation of the sign: this relates to the meanings we associate with a sign. So, a tree might **connote** nature, or something natural.

A media producer could use a tree or leaf to encode this kind of meaning. For example, an advertisement for a cleaning product containing natural ingredients might feature a picture of a leaf. Similarly, an oak tree gives specific connotations of strength and power – as oak trees grow to be large, tall and solid – and stability and endurance – as oak trees can live for many hundreds of years.

Connotations are often linked to culture. The oak tree has symbolic meaning in many cultures. The 'royal oak' is important in British history, for example, as it is the tree in which the future king, Charles II, hid during the Civil War. An oak tree could be used to connote history and tradition in a British media product, but an audience from a different culture might not understand this.

Many media products are **polysemic**; they communicate different meanings and so can be decoded in a variety of ways. As noted above, a picture of an oak tree has many connotations and different audiences might interpret the same image in different ways. In addition, while you might begin by analysing each element of a product separately, you will need to consider the combination of those elements and the meanings communicated by the product as a whole.

An oak tree carries symbolism and can connote many different meanings.

Activity 1.1

Look at each of these four images:

- What is the denotation of the image?
- What are the connotations of the image?
- How might a producer use the image to communicate polysemic meanings in a media product?

Key Term

Mise-en-scène
The manner in which all the visual elements are placed within a frame or product, including the setting or background, props, costume and gestures.

Quickfire 1.1

What props might you expect to see in a TV crime drama?

Analysing Codes of Media Language

The main **codes** that apply across a range of different media forms are outlined below. The specific conventions of media language that apply to print products are discussed in Chapter 3, and those that apply to audio-visual and online products are explored in Chapter 5.

Visual codes

Visual codes are the elements that we see in a media product. All the media forms you will study, except radio, have visual codes that you can analyse. Visual codes relate to the images in media products, but also to elements such as the background on a magazine cover, logos and graphics. It is important to consider all aspects of the **mise-en-scène** when analysing a media product:

- **Colour** palettes are used by media producers to encode meanings and can communicate powerful messages. There are many connotations associated with different colours: for example red can suggest passion or danger, while blue usually connotes calm. Colour can also be used to establish the mood and atmosphere in a media product. Yellows and oranges, for example, suggest warmth, whereas blues and greys are considered to be colder colours.

- **Location** is very important to help an audience to understand where the product is set. The setting can also communicate messages.

- **Gesture codes** are how people express themselves through their posture and body language. Gestures can convey emotion, often in combination with facial expressions. Shaking a fist, for example, implies anger, aggression and the intent to hurt.

  - **Facial expressions** communicate meanings that are easily recognised. A sad, surprised or angry facial expression, for example, will help an audience to understand the emotion someone feels.

- **Props** can communicate messages about people and certain types of prop can signify a genre, such as guns in the action genre.

- **Dress codes**, including clothing, hair and make-up, convey messages about people in a media product, for example:
  - If a person is dressed smartly, it might suggest that they are neat and tidy, or that they care about their image.
  - A business suit might connote that a person has a responsible and well-paid job, that they are professional.
  - A particular style of clothing could identify a person with a social group. Ripped T-shirts and leather jackets, for example, are associated with 'punk' culture and could be used to connote rebelliousness.
  - Typically fashionable clothing might suggest that a person wants to 'fit in' and follow the latest trends.
  - Hair and make-up can also be used to convey elements such as personality or social status. Edward Scissorhands' wild hair, for example, connotes his troubled mind, and pale make-up suggests he has been shut away from society. The scissorhands are a sign that he was unloved and they form a barrier between him and people who often see him as a threat, while he is actually a sensitive, gentle young man.

In this image from *The IT Crowd* set episode, Moss is smartly dressed to connote he is professional, while the checked shirt and brown tie are quite old-fashioned.

Analysis of visual codes in a set product: Quality Street advert

This advert for Quality Street uses bright colours to connote the pleasure of eating the chocolates.

The two main females' dress codes match the colours of the sweet wrappers: the female on the left wears red, green and white, similar to the strawberry chocolate, while the female on the right wears a long red dress and has golden hair, reflecting the Harrogate toffee. This connotes that the man in the image is making a decision about which female to choose, as well as which chocolate.

The man wears a pinstriped suit and tie: formal clothing typical of the 1950s.

The couple in the gold picture frame wear clothing that connotes history and upper-class status and further connotes that the chocolates are a luxury.

You will study this print advertisement for Quality Street from the 1950s.

What a delicious dilemma!

18 delightfully different toffees and chocolates in

Mackintosh's 'Quality Street'

CHOCOLATE STRAWBERRY CUP
Strawberry jam and cream encased in milk chocolate.

HARROGATE TOFFEE
The delicious, smooth toffee with a most distinctive flavour.

CHOCOLATE TOFFEE FINGER
Delicious toffee covered

This close-up might connote positive emotion and confidence.

This long shot establishes the location and shows the players around the ball to convey the action and communicate excitement.

Technical codes

Technical codes are the ways in which media products are constructed using technical equipment such as cameras. Most **contemporary** media products are created with digital technology. Technical codes include the type of camera shot and the use of lighting. Print products also use technical codes of layout and design and use of typography. Audio-visual products also use technical codes of editing and sound.

Camera shots

The shot used in a media product can communicate a range of information. First, it is important to be able to identify the type of shot:

- **Close-up**: The subject takes up most of the frame. A close-up of a character's face shows their feelings and can help the audience to understand or empathise with the character.
- **Extreme close-up (ECU)**: The subject is very large and shown in detail; this suggests importance. An ECU might be used to demonstrate a product in an advert, for example, or to draw attention to a significant object in a television programme.
- **Medium close-up**: This shows a person from the chest upwards. This type of shot is used frequently in television as it replicates the way we see people when we are close to them in real life.
- **Long shot:** This shows a person, group or location in full. It can establish information about a character or location and might connote meanings about the action, for example that a character is in danger.
- **Low-angle shot**: The camera is placed at a low level and looks up at a character or object which therefore appears large and dominant. An extremely low-angle shot looking directly upwards is called a worm's-eye-view shot.
- **High-angle shot**: This is where the camera is placed at a high level and looks down on a character or object, which appears small and insignificant. An extremely high-angle shot looking directly downwards is called a bird's-eye-view shot.

This extreme close-up of a watch face might connote the significance of time passing if, for example, a major deadline is about to be reached.

This low-angle shot makes the skateboarder look powerful and skillful.

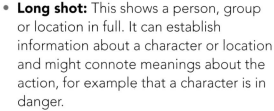

This high-angle shot of a city might connote that the institutions in the buildings are important, but the humans are insignificant.

Lighting

It is important to consider the use of lighting in media products. There are four main parts to lighting:

- **High key**: use of a **key light** and many **filler lights** to create bright lighting with few shadows. A magazine cover will often use high-key lighting to highlight the cover model.
- **Low key**: use of a key light but fewer filler lights to create shadows and contrast between light and dark. A thriller might use low key-lighting to create a sense of mystery.
- **Artificial lighting**: use of electric lighting, often in an indoor setting or studio.
- **Natural light**: use of daylight, in an outdoor setting or from a window.

Lighting is also used symbolically: bright light is usually associated with goodness and innocence, whereas darkness connotes sinfulness and evil.

Language codes

Nearly all media products use language – words – to create meanings:

- **Written language** is used in print products, including headlines in a newspaper, magazine articles and slogans in advertisements. This is explored fully in Chapter 3.
- **Spoken language** is used in audio-visual products, for example dialogue or narration in a television programme. This is explored in Chapter 5.

The use of language is a key way in which media products address, or speak to, their audiences. Some products use a very friendly, informal mode of address, while others are more distant and formal.

Genre

Genre is a way of categorising media products. The concept often relates to film and television, but can be applied to many media forms and products. A genre is defined by a set of codes and conventions used in its products.

Generic products are defined by a set of elements that are repeated across them. This **repertoire of elements** includes:

- **Visual iconography**: The particular visual codes associated with a genre. A poster for a horror film, for example, is likely to make use of an isolated setting, possibly including a 'haunted' house, a dark colour palette and low-key lighting.
- **Technical codes**: Different genres use technical codes in specific ways. Television dramas, for example, tend to feature many medium-close-up shots to establish the characters and their relationships. A dance music video will usually have fast-paced editing that matches the beat of the music.
- **Narrative**: This is the way in which the story is told. Specific narrative techniques are used in different genres. A newspaper article, for example, will usually begin with a lead paragraph that summarises the issues. Narrative is discussed in detail below.
- **Characters**: Most genres have an expected set of character 'types'. Crime dramas, for example, will often feature a troubled police officer who solves the crime, whereas sitcoms often include a character who is trying to improve their social status.

Key Terms

Key light
The main light that shines directly on the person or object in the frame.

Filler lights
Additional lights placed around a person or object to reduce shadows.

Repertoire of elements
A set of codes and conventions that are used in products from the same genre.

Quickfire 1.2

List three conventions used on the front covers of fashion magazines or music magazines.

Stretch and Challenge 1.2

Look at a range of film posters and identify their genres.

Key Terms

Familiar conventions
Elements that we would expect to see in a particular genre. (A convention of a television soap opera is the setting of a pub where characters regularly meet.)

Unexpected elements
Conventions that we would not necessarily expect to see in a genre to add an element of surprise or develop the genre.

Technological developments
New technologies that enable media producers to create products in different ways, sometimes leading to changes in a genre.

Subgenre
A more specific genre within a broader genre.

Hybrid
A combination of two or more different genres in the same product.

Disruption
An event or action that interrupts the narrative.

Conflict
A clash between two characters or groups of people.

Linear narrative
A narrative structure where all of the events happen in logical order, one after the other.

Cause and effect
Where one event causes another event to happen, such as a robbery causing the victim to have nightmares.

Stretch and Challenge 1.3

Look at a range of DVD covers for television programmes. Can you identify any hybrid products?

Theoretical perspectives on genre

A product in a particular genre will usually use **familiar conventions** as well as some **unexpected elements**, as argued by theorist Steve Neale. This helps to make the product unique and ensures that audiences do not become bored with the same conventions. Audiences benefit from genre conventions as they know what to expect and enjoy the familiarity of consuming products in their favourite genres. Genres are also important to media industries as their appeal to specific audiences helps to guarantee the success of a product.

Genres do not stay the same. They change over time for a number of reasons:

- Genres need to develop in order to maintain the interest of audiences.
- **Technological developments** allow producers to use new visual and technical codes. The Bond film posters set products, for example, demonstrate technical developments from hand-drawn imagery to layered photographic images.
- **Social and cultural contexts** also influence genres, which might develop to reflect issues and events occurring in society at the time. Contemporary crime dramas, for example, reflect developments in forensic science when crimes are being solved.

Many genre categories are quite broad, so **subgenres** often develop. These break a genre down into subdivisions that have their own conventions. Rock music, for example, has many subgenres, including grunge, progressive rock and alternative rock. Another way in which genres can develop is when conventions from two or more genres are used in the same product, called a **hybrid**. Hybridisation can breathe new life into a genre by creating something fresh and unexpected. It can also widen the audience for a product. A clear example of a hybrid film is *Cowboys and Aliens* (2011), which combined science fiction and western genre conventions.

Narrative

We are all familiar with the concept of a story. We read, hear and tell stories many times every day. All media products contain an element of storytelling or an account of events, for example a newspaper article. When we study narrative, however, we need to analyse how the story is told by considering how the events are ordered and which characters are shown to be the most important in the story.

Structure

Most narratives are based on some form of **disruption** or **conflict** that has to be resolved. The way in which these elements are organised and put together can vary depending on the form, genre and the individual product.

Some narratives start at the beginning of a story and move chronologically through the events to the end. This 'beginning–middle–end' structure is called a **linear narrative**. It is easy to follow as everything happens in the 'right' order. In this type of narrative, each event usually happens as a result of another. This is called **cause and effect**, so the structure seems logical.

Tzvetan Todorov was a Bulgarian theorist who studied classic fairy tales and folk stories. His theory of narrative states that the following stages will occur:

- **Equilibrium**: At the beginning, everything is calm and balanced; there is no conflict.
- **Disruption**: An event or problem occurs to upset the balance.
- **Recognition**: The characters realise that there is a problem.
- **Resolution**: The problem is solved.
- **New equilibrium**: Everything returns to a state of balance.

Some media products, however, adopt a different approach to narrative. A **non-linear narrative** might begin part-way through a story or even at the end and then explore earlier events. **Flashbacks** or **flashforwards** might be used to help structure the narrative. This allows producers to hold information back from the audience, which might be revealed later on, and this can create intrigue and suspense. Crime dramas often begin with a murder and then work backwards to reveal information about why and by whom the murder was committed.

Many products, even those with linear narrative structures, avoid revealing everything about a character or story at the beginning. Producers might offer some details and drop hints about what is to come, but leave some elements of mystery to keep the audience guessing. This is an example of an **enigma code**, a narrative code outlined by French literary theorist Roland Barthes. It engages the audience and encourages them to actively participate by trying to solve the 'puzzles' in the narrative.

A film poster is likely to use enigmas to 'hook' the audience in and encourage them to look out for the trailers and watch the film.

Many fairy tales have a clear linear narrative.

 Quickfire 1.3

Think of a television programme that follows Todorov's narrative structure.

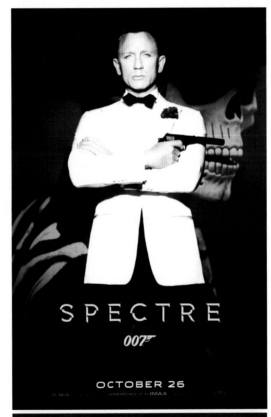

SPECTRE
007
OCTOBER 26

You will study a poster similar to this one for the Bond film *Spectre*.

Key Terms

Equilibrium
A situation where everything is calm and settled; there is no conflict.

Resolution
When problems or disruptions are solved, or conflicts have been settled.

Non-linear narrative
A narrative where the events do not happen in chronological order.

Flashback
A scene where the narrative jumps back in time to show a past event.

Flashforward
A scene where the narrative jumps forwards in time to show a future event.

Enigma code
A mystery or puzzle. Media products often don't tell all elements of the narrative at once, but withhold information to keep the audience guessing.

 Quickfire 1.4

What enigmas can you identify in the *Spectre* poster above?

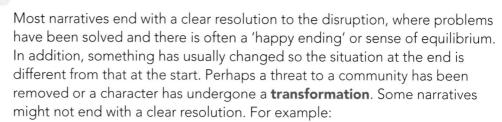

Key Terms

Transformation
A major change. Characters are often transformed as a result of events that occur in the narrative. (A character might change their lifestyle after a health scare.)

Cliff-hanger
A structural device where the narrative is paused at a tense or exciting moment, which encourages the audience to watch the next episode.

Quest
A mission that a hero has to undertake or a goal that they need to achieve.

Protagonist
The main character in a narrative; also the hero in many narratives.

Antagonist
A character who is in opposition to the protagonist; also the villain in many products.

Top Tip

Propp's theory of narrative is one of the two key theories you need to know. (The other is Blumler and Katz's Uses and Gratifications theory, see page 34.) Learn the main points of the theory and try to apply it to all the media products you study.

Quickfire 1.5

Name three media products where the hero defeats a villain.

Most narratives end with a clear resolution to the disruption, where problems have been solved and there is often a 'happy ending' or sense of equilibrium. In addition, something has usually changed so the situation at the end is different from that at the start. Perhaps a threat to a community has been removed or a character has undergone a **transformation**. Some narratives might not end with a clear resolution. For example:

- A news story might be ongoing, so a report on a particular day will not have a definite ending.
- An episode of a TV drama series might end on a **cliff-hanger** to encourage the audience to watch the next episode in order to find out what happens.

Theoretical perspectives on narrative

Key Theory 1: Propp's theory of narrative

Vladimir Propp was a Russian theorist who studied the narrative structure of Russian folk tales and identified similar features in them. Key elements of his theory, presented in his book *The Morphology of the Folktale* in 1928, are:

- There are 31 key stages in narrative structures, including:
  - A villain deceives a victim
  - A hero is dispatched on a **quest**
  - The hero is given a magical power or object
  - The villain is defeated
  - The hero marries the 'princess'.
- There are eight main character types that appear in narratives:
  - Hero – the main character or **protagonist** who drives the narrative forward and determines the outcome
  - Villain – the **antagonist** who acts in opposition to the hero and creates the disruption or conflict
  - 'Princess' – often marries the hero and so can be seen as a 'prize'
  - Father of the 'princess'
  - Donor – gives the hero an important item or object
  - Helper – assists the hero in the quest
  - Dispatcher – sends the hero on the quest
  - False hero – claims to be a hero but is actually dishonest.

Superman is an iconic superhero character and a typical Proppian hero.

Propp's theory was based on traditional folk stories, but his ideas show that there are key stages of narrative and character types that are found in most stories. Many contemporary narratives will feature some of these elements, but it is important to remember that every media product will be different, so similar narratives will not always have the same features.

Another key element of narrative relates to the conflict at the heart of the story. Many narratives are constructed around **binary oppositions**. This is a theory that was developed by Claude Lévi-Strauss, a French theorist who proposed that narratives may be structured around pairs of opposing forces. These could be characters, for example hero versus villain, but they can also be more **abstract concepts**, such as good versus evil, or humans versus nature. One of these will usually triumph over the other in a narrative, and this communicates messages and viewpoints about the world. For example 'good' usually conquers 'evil' as the message reinforces society's view that this is the right or 'natural' thing to happen. It also constructs a positive view of the world that provides the audience with a reassuring 'happy' ending. Many narratives are based around a conflict between a hero and a villain. In many, but not all, cases the hero will win.

Key Terms

Binary oppositions
Pairs of 'opposites' (characters or abstract ideas) that come into conflict within a narrative. The outcome of the conflict can communicate messages, for example that the hero 'should' defeat the villain and restore equilibrium.

Abstract concept
An idea, such as beauty or happiness, rather than a physical object or something that exists.

Stretch and Challenge 1.5

Can you think of any media products where a hero has failed?

Activity 1.2

Analyse the narrative elements in the poster for *The Man with the Golden Gun*.

- What stories or elements of narrative are shown? (For example, a fight between two characters.)
- Which of Propp's character types can you identify? How are these signified?
- What enigmas does the poster create? What questions might you ask about the narrative?
- Are there any examples of binary oppositions?

Representation

Key Terms

Construct
Put elements together to create a media product.

Version of reality
A particular view or interpretation of actual events. (Different newspapers will report different elements of the same event to denote their version of what happened.)

Selecting and combining
Choosing elements to include in a product and putting them together in particular ways to communicate meanings. (Selecting an image and combining it with a caption will communicate a message.)

Mediation
The way in which media producers interpret and re-present aspects of reality to audiences.

Purpose
The aim or intention of the product. (An advert's purpose is to persuade; a sitcom's purpose is to amuse.) Purpose also relates to the reasons why media producers select particular elements of media language to communicate their intended meaning.

Point of view
This relates to whose perspective or ideas are shown in the product. Point of view can be shown in different ways, for example the positioning of the camera or the use of language.

Gavin Bond / GQ © The Condé Nast Publications Ltd

Representation is the way in which people, places, issues and events are portrayed in the media.

You will study and analyses the representation of social groups in relation to gender, ethnicity and age, for example the representation of women in the Quality Street and *This Girl Can* advertisements.

An **issue** is a specific topic represented in a media product, for example an environmental topic such as climate change or a social subject such as drug abuse. The newspaper set products include specific issues that you will need to analyse, but issues feature in many of the other set products, including the *Pride* magazine cover.

An **event** is something that happens in the world. It might be expected, for example a political election or a royal wedding, or unexpected such as an earthquake or terrorist attack. Events are reported in newspapers and other news media, and other products might also depict them, for example the set *GQ* magazine cover.

Theoretical Perspectives on Representation

Media producers **construct** representations of individuals, groups, issues and events using media language. As the theorist David Buckingham has argued, the media do not simply present a picture of the real world, they re-present **versions of reality** by **selecting and combining** different elements of media language, as you might see in the images and text of a newspaper article. This process is called **mediation**. It is really important to think about how media products interpret and present aspects of reality, especially in news media where actual events are being shown.

Representations are constructed by media producers for a particular **purpose** and they communicate messages and **points of view** about the world. Media producers have considerable power, as their representations are consumed by audiences who could be influenced by them. It is important to think about who or what is being represented and to consider the context and who is constructing the representation.

Media industries have traditionally been controlled by powerful groups of people, such as educated, wealthy white males. As a result, certain social groups, including women, minority ethnic groups and people with disabilities, have often been under-represented or misrepresented in the media. The media industries do reflect changes in society: many organisations now have a more diverse workforce and many contemporary media products represent a wider range of social groups in a more positive way. Nonetheless, there are still areas of the media where minority groups are under-represented.

When you analyse representations, it is important to be aware of the choices made by producers, so you should always consider the following:

- What is the purpose of the product? This can affect the way representations are constructed. A cosmetics advert might construct an image of a 'perfect' woman as the purpose is to sell the product.

- What elements have been selected? What has been left out? Media producers make decisions about how to construct representations. They choose what to include and exclude in the product. This means that certain groups might be excluded. There are, for example, relatively few representations of people with disabilities in the media.

- Whose point of view is taken? This is important as it **positions the audience**. We might be shown the point of view of a particular character in a narrative, while news stories might take a particular viewpoint. The set newspaper front page of the *Sun*, for example, uses the phrase 'You tell him' to show that it is reflecting the viewpoint of a *Sun* reader.

- What messages does this representation communicate?

Analysis of representation in a set product: *This Girl Can*

- **Purpose**: *This Girl Can* is a promotional campaign produced by Sport England. Its aim is to encourage women and girls to become active and take part in sport.

- **Selection**: The image is of a young white female in an exercise class, accompanied by the slogan 'Sweating like a pig, feeling like a fox'. The female is not a celebrity, rather she is constructed as an 'ordinary' woman. She is wearing unbranded sports clothes and has her eyes closed. There are no men in this poster, as the campaign specifically targets females.

- **Pont of view**: The woman's point of view is presented, suggested by the image and the slogan.

- **Messages**: Being active makes you feel good and it is OK for a woman to enjoy exercise and get 'sweaty'. The representation is quite different from many images of 'perfect' females shown in the **mainstream media**.

 Quickfire 1.7

How do two newspaper front pages show different versions of the same event?

 Stretch and Challenge 1.6

Write two paragraphs discussing your findings to Quickfire 1.7.

Top Tip

Ask these key 'what' and 'who' questions every time you analyse the representations in a media product.

 Key Terms

Position the audience
Using aspects of a media product to put us in a specific place from which we experience the text. (A photograph can position us outside a window looking into a building, so we feel like an 'outsider'.) We can also be positioned in a way to accept an idea or point of view.

Mainstream media
Products that have mass appeal for a wide range of audiences, such as pop music videos, television soap operas and the dominant newspapers.

This picture shows one of many powerful, groundbreaking images produced as part of the *This Girl Can* campaign.

Stereotypes

A stereotype is an oversimplified image of a particular type of person or social group. Stereotypes categorise groups of people by a narrow range of superficial and often negative attributes. They can become 'fixed' when we recognise and identify a group of people by these traits. A stereotype of students, for example, is that they like to party more than study. While there might be some truth at the heart of a stereotype (many students do enjoy partying), it is limiting and potentially damaging to assume that every person in a particular group is the same (most students also work very hard). Typically, the groups of people who are stereotyped are in the minority and have limited **power** in society.

Teenagers are often stereotyped as being uncommunicative and interested in social media, as shown in this scene from the BBC sitcom, *Outnumbered*.

Stereotypes are a useful tool for media producers as they can communicate a lot of information very quickly and give an audience a recognisable type of individual or social group. Some comedies also use stereotypes as they can be an effective way of generating humour. Stereotypes can change over time. Gender stereotypes, for example, have developed as male and female roles have changed in society. It is important to consider to what extent media products **uphold** or **subvert stereotypes**.

Gender

Gender relates to the attributes and behaviour that we associate with being male and female. In Media Studies, we analyse the ways in which producers construct representations of **masculinity** and **femininity** in media products.

Men have, traditionally, had more power than women in society and this has been reflected in the media. You will see some clear evidence of this in the historical products that you study. While there are clear biological differences between the sexes (men are physically stronger for example), many gender differences are cultural. Men have tended to go out to work, for example, while women have had a more domestic role.

There are many attributes associated with masculinity and femininity, and many of these reflect the fact that men have, historically, been more dominant in society:

- Men are frequently shown to be tough and strong, and also rational and unemotional. In contrast, women tend to be represented as being weaker and more emotional.

- Ideas of physical attractiveness in males are often linked to physical strength and muscularity. Attractiveness in females is typically associated with beauty and a slender body image.
- Women are stereotypically represented as home-makers and mother figures, whereas men tend to leave the home to go to a manual or professional job.
- Linked to this idea, women are typically shown as being dependent on other people, typically a man. Men are often represented as being more independent and less reliant on others.
- There are also many stereotypical interests associated with each gender, for example men enjoying cars, sport and rock music; and women being interested in fashion, beauty and romantic comedies.

Changes in society affect the way that gender is represented in the media. As a result of the **feminist movement**, women have gained more power in society. Men's roles have also changed. In the past, a man tended to be the main or sole breadwinner in a family, but this is no longer the case for many men. There is now much more equality between men and women in society and there are less clear boundaries between masculinity and femininity. Many men care about their appearance and are interested in fashion and grooming products, which would have been considered stereotypically feminine traits in the past. Some contemporary media products reflect these changes, for example:

Women have traditionally been represented in domestic settings.

- Women appear in professional roles, such as lawyer Zoe in *Luther* and Vice President Selina Meyer in *Veep*.
- Women are shown to be independent and powerful, as in Katy Perry's video for 'Roar'.
- 'Strong' men are able to show emotion, for example Luther, and John Watson in *Sherlock*.
- Male characters work in traditionally 'female' professions such as nursing, for example Fletch in *Holby City*.
- Elite sports men appear in advertisements for cosmetic products, such as the Nivea campaign featuring Liverpool footballers.

Despite this, many gender stereotypes are still used by media producers to communicate messages to audiences.

Theoretical perspective on gender representation: feminist approaches

Feminist approaches to Media Studies argue that the media are included in the discrimination against women in society. There is more gender equality in society today, but many of the media industries are still dominated by men: fewer than ten per cent of film directors are female, for example. This impacts on the representations of females in media products, and women are under-represented in many areas of the media. The vast majority of television adverts, for example, use male voiceovers.

Key Term

Feminist movement
The move towards women gaining equal rights in society. The 1960s was a particularly significant period when many campaigns and new laws gave women more equal rights and greater freedoms.

Quickfire 1.9

How do the historical products you have studied reflect traditional gender stereotypes?

Stretch and Challenge 1.7

Try to identify some other stereotypes associated with men and women.

Key Terms

Passive object
A character who does not take an active role; events happen around them and they have limited involvement in the narrative.

Active subject
A character who makes things happen and moves the narrative forward.

Male gaze
The person who is looking (usually at a female) is assumed to be male; the audience sees the females through male eyes.

Baby boomer
A person born just after the Second World War (between 1945 and 1960), when there was a big increase in the population as men returned from the war and couples began to have children.

Grey pound
A term used to describe the disposable income that older people have to spend on items for themselves, such as holidays.

In addition, when women are present, they are often represented as **passive objects** rather than being **active subjects** who drive the narrative forward. This idea is presented in Laura Mulvey's Male Gaze theory (1975), which she developed in relation to women in Hollywood films. Mulvey argued that women are usually represented as objects of a **male gaze**: the protagonist, and the expected audience, is male and looks at the female as an object of desire.

The poster for *The Man with the Golden Gun* is an example. It features the 'Bond girl' stereotype. The visual codes of bikinis, long flowing hair and provocative gesture codes suggest that they will be sexual objects rather than active protagonists in the film.

Age

You will study the way in which people from different age groups are represented in media products. There are various attributes associated with: younger age groups (children and teenagers), adults (younger adults and middle-aged people) and older age groups that might be used in media products. Adults are in the majority in society; they tend to have the most power and produce most media products. Younger and older people are arguably less powerful and are more likely to be negatively stereotyped:

- Children are often shown to be weak or vulnerable and in need of protection.
- Teenagers are frequently represented as being 'stroppy' and antisocial, for example the hoodie-wearing rebellious youth stereotype.
- Older people might be depicted as frail, lonely or forgetful; stereotypes include the 'grumpy old man'.

This advert for Shreddies depicted stereotypically caring 'nannas' who 'knitted' the breakfast cereal.

Recent years have seen a wider range of more positive representations of older people. This reflects changes in society as there is an ageing population and many people are healthier and living longer. The **baby boomer** generation (born shortly after the Second World War) are now in their 60s and 70s, and many have high levels of disposable income, so advertisers often target the **grey pound**. Older people are increasingly represented in the media as being active, working and enjoying leisure activities. Nonetheless, the mainstream media is still dominated by representations of younger adults, especially in relation to images of health and attractiveness.

Some publications, such as the *Guardian* and *Good Housekeeping*, regularly feature 'all ages' models in their fashion pages, which subverts stereotypes of older women.

Ethnicity

The media play an important role in constructing and communicating representations of ethnicity. Ethnicity relates to a person's national, cultural or religious identity. People from many different ethnic backgrounds live in contemporary Britain: it is a multicultural society. Historically, however, Britain was less diverse and people from **minority ethnic groups** have tended to be, and are still, under-represented in the mainstream media.

There are also many examples of misrepresentation and stereotyping of ethnic minorities. Theorist Stuart Hall argued that representations often focus on 'otherness', for example, emphasising difference or foreignness, such as:

- exotic people from a different culture, for example in an advert for a luxury holiday (this can be positive as well as negative)

- threatening or dangerous people:

  - villains in a television programme or film

  - immigrants to Britain represented negatively on a newspaper front page

  - antisocial young people (linked to youth stereotypes) in the news and in fictional products

- victims, as in adverts for charities working in developing countries.

You will see positive changes over time when you compare historical products (such as *The Man with the Golden Gun* poster) with contemporary ones (such as modern film posters, *Pride* magazine or the video for Pharrell Williams' 'Freedom').

This poster in an Oxfam shop window tries to appeal to people's sense of sympathy, but its representation of people 'in need' could be seen as patronising.

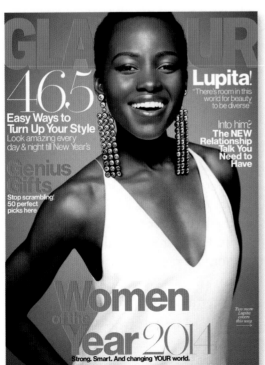
Tom Munro / Glamour © Condé Nast

The actress Lupita Nyong'o has featured on a number of magazine front covers in recent years (see page 70, too, for example), which reflects a move towards greater diversity in the representation of ethnicity. In this December 2014 issue of *Glamour* magazine, Nyong'o discussed the issue of skin colour: 'European standards of beauty are something that plague the entire world – the idea that darker skin is not beautiful, that light skin is the key to success and love.' Here she is making the point that there is a perception that lighter-coloured skin, is more beautiful than darker skin, which demonstrates that there is still a lack of equality between different ethnic groups, in society and in the media.

Quickfire 1.11

How does the poster for *The Man with the Golden Gun* construct ethnic stereotypes?

Key Term

Minority ethnic group
People of a different ethnic background from that of the majority of the population.

Key Terms

Production
The stage where a media product is constructed.

Distribution and circulation
The way in which the product is delivered to different audiences.

Consumption
The way in which the audience 'takes in' the media product, for example watching television or playing a video game.

Media Industries

The study of media industries includes:

- Production processes
- Ownership and funding
- Technology
- Regulation.

Production Processes

Media producers create products for audiences. This process includes various stages such as **production**, **distribution and circulation**. You will need to consider how these processes affect the media forms and products that you study in Component 1 Section B and Component 2. Each media form will have different production practices and methods of distribution and circulation.

A television director tracks the cameras and presenters in the studio and works with the editor to put clips together.

The **production** stage includes the processes involved with constructing a media product. Before production begins, elements such as the budget, the creative team, and the facilities and equipment, need to be in place. Media producers will plan these elements carefully to ensure that the product is created efficiently. The production phase will include the creation of content, such as photographs, footage and written copy, depending on the type of product. The content will need to be organised and structured, for example the design and layout of a newspaper or magazine, or the editing of a television programme or music video.

Distribution is the way in which media products are delivered to audiences. Increasingly, media industries are using digital methods of distribution. Digital technology is also significant to the circulation and **consumption** of media products. Many popular television programmes are now available via online subscription services, such as Netflix or HBO. Sometimes, an entire series is released on the same day, allowing audiences to 'binge-watch' rather than having to wait each time for the next episode to be broadcast.

Top Tip

It is a good idea to learn the names of the organisations that have produced the set products that you study.

Activity 1.3

Look at a two different newspapers or magazines (print copies or websites). Make notes on the following:

- Does the product include adverts?
- If so, how many?
- What products are advertised?

Ownership

Some media products are produced by large organisations such as Channel 4 (*The IT Crowd*) or News Corporation (the *Sun*). Some, however, are created by smaller, more independent companies, such as Pride Media Group, which publishes *Pride* magazine. It is important to consider who has created a media product as this is can affect elements such as the **production values** and representations that are used. As well as the media organisation, the individual people involved in production also affect the finished product and how it is perceived. For example:

- a particular actor might be recognised for a certain type of role or character
- a director, writer or producer might be known for a certain type of film or programme and style of production
- a newspaper journalist might be known to support a particular political party.

The way in which products are funded is also important to consider. Some products will have **public funding**, for example Sport England's *This Girl Can* campaign or BBC products, which are funded by the licence fee, while others will be commercially backed products. These will not usually receive public money and are likely to be funded by advertising.

Technology

Technology has an important role in the production of media texts. Recent developments in digital technology have changed the nature of many media products. Augmented reality, for example, has enabled audiences to interact more fully with video games. *Pokémon Go*, one of the set products, is an example of an augmented-reality game.

Technology also has an impact on how products are distributed and circulated, and you will need to consider this in relation to the different forms. Most magazines, for example, are now published in digital editions as well as print. Many media organisations create content that is available on different platforms, including social media sites such as Facebook and Instagram. This use of **convergence** allows media producers to reach a wider range of audiences and increase the chance of their product's success.

You will also consider the ways in which new technologies impact on the different media industries that you study.

Regulation

Most media industries are regulated by an official organisation. Television, for example, is regulated by **Ofcom**. The role of the regulator varies across different industries, but the key functions of regulation are to:

- Offer guidance to media companies about the standards or codes of practice they should follow.
- Monitor or control media organisations. This might include responding to complaints if an organisation has not followed the appropriate guidelines.

The main purpose of regulation is to protect the public, especially younger people, from unsuitable or possibly harmful media content. The BBFC (British Board of Film Classification), for example, classifies films into different age certificates in the UK. (There is more on the BBFC on page 82.)

The internet is difficult to regulate. While some online media content, such as **video on demand**, comes under the jurisdiction of Ofcom or the BBFC, much of the internet remains unregulated.

Quickfire 1.12

Why is it important to know who has produced a media product?

Key Terms

Production values
The quality of the technical elements of a product, for example the camerawork, lighting, costumes and sound. Products with a high budget are much more likely to have high production values as the equipment and materials used will be of a very high standard.

Public funding
Money that comes from the government or sources such as the television licence fee.

Convergence
The way in which products or brands are made available to audiences on a number of platforms. (*The Archers* is broadcast on radio, but listeners can also download episodes, and the website offers additional content to engage the audience.)

Ofcom
The Office of Communications, the regulator for broadcasting, telecommunications and postal services in the UK.

Video on demand
Audio-visual products such as television programmes and films that are available to stream or download from the internet.

Stretch and Challenge 1.9

Research the different BBFC age ratings for films.

Key Terms

Passive consumers
People who use media products, but do not actively engage with or question them.

Effects debate
The idea that media products might have a negative influence on an audience's behaviour.

Active audience
People who make deliberate choices about the media products they consume, and actively respond by, for example, agreeing or disagreeing with the messages in them.

Interact
The way in which audiences actively engage with media products, mainly as a result of digital technologies (examples include playing a video game and posting comments about a media product on social media).

Target audience
The group of people that a product is intended for. It might be defined by social group (age, gender and so on) or other factors such as lifestyle or interest.

Categorise
The way media organisations divide an audience so that they can target their products at specific groups.

Audiences

Media audiences are the people who consume media products. In the past, it was assumed that the audience for a media product was one large 'mass' of people who were **passive consumers** and accepted the messages that the producers encoded in the product. This led to concerns that the media could affect people's attitudes and behaviour. Several theories developed which can be grouped under the heading of the **effects debate**, where the main concern was that certain people might 'copy' violent acts seen in films or video games. More recent theories have explored the idea of the **active audience** and it is now widely accepted that media audiences consist of different groups of individuals who actively choose media products for particular reasons and respond to them in different ways. Increasingly, due to developing technologies, media audiences and users are able to **interact** with media products, often becoming active participants and even creators of media products themselves.

Many audience members have become active creators of blogs and vlogs.

Target Audiences

Media producers create products for a particular **target audience** and aim to reach that audience by constructing an appropriate product and marketing it effectively. Producers **categorise** audiences in different ways in order to position their products effectively. They use:

- **Demographics**, including factors such as:
  - Age (different industries use various age bands, but they will usually categorise audiences into younger age groups, adult audiences, and older adult audiences)
  - Gender
  - Socio-economic group, categorised by occupation and level of income. Media products might aim to appeal to, for example, ABC1s (A – senior managers and professionals, such as doctors, lawyers; B – middle managers and professionals, such as teachers; C1 – junior managers and clerical workers; C2 – skilled manual workers, such as plumbers, mechanics; D – semi-skilled or unskilled manual workers, such as retail workers or labourers; E – casual workers, pensioners, people receiving state benefits)

- **Psychographics**, including factors such as people's values and beliefs as well as their interests and lifestyles. These are often used by advertisers but can also be applied to other forms such as magazines. Audiences can also be categorised in terms of generations of people who might have broadly similar experiences and viewpoints, for example:
  - baby boomers, born in the years after the Second World War into a period of economic prosperity and growing social freedom
  - millennials, born in the 1980s and 1990s, who grew up with rapidly developing digital technologies and became adults in the early 2000s.

When you study a media product, you can usually identify the target audience from the style and content of the product. A product aiming at a youth audience, for example, might include representations of young people and will use suitable conventions to **appeal** to that audience. Some products target a very specific or **specialised audience**, such as a mountain biking magazine, while others might have a much wider target audience. Products that are aimed at a very wide audience are often described as mainstream.

While a product might have a very specific **primary audience**, it might also have other **secondary audience** groups. Women's magazines specifically target a primary female audience, but many also have a secondary audience of males who read them to find out about women and their interests.

It is also important to consider the **mode of address** that the product uses. The *Lego Movie* poster, for example, shows a Lego character running directly towards the audience with a panicked expression. This immediately **engages** the viewer and makes them feel involved with the product, which might encourage them to go to see the film.

Activity 1.4

Look at the following products:
- Who is the target audience for each product? Be as specific as possible.
- How has this audience been targeted?
- Include examples of media language and representations.

Key Term

Gratifications
Pleasures that audiences gain from consuming media products.

Quickfire 1.13

List three types of media product that provide an audience with entertainment.

Stretch and Challenge 1.11

Identify the specific gratifications that you gain from consuming your favourite media products.

Theoretical perspectives on audiences

Key Theory 2: Blumler and Katz's Uses and Gratifications theory

You need to be able to apply the Uses and Gratifications theory to your study of media products. This is an active audience theory which argues that audiences select media products that fulfil particular needs or **gratifications**. The reason why one person chooses a product might be different from another person's. People's individual needs, as well as factors such as their social background, will influence how they engage with and respond to media products.

There are four key 'uses' that we can apply to media products:

- **Information**: Audiences find out about the world through the media. Newspapers are a clear source of information, and many other media products can also be informative, such as storylines in *The Archers* about farming and the environment.
- **Personal identity**: Audiences feel that they can relate to a particular character or situation in a media product. Magazine articles that feature 'real life' stories and television dramas are examples of products that may provide a sense of personal identity.
- **Social interaction**: Audiences can engage further with a media product by discussing it with other people. This could be in person or online, for example using social media, online forums or gaming which allows audiences to interact directly with others.
- **Entertainment/diversion**: Many media products provide a sense of 'escape' from everyday life and give pleasure and entertainment.

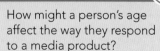

Audience Responses

As we have seen, audiences are made up of individual people who interpret the same media product in different ways. Factors that affect how we respond to media products include our age, gender, ethnicity and social background. We are also influenced by our life experiences and sometimes by the context in which we consume a product. For example, if we watch a television programme with friends, our response might be affected by their reactions.

Theoretical perspectives on audience responses: Stuart Hall's Reception theory

Quickfire 1.14

How might a person's age affect the way they respond to a media product?

You will know from your study of media language that producers encode messages into media products that audiences will decode. When audiences consume a media product they might or might not interpret the messages in the way the producers intended.

Cultural theorist Stuart Hall developed the Reception theory, which can be helpful when studying responses to media products. This theory suggests that audiences interpret or 'read' a product in one of the following ways:

- **Preferred reading**: The audience interprets the text in the way the producer intended and accepts the messages that are encoded. This is more likely to happen when the audience falls into the target audience group.

- **Negotiated reading**: The audience accepts some of the messages presented, but disagrees with others.

- **Oppositional reading**: The audience rejects the intended meaning of the text. This is more likely if the audience is not the target audience or possibly if they are from a different social background from that of the producers.

This front page of the *i* celebrated British Olympic success.

The image on the right is taken from the *i* newspaper during the London Olympics in 2012.

A preferred reading would be that Britain is a successful sporting nation, anchored by the headline 'Britain's Golden Day' and the images of sportspeople in Team GB kit and holding gold medals. The patriotic message would be fully accepted.

A negotiated reading might accept the positive message of sporting success but might feel that there are more important events than sport that should be on the front cover.

An oppositional reading might disagree that this is a 'historic' event and feel that the Olympics should not dominate the front page.

We also need to consider how audience responses will change over time. For example, *The Sweeney* was extremely popular in the 1970s, but a modern audience might be shocked and offended by the violent behaviour of the police.

Quickfire 1.15

What are encoding and decoding?

Stretch and Challenge 1.12

Look at a newspaper front cover from another date and identify the preferred, oppositional and negotiated readings.

Contexts

When you analyse a media product, it is important to look beyond the text itself and consider the background behind the product, for example when it was produced and what the world was like at that time. This helps in identifying some of the decisions that the producers made and the meanings they intended to communicate. It can also help you to understand audience responses.

The GCSE specification requires you to study the following points in relation to media contexts:

- How the product reflects the context through its use of media language, genre conventions, representations, themes, values, messages and viewpoints.

- How the product reflects the context in which it was made through aspects of its production, distribution, marketing, regulation, circulation and audience consumption.

A sign outside a filling station in the USA in April 1974.

Key Terms

Patriarchal
A situation or society that is dominated by men.

Political leaning
Supporting a particular political party (such as Conservative or Labour) or set of political ideas.

Historical context relates to the period in which a product was produced and the events occurring at the time. We are concerned mainly with texts from the past here, such as the Quality Street advert or the poster for *The Man with the Golden Gun*. Learning something about what was happening in the world in the 1970s can help us to understand some of the images and ideas included in the film poster and see how the film reflects the time in which it was made. The energy crisis of 1973, for example, is reflected in the film's plot and indicated through the solar power station and laser gun shown on the poster.

You should also consider how production processes were different at the time and how the available technology influences the product.

Social context relates to society at the time the text was produced, for example the role of women during that particular period. This will affect the representations in a media product and the messages and values it communicates. The poster for *The Man with the Golden Gun* suggests that society in the 1970s was still quite **patriarchal** as the man is dominant and the women are sexualised objects.

Cultural context concerns elements such as style, genre and technology, which will affect the product and how it is consumed. Media products are affected by current styles and genres in various forms of media or art. The style and content of *Luther*, for example, reflects the current trend for crime dramas to explore the protagonist's personal life and is influenced by thriller genre conventions as well as the police drama genre.

Political context is the way in which a media product is affected by the politics of the time, for example the political party in power and the key political issues affecting the country or world. Today, this could link, for example, to the economy and issues such as Brexit. Political context is particularly relevant to newspapers as they report on political events. Most newspapers have a **political leaning**, which might be evident on the front page in the images and language used to report a particular story.

Brexit has been an important political issue in Britain since the EU referendum in 2016.

The Media Studies Specification

OVERVIEW

The Eduqas GCSE Media Studies specification provides you with a broad programme of study through which you will gain a thorough understanding of the subject. You will:

- develop knowledge and understanding of the **theoretical framework** of media studies by studying a wide range of different media forms and products
- explore the links between different forms and products, between products and contexts, and between theory and **practical work**
- apply your knowledge and understanding of the media to a practical production in response to a brief set by the awarding organisation.

Media Forms

The forms that you will explore are:

- Advertising and marketing (print advertisements and film posters)
- Film (in relation to industry issues only)
- Magazines
- Music videos and online, social and participatory media through a single music topic
- Newspapers
- Radio
- Television
- Video games.

You will study a range of different products. Most of these will be set by Eduqas, but additional texts will be chosen by your teacher. The set products cover a variety of forms and will be produced by different types of organisation for a variety of audiences. Most of the products will be contemporary, but you will study some examples from the past and explore their historical **context**. You will draw on your existing knowledge of the media and will probably recognise many of the set forms and products that you analyse. The specification will also extend your experience of the media as you explore texts that are less familiar.

Key Terms

Theoretical framework
The basis for your study of the media, covering media language, representation, media industries and audiences.

Practical work
Tasks in which you create your own media products. (It is important to apply your knowledge and understanding of the theoretical framework to your own products.)

Contexts
The background factors that can influence a media product, for example the historical situation. These help us to understand the meanings and messages in a product.

Top Tip

Try to consume a wide range of media products on a regular basis. You could aim to discover one new product every week.

Key Term

Theoretical perspectives
Ideas that have been developed by theorists that will support your study of the media.

Contexts

The study of contexts is important to help you to understand the set products and is explained in detail in Chapter 1. You will study the following contexts:

- Historical
- Social and cultural
- Political.

Theories

Theoretical perspectives will help you to develop your knowledge and understanding of the media and will support your analysis of media products. You will study theoretical perspectives in relation to the following areas of the framework:

- Media language
- Representations
- Audiences.

There are two key theories that you need to study in detail:

- Propp's theory of narrative (media language)
- The Uses and Gratifications theory (audiences).

It is important that you understand these theories and theoretical perspectives and apply them when you study different media forms and products, as they will help you to analyse in more depth. The theoretical perspectives are explained in Chapter 1 and there is further advice on how to apply them in Chapters 3 and 5.

Skills

The specification will enable you to develop skills in analysing media products and creating your own production work.

Analysis

In analysing media products you will:

- think critically about media forms and products
- **analyse** and compare how media products construct and communicate meanings (for example how a film poster conveys information about 'good' and 'evil' characters)
- use **subject-specific terminology**. There are many key Media Studies terms that you will need to use in your written work. This will enable you to analyse products accurately and demonstrate your knowledge and understanding. Key terms are highlighted and explained throughout this book
- use **discursive writing** to show that you understand media issues and can make judgements about them.

Creation

In creating media products you will:

- develop practical skills
- apply what you have learned about media language and representations to your media production
- use media language to communicate meanings to an intended audience.

Key Terms

Analyse
Explore media texts critically, considering the messages that are communicated.

Subject-specific terminology
The specialist vocabulary that applies to Media Studies.

Discursive writing
Writing that develops an argument, makes judgements about a question and draws conclusions.

You will also have opportunities to draw together your knowledge, understanding and skills from different areas of the course. There will be the chance to demonstrate your ability in either Component 1 Section B or Component 2. Your knowledge and understanding of media language and representations will be used in your practical production in Component 3.

Quickfire 2.1

Name the four key areas of the theoretical framework.

Key Term

Print media products
Media products produced in print form, traditionally on paper, such as magazines, newspapers or film posters.

The Components of the Media Studies Specification

Component 1: Exploring the Media

Overview

This component is 40 per cent of the GCSE qualification and is worth 80 marks.

It introduces you to the different areas of the theoretical framework and provides a foundation for all areas of your studies. You will:

- study media products across a breadth of forms in relation to different areas of the framework:
  - Media language and representation in Section A
  - Media industries and audiences in Section B
- develop understanding of how contexts influence media products
- use theories or theoretical perspectives and subject-specific terminology.

Section A: Exploring Media Language and Representation

In this part you will explore a range of forms and analyse many different **print media products**. This will enable you to develop a detailed understanding of print media forms and the specific terminology, codes and conventions that apply to print products. You will explore:

- elements of media language such as visual and technical codes, genre and narrative
- representations of gender, age, ethnicity, issues and events
- contexts of the set products and how these affect the use of media language and the construction of representations.

The set products that you will study in Section A are:

Form	Advertising	Marketing	Magazines	Newspapers
Set products	Print adverts: • Quality Street (1956) • *This Girl Can* (2015)	Film posters: • *The Man with the Golden Gun* (1974) • *Spectre* (2015)	Magazine front covers: • *Pride* (November 2015) • *GQ* (July 2016)	Newspaper front pages: • The *Guardian* (4 September 2015) • The *Sun* (18 December 2013)

There are contrasting set products in each form, offering the opportunity to explore fully the media language, representations and contexts. For example:

- The set advertising and marketing products include contemporary and older examples that will allow you to explore historical and social contexts in detail.
- The set magazine covers target different audiences, which affects the use of media language and representations. *Pride* is aimed at a specialised female audience, while *GQ* targets a larger male readership.
- The set newspaper front pages are from different types of product (a broadsheet and a tabloid) produced by different organisations, which will enable you to explore political contexts.

In addition to these products, further examples will develop your knowledge and understanding of the theoretical framework and allow you to practise your analytical skills.

Section B: Exploring Media Industries and Audiences

Here you will study different areas of the framework and focus on issues relating to industry and audience. You will explore:

- areas of industry including production processes, ownership, technologies and regulation
- the audience, including audience categorisation, target audiences and responses.

Section B set products are:

Form	Film (media industries only)	Newspapers	Radio	Video games
Set product	*Spectre* (2015), cross-media study	The *Sun*	*The Archers*	*Pokémon Go* (2016)
What will I study?	• Selected pages of the official website • Extracts of the film in relation to industry	• One complete edition • Selected pages of the website	• One complete episode • Selected pages of the website	• Selected pages of the website • Extracts of the game in relation to industry and audience

Pokémon Go is the set video game product in Section B.

As you will see, most of the set products are in different forms from those in Section A. Newspapers are studied in both A and B. Film is only studied in relation to media industries, to ensure that there is no overlap with Film Studies. You will explore pages of the film's website, but will not undertake any analysis of the film. All other forms are studied in relation to industries and audiences. Your teacher will select specific elements of each product for you to study.

Component 2: Understanding Media Forms and Products

Overview

This component is 30 per cent of the GCSE qualification and is worth 60 marks.

Component 2 builds on your studies from Component 1 and will deepen your knowledge and understanding of the theoretical framework. You will study **audio-visual** and **online media products** in depth, analysing media language and representations, as well as exploring industry and audience issues.

You will study both of the following topics:

- **Television**: crime drama or sitcom. Your teacher will choose one for you to study.
- **Music**: music video and online media. Your teacher will select specific music products from the options set by Eduqas.

You will study each topic in relation to all areas of the theoretical framework:

- Media language: how media language communicates meanings in the different forms
- Representations: how the media re-present the world and convey messages and viewpoints
- Media industries: how products are funded, produced and distributed
- Audiences: how products target their audiences and how audiences respond to the same product in different ways.

You will also study contexts and develop your ability to apply theoretical perspectives to the set products.

Section A: Television

In this section you will study one television genre in depth. Through the detailed analysis of two set products you will explore:

- genre codes and conventions, and how these change over time
- specific representations in the genre products
- the financial importance of the genre to the media industry
- developments in online broadcasting
- the popularity of the genre with audiences; the appeal of the products
- how audiences consume and respond to the products
- how media language, representations and themes in the products reflect their contexts.

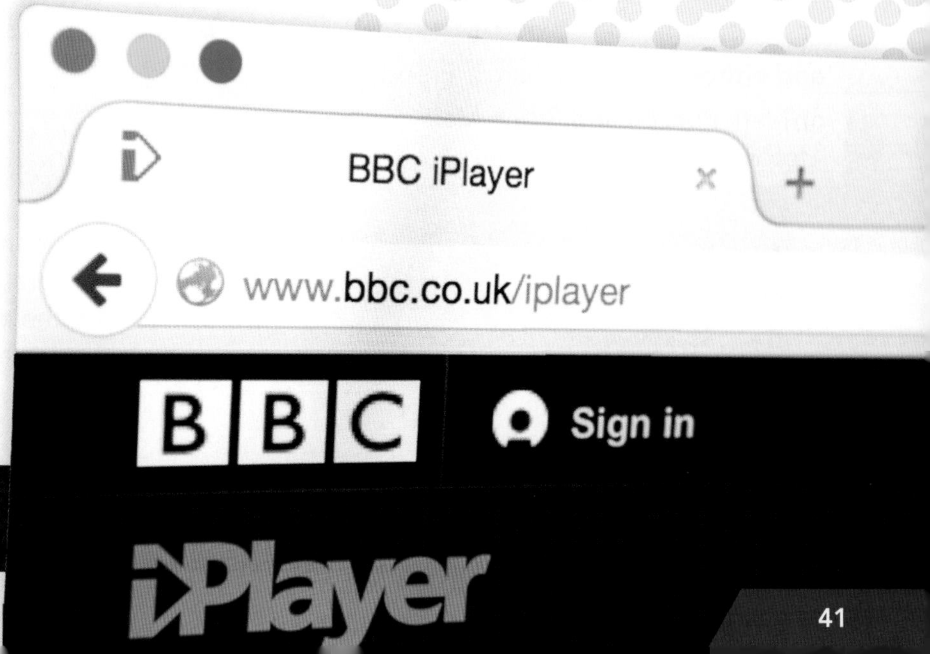

BBC iPlayer
www.bbc.co.uk/iplayer

BBC Sign in

iPlayer

The BBC's iPlayer on-demand service is one of several ways in which audiences can access television programmes.

The options for the television genre topic are:

Option 1: Crime drama	Option 2: Sitcom
Luther, Series 1, Episode 1 (2010) **plus** a ten-minute extract from: *The Sweeney*, Series 1, Episode 1 (1975)	*The IT Crowd*, Season 4, Episode 2: 'The Final Countdown' (2010) **plus** a ten-minute extract from: *Friends*, Season 1, Episode 1 (1994)

You will study one complete episode of the contemporary product. Your teacher will choose an extract from the older programme for you to analyse.

Section B: Music – Music Video and Online Media

Section B is an in-depth study of music where you will analyse the following contemporary products in relation to all areas of the theoretical framework:

- Two contemporary music videos
- The artists' online and social media platforms.

You will also analyse one music video from the past in relation to media language, representations and contexts.

The music topic will enable you to explore:

- connections between the different forms (music videos and online media)
- how context affects media language and representations in music videos
- the importance of convergence to the music industry
- the way that music is marketed through different platforms, including websites, social and participatory media
- the appeals of music products and audience interaction and participation.

The options for the music topic are:

Contemporary music videos	Music videos from the 1980s and 1990s	Online, social and participatory media
Two music videos from the following options: **Either** Katy Perry, 'Roar' (2013) **or** Taylor Swift, 'Bad Blood' (2014) *and* **either** Pharrell Williams, 'Freedom' (2015) **or** Mark Ronson and Bruno Mars, 'Uptown Funk' (2014)	**One** of the following music videos: **Either** Duran Duran, 'Rio' (1982) **or** Michael Jackson, 'Black or White' (1991)	**Either** katyperry.com **or** taylorswift.com *and* **either** pharrellwilliams.com **or** brunomars.com

You will study the music videos and online media in relation to two contemporary artists. Online, social and participatory media includes the artist's website, their Facebook and Twitter pages, and other relevant social media.

Taylor Swift is one of the set artists for Section B of Component 2.

Component 3: Creating Media Products

Overview

This component is 30 per cent of the GCSE qualification and is worth 60 marks.

This part of the assessment is non-exam. It will be internally assessed by your teachers and moderated by Eduqas. You will be required to:

- create media products for an intended audience
- apply knowledge and understanding of media language and representations in order to communicate meanings.

The production brief

Eduqas set the production **briefs** and these will be released on 1 March in the year before you are assessed. Your teacher might set a particular option or offer you a choice of briefs. The set production briefs change every year, but the following forms will always be offered:

Form	Brief
Television	An audio-visual sequence from a new television programme **or** a website to promote a new television programme
Music marketing	A music video to promote a new artist or band **or** a website to promote a new artist or band
Film marketing	Print-based marketing material for a new film
Magazines	A new print or online magazine

The production briefs will provide:

- the genre for your production
- the intended audience for your products
- specific requirements, for example the length or quantity of the work and elements that must be included.

You will respond to the brief by creating your own ideas and showing that you can appeal to the target audience. It is important that you include all the elements stated in the brief.

In order to create a successful production, you will need to:

- undertake research, such as analysis of similar media products and potential audiences
- plan your production carefully
- complete a **Statement of Aims** – this will be assessed along with your product
- create your media product.

Your full production, including research and planning, should be completed in a period of no more than 12 weeks.

Key Terms

Brief
The production task (set by Eduqas), including details of all the elements you need to include. (All learners following the Eduqas specification will complete one of the set briefs for the year in which they are assessed.)

Statement of Aims
A short piece of writing you must submit with your production, which should outline how you will apply your knowledge and understanding of the theoretical framework to your media production.

Top Tip

Make sure you plan your production carefully and stick to the deadlines set by your teacher.

Component 1: Exploring the Media

OVERVIEW

Component 1:

- introduces you to the theoretical framework for studying the media
- develops your knowledge and understanding of:
  - Media Language and Representation (Section A)
  - Media Industries and Audiences (Section B)
- develops your ability to analyse print media products
- considers how contexts, for example social and historical, can influence media products
- introduces you to some of the theoretical perspectives of Media Studies
- extends your use of subject-specific terminology.

You will study a range of media forms in Component 1:

- Section A, Media Language and Representation:
  - Advertising and marketing
  - Magazines
  - Newspapers.
- Section B, Media Industries and Audiences:
  - Newspapers
  - Radio
  - Video games
  - Film.

Section A: Exploring Media Language and Representation

Overview

In this section you will analyse how print media products communicate meanings to audiences. You will study products set by Eduqas (see page 39) and analyse at least two further examples in each form to develop your understanding of codes and conventions and enable you to practise and improve your analytical skills in preparation for the examination.

Exploring Media Language

When analysing media language in the set products and additional examples you will need to explore:

- how the selection and combination of elements communicate meanings in different media forms and products
- how technology influences media language

- the codes and conventions of media forms and genres
- how **intertextuality** is used to communicate meanings
- the denotation and connotation of elements of media language
- theoretical perspectives on genre and narrative.

Exploring Representation

When analysing representation in the set products and additional examples you will need to explore:

- how representations of events, social groups and ideas are constructed
- the way in which media producers represent aspects of reality
- different ways in which stereotypes are used in the media
- how representations convey viewpoints, messages, values and beliefs
- the social, historical and cultural contexts of representations
- audience interpretations of representations
- theoretical perspectives on gender and feminist approaches.

Introduction to Analysing Print Media Products

When you analyse any media product you will need to consider its form and genre in order to identify specific codes and conventions. It is also important to think about the target audience, the purpose and the context of the product. You will examine a range of print products in Component 1, from a variety of forms and genres, and with different audiences, purposes and contexts. There are some features that are common to all print forms and genres, however, that you can use as a starting point when analysing any product.

Key Term

Intertextuality
Where one media product includes a reference to another media product. (Taylor Swift includes sequences in 'Bad Blood' that are similar to familiar action films. The audience might recognise these references and make connections.)

You will explore film posters and newspaper front pages as part of your print media analysis.

House style
The consistent use of elements such as colour, design, typeface and language to create a clear brand identity for a product.

Foreground and background
The foreground relates the front of an image, the part that appears closest to the audience. This usually has prominence, so what is placed here has greater importance than the background, the part that appears to be further away from the viewer.

Brand identity
The image of a particular product or company, and the values associated with it. (The Asda brand is associated with good value for money, reinforced by the 'Asda Price Guarantee' that features in advertising and on displays in store and so on.)

Masthead
The name of a newspaper or magazine, usually positioned prominently at the top of the cover or front page.

Quickfire 3.1

Which newspapers use a serif font for the **masthead** and which use a sans-serif font? What might this connote about the newspapers?

Codes and conventions of print media products

- **Layout**: how visual elements are arranged on the page. Consider how images, graphics and text have been combined and which of the elements are placed in prominent positions.
- **Design:** the visual and technical elements that contribute to the style – perhaps **house style** – of a print product, including the choices of typography, colour and images.
- **Technical codes**: camera shots used in photographs; lighting; editing, for example layering of images or digital manipulation such as airbrushing.
- **Images**: photographs, illustrations and graphics, such as icons and logos. Consider the type of images used and where they have been placed on the page. A photograph, for example, could be a cover model on a magazine or an event depicted on a newspaper front page. Consider what is in the **foreground** and **background**, and why.
- **Visual codes**:
  - Colour palette: Colour communicates meanings in a media product as different colours have particular connotations. White is often associated with innocence, for example, so a 'good' character, or 'hero' might be dressed in white. The colour design is important to the style of a product, as a dark colour palette will create a very different mood compared with a pale colour scheme.
  - Dress codes, hair and make-up
  - Gesture codes and expressions
  - Setting/location of images and use of props.
- **Typography**: the style and size of font used. This can communicate messages about the product and the **brand identity** of the organisation that has produced the product.
  - A serif typeface features small decorative lines, or serifs, at the end of the lines forming each letter, such as Times New Roman. Serif typefaces might be considered to be more formal and traditional.
  - A sans-serif typeface does not feature these lines and might be considered to be more contemporary.
  - The size and styling of the font is also important; for example, does the text 'lean forward'? This might be interpreted as indicating a forward-looking, modern, product.

- **Language codes:** the wording used in the written **copy** on a print product. Consider how this communicates meaning:
  - Is the language **formal** or **informal**?
  - Does the product include **specialist lexis**?
  - Are linguistic devices used, such as **alliteration**, **personification**, and **metaphor**, to add emphasis and impact to a print product?
  - Does the product include **emotive language**?
  - Are **imperatives** used?

- **Mode of address:** how the product communicates with the audience. Some products will use a **direct mode of address** to engage the audience and make them feel involved with the product. Some products adopt a more formal, indirect mode of address.

- **Anchorage**: the way in which written text is used to secure or solidify the meaning of an image, such as a caption for a newspaper photograph.

- **Narrative**: the 'story' constructed through the text and images. A newspaper article might report a complete story, while an advert might establish elements of a narrative situation or characters to communicate meanings.

Quickfire 3.2

How does this cover of *Harper's Bazaar* use imperatives?

Stretch and Challenge 3.1

Select some different print products and identify the use of codes and conventions listed above.

Top Tip

Make a list of the key subject-specific terms relating to each topic and try to use them every time you analyse a media product.

Key Terms

Copy
The written text in a printed publication.

Formal language
Using an indirect mode of address and possibly more complex vocabulary. (A broadsheet newspaper is likely to use more formal language than a tabloid.)

Informal language
Using a more direct mode of address and possibly more colloquial, or slang, terms. (A gossip magazine is likely to use informal language.)

Specialist lexis
Language relating to a specific topic or subject; the use of specialist lexis assumes that the audience brings a level of subject knowledge.

Alliteration
Where several words in a phrase or sentence begin with the same letter or sound to add emphasis.

Personification
Giving objects or ideas human qualities, such as Old Father Time. Personification can communicate meaning by helping an audience view an idea or object in a certain way.

Metaphor
A comparison between two unrelated objects to communicate a particular meaning. Describing a person as a 'rock', for example, connotes that they are very reliable and supportive.

Emotive language
Descriptive language that aims to generate an emotional response, such as sympathy for a character or shock at a news item.

Imperatives
Command words such as 'Read this'. Magazine covers in particular often feature imperatives as a persuasive technique.

Direct mode of address
Where the product seems to speak directly to the audience, for example by using personal pronouns such as 'we' or 'you'.

Print Advertising

Advertising is a media form that aims to draw attention to a product, service or issue. It is a huge global industry and is very important to the British economy. Advertising also provides a major source of income to other media industries, especially television, magazines and newspapers. We encounter advertising in different forms and places, often many times each day and sometimes without even realising. It is therefore important for the producers to make an advert eye-catching and memorable, as an audience does not usually actively choose to engage with an advert and might only see it for a few seconds as they pass by a bus shelter or read a magazine. **Advertising campaigns** might involve television and radio adverts, print advertising (such as billboard posters and magazine pages) and, increasingly, digital advertising. You will study print adverts in detail in Component 1 Section A.

Aims of advertising

All adverts aim to communicate a clear message about the product, service or issue. Depending on the type of campaign, an advert might also intend to:

- raise awareness (of a new product or an issue for example)
- inform or educate (as in a public awareness campaign)
- persuade audiences (to buy a product or donate to charity for example)
- create a **unique selling point**.

Activity 3.1

Create a log of all of the advertising you encounter in one day. This might be television and radio adverts, posters on public transport or digital displays outdoors, print adverts in magazines, and digital advertising on the internet or on your mobile phone.

Stretch and Challenge 3.2

Select one of the print adverts you logged in Activity 3.1 and analyse it using the list of codes and conventions of print products.

Quickfire 3.3

Why is it important for an advert to show a product's unique selling point?

Key Terms

Advertising campaign
An organised advertising strategy, possibly using a range of different media platforms, to achieve a specific purpose, such as a series of adverts to launch a new perfume or a sequence of adverts for a department store in the lead up to Christmas.

Unique selling point
Something that makes a product stand out from competitors' similar products. Advertisers aim to communicate the 'unique' nature of the product to persuade the audience to buy or use it.

Consumer goods
Physical products for purchasing, such as food, cars and cosmetics.

Services
Non-physical products, such as car insurance, health provision or mobile phone contracts.

Brand
The name of a product or the manufacturer of the product, established through a trademark or logo that is recognisable to an audience, such as Heinz, BT, Reebok.

Aspiration
The desire for a higher level of success or material wealth. Adverts often create aspirational lifestyles, such as a really clean and tidy home or a sophisticated party.

Identifying different types of advertising

Advertising can be split broadly into two types: commercial and non-commercial.

Commercial advertising has the aim of making money by promoting **consumer goods** or **services**. This type of advertising generally focuses on persuading an audience to make a purchase. The advert will also aim to communicate a message about the **brand**. If the product is already well known, the advert might aim to reinforce the existing image of the brand to fulfil audience expectations and encourage their loyalty to the brand. It can be argued that this type of advertising creates a sense of need or desire in an audience, often creating a sense of **aspiration**, in order to persuade them to buy a product.

Non-commercial advertising includes public information drives, such as the government's 'Think!' drink-driving campaign, and charity messages. Some campaigns might simply aim to inform the audience of an issue, but many also intend to persuade the audience to donate money to a charity, for example, or to change their behaviour in some way, such as giving up smoking. This type of advertising might use methods such as direct appeals or even **shock tactics** to communicate the message. Charity advertisements, for example, often depict images of suffering to convey a strong message about the need for action. Some adverts use different techniques to defy expectations or prompt audiences to think differently about an issue. Non-commercial adverts might also seek to represent true aspects of reality rather than constructing an aspirational world.

Top Tip

When you read a magazine, take note of the different types of adverts included. Identify how they communicate ideas to the reader.

Key Term

Shock tactics
Using elements of media language to shock the audience and create a strong particular reaction. (An image of a war zone in a charity message might make the audience want to help and so donate money to improve the situation.)

Quickfire 3.4

What adverts have you seen that use shock tactics?

Advertisers use many tools to promote a brand and transmit the messages associated with it.

Key Terms

Logo
A simple design that makes a product recognisable and communicates information about the product or brand identity. (The National Trust logo features oak leaves and acorns, which relates to the organisation's work as a conservation charity and promoter of outdoor spaces. The Nike logo is the recognisable 'swoosh' that suggests action and movement, relating to the company's sports products.)

Slogan
A short, punchy phrase that communicates key ideas about a product or issue.

Hyperbole
Exaggerated language to create emphasis.

Wordplay
Using a word that has more than one meaning, or adapting the spelling or meaning of words, often to humorous effect.

Have an egg-cellent day!

Quickfire 3.5

What other types of advert use soft-sell techniques?

Codes and conventions of print advertising

In addition to the main codes of print products detailed above, there are some common conventions specific to print advertising. These vary according to the genre and purpose of the advert as you will see when you study the examples in the next section.

The product or issue being advertised or promoted is likely to include:

- name of the product/brand
- **logo**
- **slogan**
- details of the product or issue, for example technical specifications of an electrical product or explanation of a particular situation in a charity advert.

An advertising **hard sell** will feature a product or issue prominently and there is a clear and direct message.

In a **soft sell**, the product is often less prominent but an ideal lifestyle is created in order to present and push the product. A car advert, for example, might feature a happy couple driving through a beautiful landscape. This can create a sense of aspiration in the audience.

Images like this in a car advert suggest an aspirational lifestyle.

Advertising **language** makes use of:

- facts and information
- persuasive vocabulary, including **hyperbole**, imperatives and emotive language, to draw attention to the product
- **wordplay** to communicate a message quickly and memorably.

Modern advertising often makes reference to other media products, perhaps from different forms or genres, that audiences can identify. This **intertextuality** helps to communicate a message quickly and memorably.

Alongside these tools, the thinking behind an advert needs a **concept**: a clear idea for the advert that will communicate the image of the product and/or the brand.

Catching up with old friends is special to Ginnie and Chris
For special days out in the South West visit nationaltrust.org.uk/southwest

National Trust

How intertextuality is used in advertising: the National Trust

The National Trust is a charity that looks after many historic properties, gardens and wild spaces in Britain.

This advertisement uses an intertextual reference to the iconic 'I love NY' logo that has become a very popular cultural image. The 'I love/heart…' logo was designed in the 1970s to advertise tourism in New York but has since been used in relation to many other products and places.

Historical Advertisements

The current set product is a 1950s advert for Quality Street and you will need to analyse this in detail. It is important to examine other historical adverts in order to develop your knowledge of genre conventions and your understanding of how contexts can influence media products, particularly in terms of representation. Analysing older examples of advertising will also help you to identify how the genre has developed over time and how changing technologies have affected media language.

Many early-20th-century newspapers featured small advertisements like these, with emphasis on the text and only simple line illustrations. They were often in black and white or added just one colour.

Activity 3.2

Why do you think the National Trust has used this intertextual reference? How is the meaning of the logo anchored by the image in the advert? Write a paragraph analysing how intertextuality has been used in this product.

Top Tip

Get into the habit of annotating the details of print products with subject-specific terminology. This will help you to prepare for the 'unseen' analysis in the examination.

Analysing an example: Coca-Cola advert, 1960s

Come on - let's have a 'COKE'!

Coca-Cola is real refreshment for everybody—
any time of day. Out and about, or at home with the
family, it's always the right time and place for 'Coke'.
Pure and wholesome, delicious and refreshing
Coca-Cola is unlike any other drink in the world.
Enjoy 'Coke' whenever you feel like a 'break'—
and return to work (or play)
wonderfully refreshed!

Drink
Coca-Cola
'TRADE MARK REG.'

Call it 'Coke' or Coca-Cola
it's the same delicious drink

'Coca-Cola' and 'Coke' are the registered trade marks of The Coca-Cola Company

The producers of this advert selected and combined codes and conventions to convey meanings, messages and values.

Media language

The familiar Coca-Cola logo (already a well-known brand) is prominently positioned next to an image of four iconic bottles, visually presenting the product.

The slogan 'Come on – let's have a COKE' emphasises the brand name. The use of 'let's' aims to include the audience and make them feel close to the brand.

The layout is quite crowded, a more common convention in older advertising, and includes a detailed illustration and a large amount of written copy.

The images and language construct a narrative, placing the product in a context. The characters have been playing tennis and the drink provides refreshment. The slogan 'Come on…' seems to be a quote from one of the characters, which brings the narrative to life.

The advert features drawn images rather than photographs. This reflects the period in which it was produced – when this type of image was common – and the technology available at the time.

The colour palette is pale and light, allowing the bright red of the logo and the slogan to stand out. This use of red emphasises the 'Coke' brand and is consistent with its house style.

The language uses many codes typical of the advertising genre:

- An imperative, 'Drink Coca-Cola', to sell the product
- Alliteration, 'real refreshment… delicious drink', for emphasis. The adjectives 'refreshing' and 'delicious' have often been used in advertising for Coke.
- Descriptive adjectives such as 'pure' and 'wholesome' stress the benefits of the drink, and together with the representations of the fit people in the illustration, anchor the message that Coke is nourishing.

Representation

The dominant main image is of a young, stereotypically attractive female.

Visual codes are clear: a fitted white tennis dress, short hair, make-up and racket construct a representation of a healthy, sporty, feminine woman.

The images construct representations of active females, but the males seem dominant. The umpire is male. A male arm is foregrounded on the right-hand of the page, holding or pulling the female, whose gaze is directed towards him. This connotes that the women have less power than the men.

Quickfire 3.6

What messages about the Coke brand does the logo communicate?

Quickfire 3.7

What are the connotations of the colours red and white in this advert?

Social and historical context

This advert reflects the prosperous period after the Second World War when people enjoyed increased leisure time and had disposable income to spend on activities such as belonging to a sports club.

The 1960s was a time of great social change as both the feminist and civil rights movements were gaining momentum, leading eventually to a greater degree of gender and racial equality. Nonetheless, this advert constructs a representation of a group of white, middle-class characters where the males seem dominant, reflecting more traditional and stereotypical views of the world.

Analysing an example: Morris Oxford advert, 1959

The advert is for a family car and is aimed at couples, incorporating elements of hard- and soft-sell techniques. Brand values are established: comfort, safety, good design.

Media language

The layout divides the page into thirds.

The grey colour palette is typical of the period, when adverts were not always printed in colour.

The slogan: 'Who says dreams never come true!' is aspirational as the car is a 'dream', but connotes that the dream car is achievable. This **rhetorical question** engages the audience and encourages them to think about whether they could also afford the car.

This idea is reinforced in the more detailed copy 'This is where dreams-for-two come true…'. The aspirational nature of the product is reinforced by hyperbolic language: 'superb', 'finest'.

The image of the couple reinforces the idea of the dream. They are looking off the page as if wistfully imagining their new car. The use of fading and light and shadow creates a romantic atmosphere and connotes a narrative where this couple are planning an ideal future for their family, a situation that an audience might identify with.

Activity 3.3

The Coca-Cola website states that the brand in this period was associated with 'fun, friends and good times'. How are these values shown in the language in the advert? Find a recent Coca-Cola advert and compare the values. Write a paragraph summarising your ideas.

This is the new Morris Oxford! This is where dreams-for-two come true in one dramatically beautiful car:

For her . . . her kind of car for *their* family: luxurious, sensible, safe. Long, low lines and gayer colours, with wide-vista vision and sofa-soft seats in its big bright interior.

For him . . . his sort of car for *their* means: sparkling performance with economy, superb roadholding—and the finest features and value ever built into a Morris.

Who says dreams never come true!

* Long, low lithe . . . beauty from end-to-end.
* Fashion-plate colours and duotones.
* Big-muscled performance . . . with economy.
* Full family comfort.
* Panoramic-plus vision all round.
* 'Safety Drive' features for family confidence.
* Holiday-size luggage trunk.

ALL THIS—AND MORRIS VALUE TOO!

 Together . . . you'll choose the

"QUALITY FIRST"
NEW MORRIS OXFORD
SERIES V

PRICES FROM £575 (PLUS £288.17 PURCHASE TAX)

Twelve Months' Warranty and backed by B.M.C. Service—the most comprehensive in Europe.

MORRIS MOTORS LIMITED, COWLEY, OXFORD
London Distributors: Morris House, Berkeley Square, W.1.
Overseas Business: Nuffield Exports Ltd., Oxford and at 41-46, Piccadilly, London, W.1.

Activity 3.4

What similarities and differences can you identify in the layout and design of the Morris advert compared with the Coke advert? Why do you think the producers have constructed the layout in this way?

Key Term

Rhetorical question
A question that does not require an answer as the answer is implied, which is used to create a particular effect and involve the audience as they 'know' the answer.

Quickfire 3.8

Why do you think many historical adverts included a large amount of written copy compared with contemporary examples?

Activity 3.5

The written copy of the Morris advert is split into 'his' and 'hers', for example:

- 'Her kind of car for *their* family: luxurious, sensible, safe'.
- 'His sort of car for *their* means': 'roadholding', 'economy', 'value'.

How does this text reinforce gender stereotypes? How does the use of gender stereotypes reflect the social context of the period?

Stretch and Challenge 3.3

Research Britain in the 1950s in a little more detail. This will also help you to contextualise the set product.

Quickfire 3.9

Find examples of other adverts that include rhetorical questions. Why have they been used?

Quickfire 3.10

What is the brand identity of the Fiat 500?

Representation

The image of the man and woman constructs a representation of a middle-aged couple, the target audience for the product. The advert implies that they have children, reinforcing stereotypes of a traditional family.

The female is positioned behind the male and she is looking up, smiling and gazing at the male as he gazes into the distance. This connotes that the female depends on the male to buy and drive the car, while the male is more independent and in control, reflecting stereotypical gender roles.

The notion of the couple is maintained throughout the advert with phrases such as 'dreams-for-two' and 'together… you'll choose'. This upholds traditional values and stresses that the car is suitable for both partners.

The description of the car at the bottom of the advert incorporates gendered language to personify the car. 'Lithe… beauty from end to end' suggests a feminine aspect to the car while 'big-muscled performance' is much more masculine, extending the appeal to both males and females.

Social and historical context

The advert reinforces many dominant messages and values of the period in which it was produced. At the time, women were more likely to be housewives and mothers while their husbands worked and controlled the family finances.

The advert was produced in 1959, a time when Britain was becoming more prosperous after the war. The economy was strong, jobs were plentiful and, as a result, many families were able to buy consumer goods such as cars for the first time. So, the idea communicated in the advert that the Morris Oxford is an affordable dream or luxury, clearly reflects the historical and social context.

Contemporary Advertisements

Adverts today use many codes and conventions similar to those in the historical examples, but there are clear differences. The following examples demonstrate stylistic developments in the genre, due in large part to the availability of new technologies. You will notice a difference in elements of media language, such as more varied colour palettes, modern typography and edited images. The context is also important too, as many of the representations and messages reflect modern society and culture, and the adverts often address their audiences in more informal and direct ways. Contemporary advertising campaigns tend to feature representations of a wider range of social groups, showing diversity and greater equality in society.

Analysing an example: Fiat 500 adverts, 2014

Media language

The adverts use the format of a style feature from a magazine. This intertextual referencing is designed to appeal to a young, fashion-conscious audience.

The two adverts use a similar layout but are clearly aimed at different audiences – male and female. There is a strong central image and some detailed information about each car in the copy, similar to a fashion article.

The Fiat logo is placed bottom right, which is a prominent position on the page, but does not dominate. '500 Spring/Summer Collection' references the fashion theme and the bright colours also connote summer.

At the end of the paragraph of information about each car there is a further intertextual reference to the fashion feature genre: 'monogrammed socks model's own'. This creates humour, as the items are not actually visible.

The typeface selected for the slogans is a modern white, sans-serif font that is rounded and bold – it stands out from the coloured background and connotes informality, reinforcing the brand identity.

The image of the car is central but in the 'Sport Up' advert it is partly behind the male, while in the 'Life's Too Short' version the female is sitting on it. The message seems to be that the car is an accessory to these people's lives and is important to their image, reinforced by the slogan 'Life's too short to wear a boring car'.

'Life's too short…' is a common phrase in contemporary culture, reflecting a philosophy of making everything in life count and 'seizing the moment'. Here, the phrase is used to 'justify' the choice of a fashionable or exciting car. This also relates to women's magazines, in particular, which often offer advice and positive messages along these lines.

Quickfire 3.11

List the intertextual references in the two Fiat 500 adverts.

Quickfire 3.12

Find these adverts online to see them in detail. How do they use hard- and soft-sell techniques? Give examples.

Activity 3.6

- List all the similarities and differences between the Fiat 500 adverts and the Morris advert from 1959.
- Summarise the key ways in which the genre of car advertising has changed.

Use of media language to construct representations of gender

Advert	'Life's Too Short to Wear a Boring Car'	'Sport Up'
Audience	Female	Male
Colour palette	Feminine, warm colours – purple, orange, bright yellow car.	Masculine, cooler colours – turquoise, green, bright red car.
Model	Young, tall, slender female, aspirational figure but also relatable.	Young, slim, dark-haired male, relatable figure, not a celebrity.
Dress codes	1960s/70s-influenced fashion in a black and white colour palette set against a brightly coloured background. This is reinforced by the feminine swirls on the hat, large sunglasses and large flowers on the top.	Red, white and blue colour palette. Clothes are fashionably bright and sporty, e.g. red and white trainers. The hat is stylish and has possible references to film stars from the gangster genre.
Slogan	• Long, informal and chatty to engage the female target audience. • The selection of the verb 'wear' directly references fashion.	Short and punchy to engage the male target audience, mentions sport.
Language	• Multiple informal references to the 1970s theme, e.g. 'rocking the retro vibe', 'old skool'. • Use of the adjective 'yummy' is quite childlike and alliterative with the word 'yellow', connoting girlishness and playfulness. • Limited technical terminology; many features of the car are linked to design or colour. • Use of hyperbole – 'super-smooth pool ball design gear knob', 'super low emissions' – is persuasive and reinforces the positive features of the car.	• Informal sporting references, 'Dirk is so game-on' to anchor the meanings in the images and slogan. • The use of the popular phrase 'take… to the next level' connotes a sense of achievement and exclusivity. • Technical terms, e.g. '16" alloy wheels' and 'CO_2 emissions'. • Many persuasive hyperbolic terms to 'sell' the image of car – 'sleek… stunning…' – and sport features, such as the spoiler, are emphasised.
Representation	• The name 'Sandra P' possibly references the character Sandy in the popular 1978 film, Grease, which featured a song 'Sandra Dee'. • The female is passive, posing on her car, with an open posture and smiling widely.	• The name 'Dirk' is hard and monosyllabic, connoting masculinity. • The male is active, jumping in mid-air with wide open posture and an enthusiastic smile.

Quickfire 3.13

Describe the mode of address in the Fiat 500 adverts.

Theoretical perspectives on representation, and feminist approaches

The gender representations in the Fiat adverts conform to stereotypes in many ways: for example the female conforms to stereotypical ideas of an attractive woman who is interested in fashion whereas the male is sporty and active. The use of more technical language in 'Sport Up' reinforces messages that males are more scientific and technically minded. The use of fashion/design terms in 'Life's Too Short' implies that females are more interested in image.

The adverts demonstrate a progression from the Morris Oxford advert as the female (as well as the male) is independent, owns her own car and is self-reliant, subverting many traditional stereotypes. Nonetheless, the female is passive in comparison with the male and is pictured posing on the car in a way which can be seen to objectify her, although not in an obviously sexual way. This reinforces the idea that women are often represented as passive objects in the media while men are shown to be active.

Analysing an example: Nike *Greatness* campaign

This UK campaign for Nike was launched in the run up to the 2012 London Olympics. It featured various Nike-sponsored British athletes who have achieved success in different sports, including athletics, cycling and basketball. The adverts communicate a message about what it takes to achieve greatness, such as dedication and hard work.

GREATNESS IS THE GIRL NEXT DOOR.

@SHAKESDRAYTON
#MAKEITCOUNT

Stretch and Challenge 3.4

Find other examples of adverts that represent both males and females, and compare the ways in which they construct representations of gender. Use the grid on page 56 to structure your notes.

Key Term

Montage
A collection of different images edited together in one place. Meaning will be communicated through the selection of the individual pictures as well as the overall effect.

The Nike logo appears below the slogan, athlete's name and hashtag, almost as a tick endorsing the message and the athlete. There is no other obvious reference to Nike – no products are prominently displayed – but the 'swoosh' logo is shown on one shot of the athlete's vest. The focus is firmly on the athlete, who reinforces the brand identity.

The main image is a **montage** of images of the sprinter Perri Shakes-Drayton. The athlete is shown in action, moving from right to left, towards the slogan.

Technical codes of lighting draw attention to her muscles, connoting physical strength, and to her determined expression. This creates a powerful representation of a young black woman.

The campaign as a whole constructs positive representations of the athletes, who are shown in active postures, to be focused, strong and determined to achieve. The campaign includes male and female athletes of black and white ethnicity, reflecting diversity in contemporary society and suggesting a message of equality in sport.

Activity 3.7

- How do elements of layout and design, including the use of colour, communicate meanings in the Nike advert?
- Why have these specific images been selected? What representation of the athlete do they construct?
- What messages and values are encoded in the slogan and the hashtag 'Make it count'?

Write up your notes in a piece of discursive writing.

Analysing an example: *This Girl Can* campaign, 2015 onwards

Context

This Girl Can is an example of an awareness-raising promotional campaign, aiming to encourage women to get involved with sport and physical activity. It is not selling a product or service, so the techniques used are very different from adverts for consumer goods. You will need to analyse the set poster in detail and it will also be helpful to analyse further examples, such as the one below, to develop your understanding and skills.

The campaign was launched by Sport England, a public body sponsored by the government's Department for Digital, Culture, Media and Sport. Sport England's research revealed that women take part in sport much less frequently than men. The website, thisgirlcan.co.uk, states, 'We want to help women overcome the fear of judgement that is stopping too many women and girls from joining in.' This fear of judgement could relate to women's concerns about their appearance or their lack of skills and ability to succeed at sport. The campaign includes television and print advertising featuring real women and targets a wide female audience. There is also a social media campaign and a website that tells the stories of how the women featured in the adverts became involved in sport.

Media language

The layout and design of the advert is clear and uncomplicated, focusing on the main image and the direct message of the slogan. This reinforces the fact that these are real women, and aims to create a sense of audience identification which might encourage the viewer to take up sport.

Technical codes: The shot directs attention to the central female as she is in focus; the tennis ball and the top of the net are included in the frame to establish the setting, but are blurred.

Visual codes: The tennis player wears trousers and a T-shirt, implying that specialist sportswear is not necessary. Her T-shirt is pink, she is wearing hooped earrings and her nails are painted, connoting femininity, which is not stereotypically associated with sport.

The slogan adopts the convention used by many advertising campaigns of using a familiar phrase in a new, thought-provoking and humorous way to encourage the audience to think about the message of the advert.

Stretch and Challenge 3.5

Research the *This Girl Can* website to find out more about the background and context of the campaign.

Quickfire 3.14

Describe the type of font used in the *This Girl Can* slogan. Why do you think it has been chosen?

Activity 3.8

What techniques does the 'Talk to the backhand' poster use to encourage females to become involved with sport? Compare this advert with the set *This Girl Can* advert. List the similarities and differences.

Representation

The representations across the *This Girl Can* campaign subvert many stereotypes of sportspeople, who are often shown to be young, muscular and athletic. *This Girl Can* creates positive representations of 'ordinary' people who take part in sport, communicating the message that it is not necessary to conform to the stereotypes of elite sport in order to participate.

The campaign includes representations of different age groups, ethnicities and abilities, and includes social groups that are often under-represented in the media. 'Talk to the backhand' features wheelchair tennis players, for example, demonstrating the inclusive nature of sport.

The adverts select and construct representations of women where the focus is on engaging in activities, rather than competing. The message is the importance of taking part, with no pressure to achieve a particular goal. This reinforces the brand values of *This Girl Can* and creates a message of empowerment.

Cultural context

'Talk to the backhand' references 'Talk to the hand', a phrase that became popular in the 1990s as a way of rejecting, or refusing to listen to, what another person has to say. It is often accompanied by a gesture of putting a hand in front of another person's face to emphasise the point. Here, the phrase has been adapted to include a sporting term, the backhand shot used in tennis. This connotes that the woman is not going to listen to other people's judgements of her; she is participating in sport and overcoming the barriers that might prevent other women or other wheelchair users, for example, from taking part.

The positive representation of disability sport in the media has increased in recent years, especially following the success of the Paralympics in 2012 and 2016, but people with disabilities remain an under-represented social group in the media.

Analysing an example: Samaritans *Men on the Ropes* campaign, 2010

Samaritans is a charity that offers emotional support to people through a confidential telephone helpline. Anyone can call and talk to a Samaritan about any problem that is troubling them. The organisation's recent advertising campaigns have encouraged people to talk and listen to others. Many of these campaigns, including *Men on the Ropes*, have been run in conjunction with Network Rail as a high percentage of suicides occur on railway lines and both organisations want to reduce the number of these cases.

The *Men on the Ropes* campaign was launched in 2010 on World Suicide Prevention Day to raise awareness of Samaritans as an accessible source of confidential non-judgemental support available any time via the helpline. According to the press release from Samaritans, these advertisements were aimed at men between the ages of 25 and 55 as this is the social group that is most likely to die by suicide. A focus of the campaign was on working-class males as this was a group that the organisation found to be particularly at risk.

Quickfire 3.15

How does the 'I am acting my age' poster construct the representation of an older female?

Stretch and Challenge 3.6

Analyse the media language and representations in one of the other *This Girl Can* print adverts.

Quickfire 3.16

How are the polysemic meanings communicated in the title of the campaign *Men on the Ropes*?

Quickfire 3.17

What are the connotations of the use of the colour red in this poster?

Quickfire 3.18

What are the connotations of the slogan 'We're in your corner'?

Stretch and Challenge 3.7

Write a short paragraph analysing how media language communicates meaning in the Samaritans poster.

Quickfire 3.19

Why have the producers used a 'real' person in this lead poster rather than a famous, elite sportsperson?

Quickfire 3.20

Identify three stereotypes associated with boxing. How does this poster uphold and/or subvert those stereotypical ideas?

A note from Samaritans

NB: The contact number in the image has been replaced with the new free number, 116 123.
Samaritans is available round the clock, every day of the year. You can talk to them for free, any time, in your own way, about whatever's getting to you.
Call on 116 123
Email jo@samaritans.org
Visit – find your nearest branch on Samaritans.org.

In addition to the lead poster of David White, an IT contractor and amateur boxer, case studies included an international rugby referee and a former professional footballer.

The adverts subvert the traditional idea that showing emotion is a sign of weakness in men. Instead, they communicate a message that talking about and addressing problems demonstrates strength.

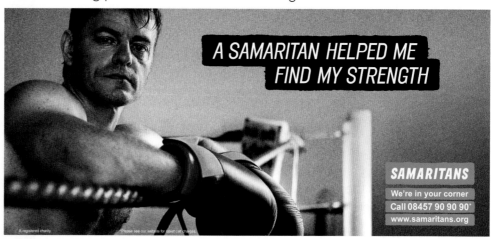

Media language

Visual codes, such as the natural lighting, dull colour palette and 'grainy' image, create a sense of realism that can help to make the advert more believable.

The selection of a 'real' person, similar to the *This Girl Can* set product, connotes that this issue can affect anyone and therefore might offer a sense of personal identification to men in a similar position.

The medium shot shows the man's serious facial expression, and the sweat on his brow denotes physical exertion but also connotes anxiety.

The use of personal pronouns to address the audience directly connotes a sense of openness and lack of judgement. The messages could help to break down the barriers men might encounter when talking about their problems.

There is no other information given about the man, creating an enigma code, and perhaps encouraging people to find out more, whether about the problems this 'masculine' man has had help with or about other issues that Samaritans can support.

Representations

Boxing is a stereotypically masculine endeavour and this male is framed from a slightly low angle to appear strong and powerful.

The slogan 'A Samaritan Helped Me Find My Strength' anchors this image. The man (David White) appears to be literally leaning on the ropes for support and has gained help from the charity to overcome problems and become 'strong'.

This representation of a physically active man is quite different from the idealised images found in many magazines and adverts for consumer goods, in order to create a realistic image appropriate to the charity campaign.

The message of this advert and the campaign is that men – including those who appear confident and powerful – need to talk and that this is not a weakness, which subverts stereotypical ideas of working-class masculinity. The purpose of the poster is to try to change perceptions of masculinity and men's mental 'strength' and encourage men to talk about issues that trouble them.

Context

The *Men on the Ropes* campaign reflects contemporary social contexts through the idea of the crisis of masculinity, as many males in society no longer have the traditional role of the main breadwinner in their homes, which can lead to low self-esteem. Many people have had money problems in recent years following the financial crisis in 2008. There were many redundancies, leaving some people suffering extreme anxiety and depression. While there is increased awareness of the importance of mental health, as well as physical health, in contemporary society there is still some misunderstanding about how this significant issue affects people, perhaps men in particular. Samaritans' work plays a key part in addressing this.

Activity 3.9

Design an advert for a new product, perhaps a chocolate bar or soft drink.
- Consider your brand – what are its values and how will you establish its identity?
- Identify a target audience.
- Design a logo.
- Write a slogan.

Then draft an advert for your product, paying close attention to:
- Layout and design
- Images
- Use of language.

Print Marketing: Film Posters

The marketing and promotion of a film includes a range of activities that will be considered in Section B as part of the study of media industries. For Section A you will study film posters in relation to media language and representation. You will examine a historical and a contemporary example and consider the way in which conventions and representations have changed over time.

A film marketing campaign aims to create a 'buzz' around the film's release to encourage audiences to watch it in the cinema. If a film is new and individual, the poster needs to clearly communicate key information about the genre, narrative and characters in order to appeal to the audience. If the film is part of a well-known **franchise**, the **distributors** will include familiar elements to draw in an audience of loyal fans, as well as trying to gain interest from potential viewers who have not seen the previous films.

Advertising for a film, especially a high-budget film from a **major Hollywood studio**, will usually include the release of different posters in a range of formats, and in different countries. The campaign might begin with a **'teaser'** poster followed by main theatrical posters nearer the film's release date.

Stretch and Challenge 3.8

Analyse the ways in which your advert from Activity 3.9 uses genre conventions and representations to communicate a message to the target audience.

Key Terms

Franchise
A series of films based on an original idea or an adaptation of, for example, a book. Recent examples include the *Star Wars*, Harry Potter and *Lord of the Rings* films.

Distributor
The company that markets the film and organises the distribution of the film to cinemas and for DVD release.

Major Hollywood studio
A large film production company such as Warner Bros. These studios have large budgets to spend on films, but also need to ensure that their films are successful and make a profit. The Hollywood film industry consists of a number of 'major' studios as well as several smaller companies.

'Teaser'
A poster or web advert that initiates interest in a film, for example, by offering an intriguing detail of the film but with little else. This 'teases' the audience and encourages them to actively look out for more information.

Quickfire 3.21

Name some other film franchises from recent years.

This poster for *Paddington 2* demonstrates many film poster codes and conventions.

Codes and conventions of film posters

Film title: The title will communicate an immediate message about the film, and the choice of typography will also convey information. When you examine a poster, consider the positioning of the title – it will usually be prominently placed.

Tagline: A short phrase or slogan that captures the key ideas or themes of the film.

Main image: This might be a single image or an edited montage of images that encapsulate key elements of the film such as the genre, characters and narrative to appeal to the target audience.

Billing block: This is the list of credits at the bottom of the poster detailing the production companies, main actors, director, writers, producers and other key roles such as music, costumes, cinematography and production design.

Star billing: Posters often feature the names of the main stars in a film as these are a major attraction to an audience.

Release date: The date for the first screenings is usually featured, but 'teaser' posters might simply state 'coming soon' or 'this summer'. This creates a sense of enigma and encourages the audience to be active in seeking out further information about the film and when it will be shown.

Company names: The production companies and distributors will be listed, usually at the bottom of the poster.

Technical information about the exhibition formats, such as 3D or IMAX, might be included, usually under the release date.

Logo: A film or franchise might have an easily identifiable logo, for example the iconic 007 logo for the Bond franchise.

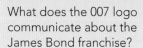

Stretch and Challenge 3.9

Find some examples of teaser and theatrical release posters for different films. Make notes of the similarities and differences between them.

Quickfire 3.22

What does the 007 logo communicate about the James Bond franchise?

Stretch and Challenge 3.10

Research and analyse further examples of the marketing campaigns for *Spectre*. Make notes on how the advertising campaign as a whole creates a 'house style' and establishes the brand values.

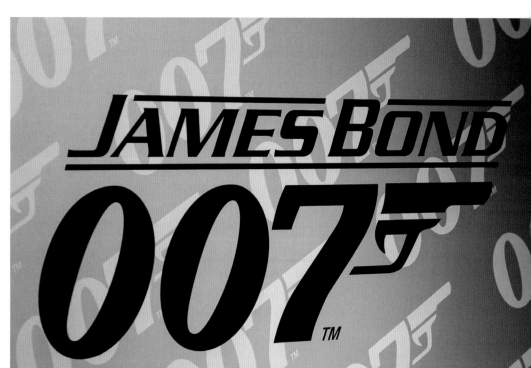

Analysing an example: *Star Wars: The Force Awakens*, 2015

Codes and conventions

Star Wars is one of the most famous franchises in film history. The original **title** is prominent and the name of the latest instalment, *The Force Awakens*, is smaller and placed between the words of the main title. Many people will recognise the *Star Wars* title, so this will attract the attention of a wide audience. Fans will be aware of the new title and its significance, having prior knowledge of 'the force'. The typeface is quite 'retro' and references the earlier films in the franchise. Yellow and black is a combination of colours that stands out on the poster.

The **main image** is a montage of characters and robots, which is similar to some earlier *Star Wars* film posters such as *The Return of the Jedi*, so will be familiar to fans of the franchise. Some of the characters are also familiar.

The sci-fi genre is clearly established through the iconography of colour, lightsabres, droids and the space setting. The active poses, explosions and guns also connote the action genre, as this film is a hybrid.

Narrative: There are connotations of binary oppositions through the use of light and dark, red and blue. This also creates enigma.

Billing block: 'Lucas Film' – large ensemble cast. While some of the actors are famous, no one is given a star billing elsewhere on the poster.

Release date: December 18 – the week before Christmas. Clearly the film is a major release or **'tentpole' film**.

Technical information: In 3D, IMAX… Technology is used to appeal, and many loyal fans might watch the film in more than one format.

Analysing a historical example: *Star Wars*, 1977

Media language

Star Wars was released in 1977. The original film is now known as *Star Wars Episode IV: A New Hope*.

The main image dominates the poster and establishes the narrative and themes of the film. The title is relatively small and placed bottom right, a prominent position on the page. The name suggests that this is a **high-concept** film with wide audience appeal.

The tagline 'A long time ago in a galaxy far, far away…' intertextually references children's stories and fairy tales. It acts as an introduction and gives us key information about the time and place in which the film is set and suggests that it might be intended for a young audience.

Quickfire 3.23

Why do film posters use enigmas?

Key Terms

Billing block
The list of the main cast and crew members, such as star actors and director.

'Tentpole' film
A very high-budget film, usually from a major producer, expecting large audiences.

High-concept
Emphasis on a striking but easily communicable central premise, designed to have wide audience appeal.

A long time ago in a galaxy far, far away...

STAR WARS

TWENTIETH CENTURY-FOX Presents
A LUCASFILM LTD. PRODUCTION
STAR WARS
Starring MARK HAMILL · HARRISON FORD · CARRIE FISHER
PETER CUSHING
and
ALEC GUINNESS
Written and Directed by GEORGE LUCAS Produced by GARY KURTZ Music by JOHN WILLIAMS

The visual codes are highly significant. The poster is dominated by a large image that is a graphical montage, and the contrast between light and dark is very striking. The **rule of thirds** can be applied as the figure of Luke Skywalker is placed on a vertical line while the ball of light is at an intersection and the light forms two clear lines at the top of the frame.

The narrative is clearly signified, supported by the title, as the light and dark connotes a battle between good and evil.

Science fiction genre conventions are used, such as the darkness connoting deep space, the other-worldly shapes, the robots and the light sabre and laser gun props. These conventions are futuristic and seem to contradict the tagline, which tells us that the story is set in the past. This creates enigma for the audience and potentially engages their interest.

Theoretical perspectives: Applying Propp's theory of narrative

Skywalker's dominant position in the frame, white dress codes and use of the light sabre all clearly establish him as the hero. The female character is also dressed in white and positioned below Skywalker as though she is being protected by him: this connotes that she is the 'princess', in need of rescue. These 'good' characters are overshadowed by the huge dark shape of the helmet of Darth Vader, connoting that he will be the villain.

These visual codes suggest that the hero is on a quest and the villain will prove to be a major obstacle that he has to overcome, a familiar feature of action films. The story of David and Goliath is possibly referenced here, while the light surrounding Skywalker and the cross shape formed by the light sabre connotes him as a saviour. These familiar elements should appeal to a wide audience.

Representation

Luke is represented as a stereotypical male hero: he is lithe, and his active posture suggests power and dominance. The open shirt reveals his muscles, reinforcing his strength and potentially appealing to a heterosexual female audience.

Princess Leia is in a more passive pose, kneeling at a lower level than the male. Her tight-fitting, low-cut dress with long splits suggest that she is an object to be looked at, with potential appeal to a heterosexual male audience.

These representations support feminist perspectives to an extent, although the fact that Princess Leia is holding a weapon suggests that she will not be completely passive in the narrative, but probably less significant than the male.

Key Terms

Rule of thirds
A framing technique – if a frame is divided into a 3-by-3 grid, objects along the vertical and horizontal lines or at the intersections have dominance.

Quickfire 3.24

Which narrative theory could apply to the use of light and dark in the *Star Wars* poster?

Activity 3.10

Compare media language and representations in the *Star Wars* posters.

Magazines

Magazines are publications that include a collection of articles on a particular topic or theme. The set products – *Pride* and *GQ* – are two front covers of print magazines, but most magazines now have an online version as well.

Magazines cover a range of genres: the set products are **lifestyle magazines**, but many other types of publication are available including fashion, gossip, music, sport and special interests.

The cover of a magazine is important as it needs to grab the attention of a potential reader in a shop or at a **newsstand**. Hundreds of different magazines are published every month and the magazine industry is very competitive, so each title has to create a clear brand identity to appeal to its target audience. The cover needs to include familiar elements to appeal to loyal readers and have features to attract new readers.

Key Terms

Lifestyle magazine
A publication that covers a range of topics related to readers' lives, such as fashion, travel, health and money.

Newsstand
A place where magazines and newspapers are displayed for sale; in a shop or at a railway station kiosk for example.

Magazines have to compete for attention in a crowded newsstand like this one in central London.

Codes and conventions of magazine covers

The main codes of print products detailed at the beginning of Chapter 3 also apply to magazine front covers:

- **Layout and design**:
  - The cover of a magazine usually features a masthead at the top of the page (centred or left) and a main central image surrounded by **cover lines**. The cover lines usually skirt around the main image but might overlap it.
  - The left-hand side is the visible section at a crowded newsstand, so it is important that this part stands out.
  - Different genres will have specific codes of layout – some magazines have much more detail and information on the front cover than others.
- **Main image:** This will relate to the genre of magazine. A cycling magazine will usually feature a cyclist, for example. Lifestyle magazines often feature a celebrity or **elite person** to appeal to readers.
- **Minor images:** Some magazine covers also feature smaller images relating to different cover lines.
- **Technical codes:** The focus is usually on the main image. Consider the type of shot, the lighting, layering of images and how this communicates with the reader. Some magazine images may be edited, in post-production to create a 'flawless' effect.
- **Visual codes:**
  - The colour palette is often important to the house style of the magazine. Many lifestyle magazines will have a different colour scheme for each edition and it is interesting to compare the Christmas edition, for example, with a summer edition.
  - The dress codes and gesture codes of the cover model on men's and women's lifestyle magazines are significant, as this is usually the main feature of the front cover.
- **Typography:** Each magazine will have a particular style of typography that reflects its house style and brand image.

Key Terms

Cover lines
The short 'headlines' on a magazine cover that give readers a brief insight into the content of the articles.

Elite person
A celebrity or person of high status that will appeal to target readers.

Quickfire 3.25

What does the typography on the *National Geographic* cover connote about the magazine?

National Geographic and *Time* are well-established brands and use a bold colour border around each front cover, which is eye-catching and recognisable.

- **Language codes and mode of address:** Many lifestyle magazines in particular adopt a direct mode of address, for example through the use of personal pronouns, questions and imperatives. The cover model normally looks directly towards the reader. This helps to involve the reader and engages them with the product.

- **Masthead:**
  - The name usually communicates a message about the magazine – for example the name *Vogue* connotes the brand values of fashion, style and sophistication through the choice of this French word.
  - The style of the masthead also conveys messages about the magazine. The *Vogue* masthead uses a classic serif font and it is always placed at the top of the magazine cover, covering its entire width. The colour used for the masthead changes to match the colour palette of the edition and reflects the idea of changing fashions.
  - Some magazines always feature the masthead in full; others will sometimes position the cover model over the masthead, which connotes that the magazine name is recognisable even if part of the masthead is covered.

- **Strapline:** A short phrase usually placed close to the masthead that communicates the brand values of the magazine.

- **Cover lines:**
  - These work like headlines that summarise the content of the main articles in the magazine.
  - They are usually placed around the main image and give readers a hint of what is inside without giving away too much information or taking up too much space.
  - They might use **exclamatives** or other linguistic techniques to attract the reader's attention.
  - Cover lines might also indicate the viewpoints and values of the magazine.

- **Puff:** A graphical feature that promotes the content of the magazine to persuade the reader to buy/read the magazine. The puff might be displayed as a banner or circle that resembles a 'sticker'.

- **Date of publication, barcode, price:** The use of these conventions will vary according to the genre of magazine and the target audience.

The *Vogue* masthead might change colour, but its font, size and position are consistent.

Stretch and Challenge 3.11

Find some examples of other magazine mastheads and analyse the brand values connoted.

Top Tip

Learn the subject-specific terminology for magazines and use this when analysing other products.

Key Term

Exclamatives
Words or phrases that 'shout out' to the reader, often using an exclamation mark for emphasis. The intended effect might be to shock or surprise the reader.

Stretch and Challenge 3.12

Conduct some research online or visit a newsagent's shop. How many men's and women's lifestyle magazines can you identify?

Set products: lifestyle magazine genre

Pride is a monthly women's magazine targeting a specialised audience of women of colour.

GQ is a monthly men's magazine targeting a large audience of men.

Women's lifestyle magazines

Women's magazines have been in existence for many years and cover a range of different subgenres including:

- 'glossy' monthlies such as *Cosmopolitan* and *Marie Claire*; fashion magazines such as *Vogue*
- weekly magazines such as *Woman* and *Grazia*
- home-focused publications such as *Good Housekeeping* and *Woman and Home*.

Each magazine will target a specific audience. Some magazines are aimed at an older or younger audience, for example, and each will have a clear sense of the socio-economic background of the readers, which will be reflected in elements such as the price and the advertising as well as the content.

Women's magazines became very popular after the Second World War and were especially successful in the 1960s when around 12 million copies of women's magazines were sold each week. There are many more magazines available now and, despite the decline in print circulation, women's magazines are still very popular.

The **codes and conventions** typical of women's magazines are as follows:

- There is often a focus on stereotypically female interests such as fashion, beauty, relationships, health, travel, cookery and home features.
- Advice columns feature in many publications and women's magazines are often described as being a 'friend' to the reader, offering positive support and guidance about contemporary life.
- These magazines are also aspirational, especially the 'glossies', and can be seen to create an 'ideal' lifestyle that women might desire to have.
- The inclusion of celebrities and features on desirable fashion items, for example, supports this idea of aspiration, and the advertising might reinforce **consumerist messages** – that readers can buy aspects of an ideal life.

Men's lifestyle magazines

Magazines for men have also been in existence for many years, but the men's lifestyle magazine came to popularity in the 1980s. At this time there were several new publications in the UK, including *FHM* and *GQ*. This can be linked to social changes as, at this time, the notion of the **new man** arose and there was a growth in the market for male fashion, styling and grooming products. These new magazines began by offering fashion and style advice to men in the way that magazines such as *Cosmopolitan* did for women.

Quickfire 3.26
Why do you think there has been a decline in the circulation of print magazines recently?

Stretch and Challenge 3.13
Look at a range of women's lifestyle magazines and identify how many include typical codes and conventions.

Stretch and Challenge 3.14
How does *Pride* magazine subvert consumerist messages?

Key Terms

Consumerist messages
Ideas that it is necessary to buy products and other goods, usually to achieve a particular lifestyle.

New man
A phrase that originates from the 1980s to describe a man who does not conform to masculine stereotypes, for example, by being willing to do domestic tasks and look after the children.

Quickfire 3.27

What typical features of a women's lifestyle magazine are shown on the set cover of *Pride*?

As time progressed, these publications developed into more general lifestyle magazines and, from the 1990s, new magazines such as *Loaded* were launched. At this time, many men's magazines gained a reputation for sexually objectifying women. Some people argued that 'lads' mags' like *Loaded* were a reaction against the feminist movement and reflected the **crisis of masculinity** as men's role in society was no longer secure.

The idea of masculinity in crisis was also represented in other media products at the time. The film *The Full Monty* explored the issue of unemployment as a group of male steelworkers are made redundant and struggle to find new identities and make ends meet. Eventually they form a striptease act, in extreme opposition to their former roles in the manufacturing industry.

However, these 'lads' mags' have been in decline for a number of years (*Loaded* closed in 2013). There are still several men's lifestyle magazines in publication, but they have not been as popular as women's magazines and, while there are many music and sports magazines aimed primarily at a male audience, there are fewer general lifestyle magazines for men.

Image used under licence from Pride Magazine

The set products: *Pride* and *GQ*

Pride is a women's monthly lifestyle magazine published by Pride Media, a British company. It has been published in the UK since 1991 and was the first ever UK monthly black publication. *Pride's* Facebook page describes it as 'a monthly lifestyle glossy magazine aimed at the aspirational woman of colour'.

It has a readership of 146 000 per month and over 60 per cent of its readers are university graduates (details from the 2015 *Pride* media pack on pridemagazine.com).

The magazine includes sections on news, entertainment, hair and beauty and fashion. The features clearly target the specialised audience and there are many empowering representations of black women. The magazine also explores serious issues that target readers might relate to.

GQ is an award-winning men's monthly lifestyle magazine published by Condé Nast, a major global magazine publisher. It was originally published in the USA as *Gentlemen's Quarterly* and launched in the UK in 1988. The magazine includes sections on fashion, grooming, culture and relationships. There are also regular features on politics, sport, cars and fitness, which could be considered stereotypically male interests. British *GQ* has a readership of over 400 000 and a **circulation** of 114 000. The average age of the reader is 34; 80 per cent of its readers are ABC1 (see page 32) (statistics from the 2018 *GQ* media pack, condenast.com).

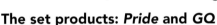

Key Terms

Crisis of masculinity
The idea that males suffered uncertainties of identity as women gained more power in society. It can also be linked to a decline in typically masculine jobs in manufacturing.

Circulation
The number of copies of a magazine or newspaper issue sold. The **readership** is the number of people who read each issue, which is usually higher than the circulation.

Stretch and Challenge 3.15

Can you identify any examples of the crisis of masculinity in other media products you have studied?

Quickfire 3.28

What typical features of a men's lifestyle magazine are shown on the set cover of *GQ*?

Stretch and Challenge 3.16

How does the set cover of *Pride* reflect its contemporary social context?

Quickfire 3.29

Why is a publication's readership usually much higher than the circulation figure?

Stretch and Challenge 3.17

Research the *Pride* and *GQ* media packs in more detail and think about how each cover appeals to the audience of the magazine.

Analysing an example: *Elle*, November 2016

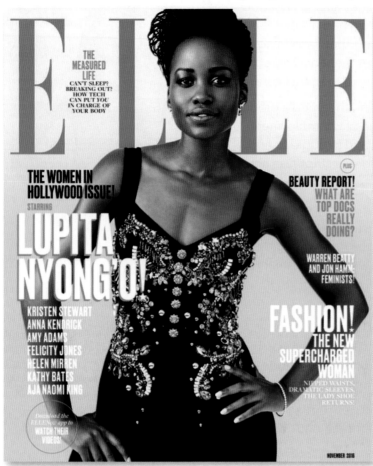

By kind permission Dan Martensen / Elle US

Media language

The layout and design is typical of a women's magazine front cover:

- The masthead covers the top third of the page, recognisable despite being partly behind the image of the cover model.
- The main image dominates the page; the straight camera shot and direct mode of address engage the reader.
- Cover lines overlap the main image, although the body is mostly visible.
- The 'puff', bottom left, encourages the reader to interact with the app.

The colour palette is red, white and black on a grey background. These are bold shades often considered to be masculine colours used here to connote female strength and empowerment.

The font used for the cover lines is sans-serif and contemporary, in contrast to the more traditional font of the masthead. This might suggest that *Elle* is moving forwards while retaining traditional values. The main cover line is larger and has a shadow for added emphasis.

The language includes many techniques to appeal to the reader: personal pronouns, rhetorical questions, exclamatives.

Representation of gender and ethnicity

The cover model is Lupita Nyong'o, featured in the 'Women in Hollywood Issue'. Nyong'o is a major Hollywood star; she won an Oscar for her role in *12 Years a Slave* and had a leading role in *Star Wars: The Force Awakens*. The publishers have selected a black cover model (most of the actresses listed are white), which is still relatively rare in mainstream lifestyle magazines.

The image represents Nyong'o as a strong, successful woman. This is connoted by her open and confident posture, especially the placing of her hands on her hips.

The dress codes reinforce this representation, as the embellishments connote luxury but the dress is not especially figure hugging or revealing. Nyong'o's hair, make-up and jewellery are subtle and she is not sexually objectified. She is represented as an attractive and powerful young black woman, a positive and aspirational **role model**.

The cover lines support the notion of empowering women. They feature stereotypically feminine topics such as fashion and beauty, but language such as 'Supercharged Woman' connotes strength and success while the 'Measured Life' feature suggests that women can take control of their bodies.

The reference to actors Warren Beatty and Jon Hamm as feminists is an intriguing cover line as both are famous for playing dominant and patriarchal characters, but this also reinforces the idea of female empowerment.

Quickfire 3.30

How does the use of language on this *Elle* cover appeal to the reader?

Key Term

Role model
A person in a position of authority or prominence who provides a good example to others.

Stretch and Challenge 3.18

How could you apply feminist perspectives to this front cover of *Elle*?

Analysing an example: *Square Mile*, 7 July 2015

Square Mile is a luxury lifestyle magazine that targets a specialised audience, primarily people who work in the financial district known as the City of London. The title of the magazine refers to the colloquial name for the City, which covers an area of approximately one square mile.

Representation of gender and ethnicity

The layout and design of the front cover suggests that the audience for *Square Mile* is predominantly male, reinforcing the traditional notion that business and finance are male-dominated industries.

The main image and cover line feature the boxer Anthony Joshua. At the time of publication Joshua was already a successful sports star, having won a gold medal at the 2012 Olympics and was beginning to make a name for himself in the professional ring.

The cover line 'The British boxing prodigy takes on the world one knockout at a time' reinforces values of patriotism, competitiveness and success that potentially reflect the beliefs of the target audience of 'City' workers.

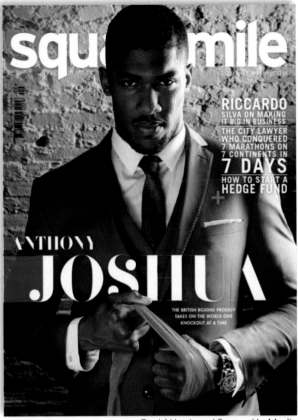

David Harrison / Square Up Media

The main image constructs a strongly masculine representation:

- Joshua's facial expression and direct mode of address suggest that he is a serious young man. He looks down slightly towards the audience, connoting superiority, while his powerful, square posture and closed fist suggest that he is poised and ready for action.

- His smartly tailored suit highlights his physique and connotes that he takes pride in his appearance. The red hand wrap is the only, but significant, visual code that denotes him as a boxer. It is pulled tight, connoting his strength. The luxury watch reinforces an image of success and wealth, likely to appeal to affluent readers of the magazine who might aspire to a similar lifestyle and appearance of success.

- The key light is positioned to the side, bathing the left half of Joshua's face in light while the right side is more shadowed, connoting that he is a successful young man and a 'bright' celebrity, but also a determined competitor in a highly physical, challenging, potentially dangerous sport.

The front cover constructs a representation of Anthony Joshua that embodies masculine stereotypes of physical strength and power, arguably demonstrating some elements of the **hypermasculine** male, but the dress codes are more typical of business than sport. Joshua is shown to be stylish and well groomed, reflecting a more contemporary notion of male identity. The cover challenges some of the negative media misrepresentations of minority ethnic groups as 'other' (villains, for example) and avoids dress codes that are stereotypical of young black men. It reinforces Joshua's athleticism and sporting prowess, communicating a positive message about a successful young British male.

Stretch and Challenge 3.19

Draft a cover for a new men's or women's lifestyle magazine. Try to include the main conventions and consider how you will represent gender.

Key Term

Hypermasculinity
Exaggerated masculinity, for example extreme strength, aggression or 'macho' behaviour that is sometimes associated with male sports stars.

Stretch and Challenge 3.20

Compare the *Square Mile* cover with the Samaritans poster on page 60.

How does the use of media language in each product:

- Convey messages about masculinity?
- Use boxing to connote meanings about emotional and physical strength?
- Reflect the purpose and context of each product?

Top Tip

Use the headings in the table in Activity 3.11 to analyse other media products in preparation for the unseen analysis in the Component 1 exam.

Activity 3.11

Analyse the use of media language on the *Square Mile* cover using a table like this:

Convention	Example	Analysis
Colour palette	*Red hand wrap, white background wall and font, blue suit.*	*The combination of red, white and blue in the colour palette connotes Britishness and patriotic values.* *Red and blue also connote the boxing ring (the colour of the ropes and 'corners' for each boxer).*
Layout and design		
Masthead		
Typography		
Image		
Language		
Mode of address		

Newspapers

In Section A you will study media language and representations in two set products: the front pages of the *Sun* (18 December 2013) and the *Guardian* (4 September 2015). You should also analyse other newspaper front pages to help you to understand the codes and conventions and see how different newspapers represent events. In Section B you will develop your knowledge and understanding of industries and audiences in relation to the *Sun*.

Newspapers are print publications that report events that are happening in the world. They are published daily in the UK (Monday to Saturday) and many also have a Sunday edition, for example, the *Sun on Sunday*. The *Guardian's* sister paper, the *Observer*, is published on Sundays. Most daily and Sunday newspapers include:

- news stories, placed on the front cover and in the opening pages
- features relating to other cultural and social topics such as entertainment, health and travel
- crosswords and other puzzles
- sports news, placed on the back pages.

Print newspapers have faced competition in recent years from the availability of news in other forms, such as 24-hour television news and online news sites that are constantly updated. It is important for the front page to capture the audience's attention and encourage people to buy the newspaper.

Newspapers are still an important source of information for many people and can influence opinion about what is happening in the world. You will need to consider the way in which newspapers represent events and issues.

Newspapers also tend to lean towards either **right-wing** or **left-wing** political views, which might be evident when they report issues and events such as Brexit and elections. It is important to be aware of a newspaper's political stance as it could affect the way in which an event or social group is represented. Newspapers go through a thorough **editorial process**, as they should ensure they publish factual information and do not include misleading or inaccurate material.

Newspapers can be categorised into different types:

- popular or **tabloid** newspapers such as the *Sun* and the *Mirror*
- **mid-market** tabloid newspapers such as the *Daily Mail* and the *Daily Express*
- quality or **broadsheet** newspapers including the *Guardian*, the *Times* and the *Daily Telegraph*.

Conventions of tabloids and broadsheets

Historically, all newspapers were produced in a large broadsheet format, but, at the beginning of the 20th century, some, such as the *Daily Mirror* were produced as tabloids, approximately half the size of a broadsheet. These became very popular as they were more convenient and easier to read.

Nowadays, most newspapers are published in the smaller, tabloid format (including the *Times*), but the term 'tabloid' has come to be used to describe the populist, 'red top' publications such as the *Mirror*, the *Sun* and the *Star*. The term 'broadsheet' is still used to describe 'quality' newspapers including the *Guardian*, the *Telegraph* and the *Times*.

Each type of newspaper has specific codes and conventions:

- **Layout and design**: A tabloid newspaper's front page will usually be dominated by images and large headlines. The broadsheet front page will also feature images and headlines, but usually also carries a substantial amount of copy relating to the main stories.

Key Terms

Right-wing
Views that are politically right of centre, for example the belief that taxes should be kept low to allow the economy to grow. The Conservative Party is a right-wing political party.

Left-wing
Views that are politically left of centre, for example the belief that wealthy people should pay higher taxes to support people who are poorer. The Labour Party is a left-wing political party.

Editorial process
Newspaper articles are carefully checked before publication to ensure that they conform to the required standards and contain accurate information.

Tabloid
A newspaper format that is half the size of a broadsheet; also refers to the 'popular' press or 'red top' newspapers such as the *Sun*.

Broadsheet
A newspaper in large format; also refers to the 'quality' press, the more formal newspapers such as the *Times*.

Stretch and Challenge 3.21

Look at the front page of a tabloid and a broadsheet from the same day and compare the use of conventions.

Key Terms

Satirise
Newspapers sometimes criticise a public figure such as a politician or celebrity by mocking them or using humour.

Image-to-text ratio
The amount of space dedicated to images compared with text. A high image-to-text ratio means that the images take up much of the space and there is less written copy.

Stretch and Challenge 3.22

Look at some tabloid front pages and try to identify examples of satire.

Quickfire 3.31

Analyse the mastheads for the *Sun* and the *Guardian*. What does each suggest about the newspaper and its brand values?

Stretch and Challenge 3.23

Research the *Sun* and the *Guardian* in a little more detail to find out about the history and target readership for each publication.

- **Headlines**: Tabloid headlines are often short and attention-grabbing, using puns or other language devices to communicate messages quickly. Broadsheets often have longer headlines that convey more information about the issue or event.

- **Coverage of issues**: Tabloids are often said to sensationalise events, identifying elements of a story to emphasise and grab the readers' attention. They might include humour and sometimes **satirise** public figures. Broadsheets are recognised as providing more in-depth coverage of stories and usually adopt a more serious tone.

- **Images**: Both types of newspaper use photographs, although tabloid newspapers have a particularly high **image-to-text ratio**.

- **Written copy**: Tabloids tend to use less copy per article. Broadsheets use more copy and give more detail and background information about issues and events.

- **Language**: Tabloids use a more informal, direct mode of address and colloquial language. Broadsheets use a more formal tone and more complex language.

What do mastheads reveal about a newspaper?

The masthead is the name of the newspaper and communicates important information about the publication and its brand values.

Daily Mail:

- Black title on white background – not a 'red top' but a mid-market tabloid.

- The crest in the middle of the masthead connotes status and tradition, indicating that the newspaper has been in publication for many years.

- This is reinforced by the gothic-style font and suggests that the *Daily Mail* upholds traditional views and values.

- The date, price and tagline are positioned below the title; the tagline 'Newspaper of the Year' reflects status and popularity.

Daily Mirror:

- White title on red background – traditional 'red top'.

- 'Daily' is in upper case 'sitting' on top of 'Mirror' (upper case M, other letters lower case).

- The sans-serif font is contemporary and informal.

- 'Mirror' connotes reporting the news is a way of reflecting what is happening in the world and might suggest that the newspaper values truth.

- Top-right of red box includes date, price and strapline 'Fighting for You'. This adopts a direct mode of address with the personal pronoun and connotes that the newspaper is on the side of the reader (also suggests class struggle as the paper is left-leaning).

Codes and conventions of newspaper front pages

The main codes of print products detailed at the beginning of this chapter also apply to newspaper front pages, but there are also conventions specific to newspapers:

- **Headline**: A phrase that captures the essence of a story. It is usually in a large font and placed in a prominent position. There are many techniques used in newspaper headlines to attract the attention of the reader, including the use of:
  - puns, exclamatives and imperatives
  - well-known phrases and intertextual references
  - other linguistic devices such as hyperbole and direct address.
- **Caption**: A brief explanation placed below an image which helps to anchor its meaning.
- **Standfirst**: The introductory paragraph or section of an article that introduces the main points of the story.
- **Trail:** There might be only the start of the story or article on the front page, with the rest continued inside. This gives space on the front page for large headlines and images and other features.
- **Anchorage** is very important on a newspaper front page. The use of captions will anchor the images and the combination of headline, copy and images will construct a message for the readers.
- **Splash**: The main story on a front page. This is usually a **hard news** story, although on some days a **soft news** story might dominate. Sometimes there is one major story that will feature on all newspaper front pages, but there are often occasions where different newspapers will lead with different stories.
- **Secondary story**: A less important story than the splash, but significant enough to feature on the front page.
- **By-line**: The name of the journalist who wrote the story.
- **Plug**: An advertisement for other items in the newspaper, often placed at the top of the front page; it might feature a promotion or details about further content in the paper.

Top Tip

Make a list of the specific newspaper terminology and use this when analysing all newspaper products.

Key Terms

Hard news
Serious news stories that have national or international importance. Topics such as politics and the economy would be considered hard news.

Soft news
Less serious news that is focused on human interest or celebrity stories. The term 'infotainment' is sometimes used to describe soft news stories.

Analysing front page conventions: *Daily Mirror*, 5 November 2008, election of Barack Obama

The **masthead** includes a poppy to signify recognition of the upcoming Remembrance Day.

The **headline** 'GOBAMA' is a pun: the red 'GO' connotes that the newspaper is supportive of Obama and the headline is punchy and informal, communicating information clearly and concisely.

Splash: The main story covers the entire front page, signifying the importance of the event. The US flag in the background clearly places the story in its geographical location. The low-angle shot of Obama and his serious expression connote dignity and strength, which constructs a positive representation and suggests, under Propp's theory, that he is a hero who has succeeded in his quest.

The **caption** 'PRESIDENT ELECT. Millions turned out for Obama yesterday' anchors the image and the headline, reinforcing the idea that he has the support of the American people.

Standfirst: 'Barack Obama was on the brink of history last night as he looked set to become the first black president of the United States.' This is a clear summary, as the results of the election have not yet been announced.

Language: Use of the noun 'history' connotes the significance of this election within a social, political and historical context. This is a major world event.

Trail: 'Full story inside' encourages readers to buy the newspaper to find out all of the details.

Representing issues and events

Newspapers re-present versions of reality. All newspapers might report the same event, but in different ways by selecting different elements. It is important to consider what has been included but also what has been omitted.

Consider how elements of media language are used to construct a representation of the event. The use of images and language, for example, communicates meanings, and elements such as narrative and character might be used. Some newspapers might focus on the personal angle of an event, while others might consider the political aspects.

The newspaper will communicate particular messages and values: no representation is completely neutral; there will always be an interpretation of the event. Think about how this relates to the newspaper and its political leaning.

Think about the audience for the newspaper and how they might respond to the representations.

Quickfire 3.32

What does the tagline 'Real News... Real Entertainment' connote?

Quickfire 3.33

Identify an example of a plug on the front page. What does this suggest about the audience for the *Daily Mirror*?

Stretch and Challenge 3.24

Summarise, in a short paragraph, how the *Daily Mirror* has represented the election of Obama. Consider the elements of media language that have been selected and combined to communicate a message.

How newspaper headlines create meanings and communicate messages: the General Election announcement, 2017

At the time of this news story, the Conservative Party was in power with a small majority but was ahead in the **opinion polls**. The newspapers reported the election announcement and the headlines communicated messages about the newspapers' interpretation of the event.

- The *Sun*: Right-wing political leaning. A dramatic headline is constructed using a familiar phrase. The use of colour is unusual but adds emphasis to the fact that the newspaper believes that Theresa May and the Conservative Party will win with a significant majority. There is anchorage: the long shot showing Theresa May in front of 10 Downing Street seems to reinforce a message that she should be Prime Minister and supports the newspaper's political stance.

- The *Daily Mail*: Right-wing political leaning. The headline issues an imperative to the Prime Minister, using emotive language, and is supportive of her decision to call the election. The language is forceful and dramatic and draws on history as well as making reference to Brexit negotiations.

- The *Daily Mirror*: Left-wing political leaning. This headline intertextually references a speech by the former Conservative Prime Minister, Margaret Thatcher. This statement will be familiar to many readers and suggests that Theresa May is having a dramatic change of mind in calling the election. The use of the red, upper case 'IS' adds emphasis. This headline constructs a more negative representation of the announcement.

Quickfire 3.34

How do the *Daily Star*, the *Guardian* and the *Times* communicate meanings through the headlines?

Stretch and Challenge 3.25

Write headlines for a broadsheet and a tabloid for a story that has happened in your own community. Use some of the techniques you have identified in newspaper products.

Key Term

Opinion poll
A survey of people's views on a particular topic, such as people's opinions on political parties, carried out by a market research company.

Activity 3.12

Analyse the media language and representations on the front page of the *Sun*:

- Note the selection of the main image and smaller images. What do these connote?
- How does the headline use intertextuality?
- What does the use of the colour purple connote?
- Analyse the use of language.
- What elements of narrative are constructed?
- What 'version' of this event is constructed through the front page?

Compare the front cover of the *Sun* with the *Guardian*. Write a paragraph outlining key similarities and differences.

Comparing representations of issues and events: royal engagement

The announcement of Prince Harry's engagement to Meghan Markle was reported on the front of most British newspapers on 28 November 2017. The couple had posed for photographs at Kensington Palace, so all newspapers had access to the same images. The papers selected different photographs to use, however, and constructed different accounts of the event through the choice of language, layout and design.

The *Guardian*:

- In contrast to most papers, it does not feature the engagement as the main story. In its story, it does not simply celebrate the engagement, but chooses to focus on a contextual angle: changing attitudes towards race in society, as Meghan Markle is of mixed race.
- This reflects the newspaper's liberal stance and concern for social equality.
- The article argues that the engagement is a positive step and the selected image showing the couple smiling brightly constructs a familiar romantic narrative and connotes a sense of optimism.

Stretch and Challenge 3.26

Choose one front page. How does the representation of the event reflect the values of the newspaper?

Section B: Exploring Media Industries and Audiences

Overview

In this section you will explore various media forms through products set by Eduqas (see page 40), although your teacher will select some of the examples that you study. You do not need to analyse the media language and representations here: you will consider key industry and audience factors, such as who owns the company that produces a product and who is the intended audience. This will enable you to understand how the media industries work, the ways in which audiences are targeted and how they respond to media products. You will also explore ways in which products develop over time and how they are relevant to present-day audiences.

Exploring Media Industries

When studying media industries in relation to the set products you will need to explore:

- how media production process and technologies impact on media products
- who owns and controls the media
- the role of convergence in modern media industries
- how media products are funded
- how the media work as profit-making industries on a global scale, and reach large and specialised audiences
- the role of regulation in the media.

Exploring Audiences

When studying audiences in relation to the set products you will need to investigate:

- how media products are aimed at specific audiences
- how audiences are categorised and targeted by media organisations
- the role of technology in enabling organisations to reach audiences and in allowing audiences to use and consume the media in different ways
- how audiences might respond to and interpret media products in different ways
- the social, cultural and political significance of media products and the functions they serve
- theoretical perspectives on audience, including Uses and Gratifications.

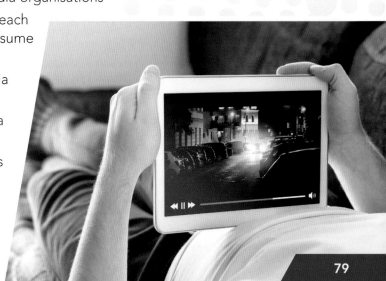

Key Terms

Vertically integrated
Owning different stages of (the film) process: production, distribution and exhibition.

Media conglomerate
An organisation that owns different types of media company. (Disney, for example, owns film and television companies.)

Syndication
Where a company sells the rights to broadcast a television programme to different channels or organisations.

Exhibition
The showing of a film in cinemas and on other platforms such as television and online.

Marketing
Promotion and advertising, including elements such as posters, trailers and online marketing including social media strategies.

Promotion
Wider activities that draw attention to the film, for example interviews with the stars and director on television or in magazines.

Film

Film is studied in relation to media industries only. You will explore the set product through key pages from the website and the marketing materials. You might study extracts from the film, but in relation to industry, for example:

- the opening credits, which will provide information about the production companies and key personnel such as the director and stars
- key sequences that relate to industry factors, such as the high production values in *Spectre*'s opening scene in Mexico City or another key action sequence.

A location shot from *Spectre*.

The film industry

The Hollywood film industry is dominated by a small number of major film studios. Many of these, such as Disney and 20th Century Fox, are **vertically integrated** companies that are part of large, global **media conglomerates**. These companies often own other media organisations, such as television channels. They have the financial power to produce high-concept 'tentpole' films, whose budgets are frequently over $200 million, as they generate profits through films and other ventures such as the **syndication** of television shows.

Stretch and Challenge 3.27

Research one of the major Hollywood studios, such as 20th Century Fox or Warner Bros. Find out who owns the studio and which other companies are part of the conglomerate.

Top Tip

Every time you watch a film, look out for the production company details. Find out a little more information about the companies involved.

Marketing

Vertical integration is important in the film industry as it allows one organisation to control the production, distribution and, in some cases, the **exhibition** of a film. Distribution is a vital stage in ensuring that a film reaches its target audience and it includes:

- **marketing** and **promotion** of the film
- organising the release and exhibition of the film in cinemas and on DVD.

The distribution budget for mainstream Hollywood films is usually extremely high and it is important that the marketing strategies are effective in order to attract the target audience and achieve high box office figures. Many films also have associated merchandise and some, such as the Bond franchise, also have **sponsorship** deals. Some films might have a soundtrack that is released as an album or associated video game. The game *Star Wars Battlefront II*, for example, was launched in November 2017 to tie in with the December release of *Star Wars: The Last Jedi*. These all help to raise audience awareness and contribute to the financial success of the film.

The marketing campaign aims to create a buzz building up to the **theatrical release** of the film. A premiere is usually held just before the release, which attracts the attention of the press, and reviews are published, which also raise the profile of the film. The opening weekend is crucial to the box office success of a film, and many films receive at least 30 per cent of their total takings in the first weekend after the release.

The release date is important because there are key times of the year when different types of film are likely to achieve success. High-budget tentpole, or **blockbuster**, films are often released in the run up to Christmas or in the summer to attract a large family audience in the holidays. Some films that are potential contenders for Academy Awards (the Oscars) tend to be released in in the run-up to the announcement of awards nominations in January.

Key Terms

Sponsorship
Paying to be associated with or have a product featured in, for example, a film. This can benefit both the film and the sponsor.

Theatrical release
The date when the film is first shown in cinemas.

Blockbuster
A major film release, usually a high-budget mainstream Hollywood film that appeals to a wide audience and achieves box office success. The term was used to describe films such as *Jaws* and *Star Wars* in the 1970s, when audiences queued around the block to the cinema.

Performance capture
A technique where digital motion-capture cameras record the movements of an actor to create a digital character on screen. This makes the character lifelike.

Quickfire 3.37

What associated products were created to tie in with the release of *Spectre*?

Technology

Many high-budget films, especially action, fantasy and science fiction films, use digital technologies such as CGI and **performance capture** to increase the visual spectacle and appeal to audiences.

Top Tip

Make a timeline of the key dates relating to the production, marketing and release of the set product.

Performance capture techniques were used to help create Andy Serkis's character Gollum in *The Lord of the Rings* and *Hobbit* films.

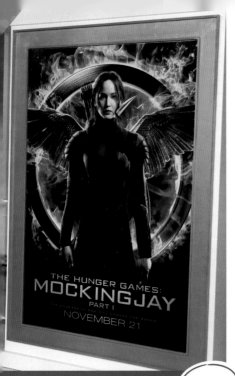

New technologies have also enabled distributors to market films in different ways, harnessing the power of the internet and social media to engage a potential audience. The promotional campaign for *The Hunger Games: Mockingjay Part 1* used **viral marketing** techniques alongside more traditional methods. Videos and posters were released on a website created for the fictional government in the film.

Viral techniques can be very successful, especially when a film is targeting a young audience who regularly use communication technology and might share elements of the marketing on social media.

The importance of the website

A website is important for many film releases, although smaller budget and independent films increasingly use social media sites (such as a Facebook page) rather than constructing a complete website. Established film franchises do usually have a website that offers:

- information about previous films they have produced and news about forthcoming releases
- clues about the narrative and characters
- marketing and promotional materials including trailers, clips, 'making of' footage and interviews with cast members and the director. This will often be exclusive, offering fans something 'extra' and building a 'buzz' around the film.
- links to a store and sale of merchandise
- possible games, quizzes and polls, depending on the type of film
- opportunities for audience interaction on, for example, forums
- links to social media platforms such as Twitter, Facebook, Instagram and YouTube.

Websites provide a way for producers to reach the audience and provide them with information and entertainment on a single platform. Websites for major film franchises such as *Star Wars* or Bond will aim to provide information for new audiences as well as offering **avid fans** a way of continuing their interaction with the brand.

Regulation

The British Board of Film Classification (BBFC) is the independent organisation responsible for rating films in Britain. Each film and DVD release is examined, and a set of BBFC Classification Guidelines is used to determine the age rating. According to the BBFC website, the purpose of classification is to protect children from 'unsuitable and even harmful content' and to provide media consumers with information about a film in order for them to decide whether or not they want to view it.

Key Terms

Viral marketing
Advertising that is distributed through non-traditional channels, such as the internet. The term relates to the idea of a virus that can spread very quickly as audiences often pass the information on.

Avid fans
Audiences who are dedicated supporters of a film franchise. They are likely to engage in much social interaction, for example discussing the film, buying merchandise and sharing information on social media.

Activity 3.13

Explore the website for Spectre: 007.com/spectre.

- What techniques are used to promote the film?
- How does the website reinforce the film brand?
- How is the website aiming to reach a large audience for the film?

Write up your notes in three paragraphs, using specific examples from the website to support your points.

The areas that BBFC examiners consider when rating a film include:

- **Discrimination**: use of discriminatory language and behaviour
- Imitable behaviour: acts that could be copied
- Violence.

The age categories for theatrical film releases include U (Universal), 12A and 15. The 12A category was introduced in 2002 when it replaced the 12 certificate (although the 12 certificate remains for DVD releases). Films that are classified as 12A are suitable for children aged 12 and over, but younger children can attend if they are accompanied by an adult. The BBFC publishes detailed information about each decision on the website, which allows parents to decide if they want their children to see a 12A film.

Age ratings can be an important factor in enabling a film to attract its target audience. For example, if producers are targeting an audience of families with young children, they will aim for a PG or U rating. The 12A rating is particularly significant here, as most 'blockbuster' films need to appeal to the widest possible audience and so, like many mainstream films, will aim to achieve this certificate.

The BBFC guidelines are reviewed regularly and updated in response to social change. A key development occurred in 1994, following the Jamie Bulger case where two-year-old Jamie was murdered by two ten-year-old boys. There were suggestions that the crime was inspired by a scene in a horror film, *Child's Play 3*. The link was not proven, but the case raised concerns about the impact of violence in the media and there was an amendment to the Video Recordings Act of 1984 to take account of this. As a result, the BBFC was required to pay special attention to the 'potential for harm' when rating videos. A film is more likely to be given a higher age rating on DVD than for the cinema release, as younger people might have access to the film in the home.

Key Term

Discrimination
In this context, discrimination refers to offensive content in a media product, for example about gender, race or religion.

Stretch and Challenge 3.28

Research the BBFC website and make notes of the key criteria for the 12A certificate.

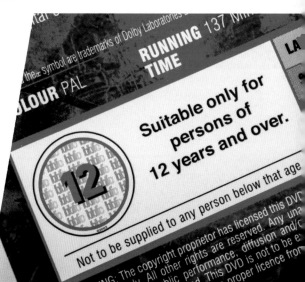

Analysing the set product: *Spectre*

The James Bond film franchise is a hugely successful global brand. The first film was *Dr No*, released in 1962, and *Spectre* was the 24th film in the series. Several actors have played the iconic role of Bond, most recently Daniel Craig. *Skyfall*, the previous Bond film to *Spectre*, was enormously successful: it took over $1 billion worldwide and became the highest grossing film of all time (in 2012) at the British box office. This meant there were high expectations for *Spectre*, which was also directed by Sam Mendes and co-starred Christoph Waltz, Naomi Harris and Ben Wishaw.

Key industry details
The production companies were Columbia (part of Sony Pictures), MGM and EON (a British company). The film was distributed by Sony Pictures.

- Sony Pictures produces and distributes films and owns film brands such as Columbia and TriStar. It is an example of a **vertically integrated** company as it owns the production and distribution stages of the process.

The Sony Pictures stand at Licensing Expo in Las Vegas.

- It is itself part of the Sony Corporation, a very large media conglomerate that produces a range of media content as well as electronic goods. Sony is also a major record label and its PlayStation is a leading brand in the video games market. These different branches show that Sony is a diversified organisation. This also allows one part of a business to link to another, for example a theme song being produced for a film.

Filming for *Spectre* took place at Pinewood Studios in Britain and on location in several countries including Mexico and Austria.

While Sony Pictures is an American organisation, Eon is a British company and there are many British cultural elements to the film: it uses a British character and institution (MI6), many of the scenes were filmed in Britain, and many of the creative people involved are British. It is therefore considered to be a UK-USA production.

Spectre had an estimated budget of $245 million. Sponsorship and tie-ins include companies and products such as Aston Martin, Omega, Belvedere Vodka, Heineken and Gilette. Many major brands paid for their products to appear in *Spectre*, and the film has been likened to a football World Cup in terms of the levels of sponsorship that it attracted. This demonstrates that the Bond franchise is seen as an iconic and far-reaching brand that other companies want to be associated with.

The film was released on 26 October 2015 in the UK. It opened in the USA on 6 November 2015 and was then released in more than 70 countries worldwide. BBC News noted that it opened in 647 cinemas in the UK, a very wide release, and broke box office records in the UK in its opening week. The total box office takings worldwide were over $880 million according to boxofficemojo.com.

Spectre was classified as a 12A certificate by the BBFC. The distributors wanted this rating and therefore reduced the levels of violence in response to BBFC feedback on an unfinished version.

The marketing of *Spectre*

There was a great deal of marketing and publicity in advance of *Spectre's* release. The range of sponsorship deals resulted in many adverts that linked the products to the film, while the official James Bond website and associated social media platforms featured regular updates.

Key marketing activities

- The 'Bond 24' announcement was made on 4 December 2014 at Pinewood Studios. Director Sam Mendes and producer Barbara Broccoli announced key details including the title of the film, the filming locations, the personnel involved, including the writers, cinematographer and cast.

Quickfire 3.38

Why do you think *Spectre* was released at the end of October?

Stretch and Challenge 3.29

Research the age certificates awarded to *Spectre* in different countries. Why might other countries have rated the film differently?

Top Tip

Read further information about the classification of *Spectre* on the BBFC website: www.bbfc.co.uk/releases/spectre-2015.

- A series of trailers were released, including a 'teaser' trailer in spring 2015 on the official James Bond website, followed by a full theatrical trailer in July and a final trailer on the Bond website in October. This pattern of marketing maintains interest in the build up to the release of the film:
  - The main theatrical trailer follows typical conventions: it is two-and-a-half minutes long and features key moments of action from the film that are tightly edited to create excitement.
  - There are many conventions of the Bond genre evident in the trailer including exotic locations, car chases, fight sequences and 'Bond girls'. The production values are extremely high and the iconic Bond theme tune is also heard.
  - The narrative picks up from the end of the last film, *Skyfall*, which will be familiar to fans. The trailer also creates many enigmas, for example about the title of the film and the antagonist, to entice the audience.
- A range of posters was issued, including 'teaser' posters and more detailed theatrical release posters.
- Aston Martin even produced a new car, the DB10, for *Spectre*, which was unveiled at Pinewood studios on the day of the 'Bond 24' announcement. This brand of luxury car has been associated with James Bond for many years.
- A series of **vlogs** was released on the official 007 YouTube page, for example a special feature on the filming of the Day of the Dead festival sequence. These behind-the-scenes features and 'making of' footage gave audiences exclusive insights into the new film in order to build anticipation in advance of the release.
- Sony released an advert, 'Made for Bond', for its new smartphone to tie in with the release of *Spectre*. The advert featured an action sequence where Naomi Harris (as Moneypenny) retrieves Bond's phone. This intertextual product is an example of **synergy**, as Sony was able to advertise both the phone and the film at once.
- The theme song is an iconic part of the Bond brand. The song for *Spectre* was 'Writing's on the Wall' by Sam Smith. It was the first Bond theme to reach number one in the British chart and, like Adele's 'Skyfall' won an Oscar for best original song. The video was premiered in October 2015.

Luxury Aston Martin cars have been linked with the glamour of Bond for many years.

Key Terms

Vlog
A video weblog that can be used to promote a media product. Vlogs might appear on a product's official website, YouTube channel and associated social media pages.

Synergy
Where different parts of the same media conglomerate work together, for example to promote a particular product.

Stretch and Challenge 3.30

Look at the range of posters on the *Spectre* website and identify how they aim to reach a global audience.

A 'teaser' poster published before *Spectre*'s release emphasises the glamour and hints at the sinister Day of the Dead setting, but gives little else away at this stage.

Newspapers

Newspapers are studied in Section A and Section B of Component 1. This is an in-depth study covering all areas of the theoretical framework.

In Section A you will analyse newspaper front pages in relation to media language and representation. In Section B you will study industry and audience issues in relation to the set product, the *Sun*. Your teacher will select one edition of the set product for you to study, and you will also explore some pages from the *Sun*'s website.

A brief overview of newspapers, including the codes and conventions of tabloids and broadsheets, can be found in Section A of this chapter (page 73).

The newspaper industry

Newspapers have been published in Britain for over 300 years. The industry has faced many challenges and several local titles have closed. In 2016 the *Independent* national newspaper became an online-only product.

Sales of print newspapers have been falling in recent years as the industry faces increasing competition from online and 24-hour television news channels. Audiences can now access the most up-to-date news on their smartphones and tablets, receive alerts and select the areas of news that they wish to consume. It is perhaps not surprising that fewer people are buying printed newspapers.

The newspaper industry has responded to this challenge by using new technologies to circulate content. Newspapers now have websites and social media feeds that are regularly updated, so readers can access the latest news. This online presence can reach a wider audience than the print edition of the newspaper, and so can possibly expand the audience beyond the intended target group.

The *Guardian*'s web content is currently free to access. Other newspaper websites require readers to subscribe.

Some newspapers, such as the *Guardian*, currently make all of this content freely available via their website and app. Some have an online subscription service so readers have to pay to access the content. The *Times*, published by News UK, has a digital edition of the newspaper that can be accessed on an app. Readers also need to pay to view the full website.

Newspapers carry advertising as this is a source of funding in addition to sales of the newspaper. Newspaper websites also have advertising, and this is vitally important to their finances, especially as print sales have fallen.

Ownership

The newspaper industry is very powerful. Newspapers communicate messages about important issues and are read by large numbers of people. In Britain, there are a small number of newspaper publishers that control the majority of the industry. News UK, which owns *the Sun* and the *Times* and is part of the international conglomerate News Corporation, is the biggest publisher. A 2015 report by the Media Reform Coalition, published in the *Guardian*, stated that the three largest companies – DMGT (publisher of the *Daily Mail*), Trinity Mirror (which published the *Daily Mirror*) and News UK – owned over 70 per cent of newspapers in the UK. This potentially limits the range of viewpoints and messages that readers receive, especially as the two newspapers with the largest circulation – the *Sun* and the *Daily Mail* – have right-wing political leanings.

Newspaper production processes

How is the news chosen?

Newspaper **gatekeepers** decide which stories to cover. There might be many factors that affect this choice, including the type of newspaper and its audience, but we can apply a set of **news values** to the decisions, as these are common factors that influence story selection.

The theory of news values was developed by Galtung and Ruge, who undertook a study of newspapers and broadcast news in 1965 and compiled a list of factors that made it more likely for an event to be covered. Although the theory was developed many years ago, the news values can still be applied to news products today:

The devastating earthquake in Nepal in 2015 was a major news story worlwide.

- **Threshold**: The 'size' of the event. The bigger the story, in terms of its importance or expected interest, and the more people it affects, the more likely it is to be covered.

- **Meaningfulness**: How relevant it is. For example, a general election in Britain would be reported in British newspapers, but an election in another country might not be as newsworthy.

- **Unambiguity**: How clear and simple the event is to report. These types of stories are more likely to be included. Complex stories, especially those that are ongoing, such as the Brexit negotiations, are more difficult to explain.

- **Unexpectedness**: If an event occurs suddenly and unpredictably, such as a natural disaster or terror attack, it is more likely to be covered due to the element of surprise. Some expected events will also be newsworthy, for example the Chancellor's Budget speech.

- **Continuity**: Once an event has been reported, there might be updates in future editions of the paper as the story develops. For example, a paper might follow the progress of a storm as it heads towards and crosses Britain.

- **Elite persons and nations**: Stories about important people (such as political leaders) and countries (such as the USA) are more likely to be reported. The engagement of Prince Harry and Meghan Markle was a major news story, but the engagement of an 'ordinary' couple would not be newsworthy.

- **Personalisation**: Stories directly affecting or involving people are more likely to be reported. Reporting of events such as earthquakes will often focus on the human angle, for example how people have been affected by the disaster.

- **Negativity**: Bad news is more likely to be reported than good news.

Key Terms

Gatekeepers
The people who decide which stories to include in the newspaper. Journalists have access to news stories from a variety of sources and newspaper editors need to 'filter' the information and select the stories to feature in the publication.

News values
A set of factors that help to determine whether or not an event is considered newsworthy.

Some events are so important that they will feature on every newspaper front cover on a particular day. These include **hard news** stories, such as the results of political elections in Britain or Europe, but also **soft news** events such as a major sporting event (Andy Murray's results at Wimbledon for example). The death of a very famous, or 'elite', person is also likely to be featured across different newspapers.

On most days, however, there are many different news events to choose from. Editors need to select the stories that they feel are most important to feature on the front page.

The death of David Bowie was reported on most British newspaper front pages on 12 January 2016.

Stretch and Challenge 3.31

Look at a range of newspapers for a particular day and apply news values to the front-page stories.

Key Terms

Phone-hacking scandal
The revelation that mobile phones belonging to a large number of people, including celebrities, politicians and 'ordinary' people, were hacked and their messages accessed by news journalists, particularly those working for the since-closed *News of the World*.

Self-regulated
An industry that is controlled and monitored by itself, not by the government. The Leveson Inquiry recommended that the newspaper industry should be free from political or government interference and that the new regulatory body should be independent.

Stretch and Challenge 3.32

Research the IPSO Editors' Code of Practice and make notes about the key areas.

Activity 3.14

On 21 November 2017 British newspaper front pages included a number of different stories:

- Brexit: reports that the 'divorce bill' could be £40 billion
- The political situation in Germany
- Cancer tests being offered in supermarket car parks
- The break-up of a British TV celebrity's marriage
- The death of a former Wimbledon tennis champion.

Consider each of these stories and decide which news values could be applied to them. The Brexit issue, for example, is ongoing and quite complex, but the chosen story focuses on a potential £40 billion bill which seems to be a clear, **unambiguous** message that has **threshold** and **meaningfulness** to a British audience.

Regulation

There have been changes in the way the newspaper industry is regulated in recent years, as a result of the **phone-hacking scandal**. The Press Complaints Commission was the regulator at the time, but was criticised for its failure to deal with the issue and was disbanded. The Leveson Inquiry set up in 2011 recommended that:

- newspapers should be **self-regulated** (as they had been before), overseen by a new independent body
- there should be a new code of standards
- the new regulator should have the power to deal with complaints about breaches of standards.

The Independent Press Standards Organisation (IPSO) was formed following the Leveson Inquiry and now regulates many newspapers and magazines in Britain. IPSO provides advice to editors and journalists, monitors standards, and responds to complaints about publications that break the Editors' Code of Practice.

The IPSO website states that this code of practice 'balances both the rights of the individual and the public's right to know'. In other words, newspapers should have freedom to publish information that is in the public interest but individual people (who might be written about in newspapers) also have the right to privacy. The Editors' Code outlines standards that must be upheld in many areas including accuracy, privacy, involvement of children and discrimination.

Overview of the set product: the *Sun*

The *Sun* was established as a broadsheet in 1964, launched with the slogan 'the newspaper born of the age we live in'. The *Sun*'s original aim was to be radical and independent; it did not intend to support any political party. The *Sun* was bought by News International, Rupert Murdoch's company, in 1969. Murdoch changed the *Sun* to a tabloid and introduced the controversial 'Page Three' feature. The *Sun* began to gain readers and overtook the *Daily Mirror* as Britain's bestselling newspaper in 1978.

The *Sun* is recognised as being an influential newspaper. It supported Margaret Thatcher's Conservative Party in the 1979 general election. It then backed Tony Blair and the Labour Party in 1997. On these occasions the party supported by the *Sun* won a major victory. In 2009 the *Sun* ran a headline 'Labour's Lost It', a pun that made reference to the fact that the party had lost the support of the newspaper. From 2010 onwards, the *Sun* has supported the Conservative Party.

The *Sun* has also received criticism, especially in response to its reporting of the Hillsborough disaster in 1989, when 96 Liverpool football fans died at an FA Cup semi-final match. The newspaper has publicly apologised for false reports made about Liverpool fans, but there was a boycott of the newspaper in Liverpool and many people in the city still refuse to read it. In 2011, the *Sun*'s sister newspaper, the *News of the World*, was closed following the phone-hacking scandal. The *Sun on Sunday* was launched in 2012.

Quickfire 3.39

What are the main differences between tabloid and broadsheet newspapers?

Newspaper industry: ownership and control

The *Sun* is owned by News UK, a company that is part of Rupert Murdoch's global media conglomerate, News Corporation. News UK also publishes the *Times* and the *Sunday Times*, and owns a number of radio stations including Talk Sport and Virgin Radio. News UK is a powerful organisation: it is the biggest newspaper publisher in the UK and the *Sun* has the largest readership of all the national papers. News Corporation owns the *New York Times* and Harper Collins book publishers, as well as several newspapers in Australia. Murdoch sold many assets, including the 20th Century Fox film company, to Disney in 2017.

The *Sun* has a right-wing political leaning and supported the 'Leave' campaign in the EU referendum in 2016. The newspaper has often raised concerns about levels of immigration to the UK and this issue featured heavily in the lead up to the referendum.

© The Sun / News Licensing

The *Sun*'s view, as in the set December front page, is that immigration should be limited.

Stretch and Challenge 3.33

Look at a copy of the *Times* (or the website). Can you identify any similarities that suggest these two products are owned by the same organisation?

Stretch and Challenge 3.34

Research the IPSO website and note down details about recent rulings on the *Sun* newspaper.

Key Term

Paywall
A system where readers pay a subscription fee to access website content. Some newspapers have introduced paywalls as a way of increasing income as print sales have fallen.

An example of regulation in relation to the *Sun*

The *Sun* newspaper and website content is regulated by IPSO. One of the points in the IPSO Editors' Code under 'Accuracy' is: 'The Press must take care not to publish inaccurate, misleading or distorted information or images, including headlines not supported by the text.' (ipso.co.uk/editors-code-of-practice/)

In March 2016 the *Sun* published an article about alleged comments that the Queen had made criticising the EU. The headline was 'Queen Backs Brexit'. IPSO upheld a complaint that the headline was 'significantly misleading'. It ruled that the headline was not supported by the text in the article, although the article itself did not break the code. The *Sun* had to publish the headline 'IPSO RULES AGAINST SUN'S QUEEN HEADLINE' on the front page and include IPSO's full adjudication on page 2.

Studying the set product: the *Sun*, industry and audience

The *Sun* is published daily in print form in the UK from Monday to Saturday. It also has a website, associated social media including Facebook and Twitter, and a mobile app. The *Sun* newspaper app is a paid-for subscription service that allows readers to download the entire print edition of *the Sun* to their tablet each day. The website is free to use. The *Sun* did introduce a **paywall** for its website in 2013, but many other tabloids retained a free website and the Sun ended the paywall in 2015. The price of the newspaper from Monday to Friday is 50p (as of March 2018).

You will study a complete edition of the *Sun*, and selected pages of the website, in order to identify key industry and audience issues. You will find industry information at the bottom of the back page of the print edition, and at the top and bottom of the website homepage. There are regular features in the *Sun* that you could consider:

- **The name and masthead**: The name reflects that most readers will buy and read the newspaper in the morning. It also connotes positivity and reliability. The masthead leans to the right, suggesting the newspaper is forward looking. The tagline (as of March 2018) 'For a Greater Britain' reflects the patriotic values of the newspaper.

- **Front page** featuring lead stories: use of familiar tabloid conventions (such as headlines that use puns and hyperbole, and large images) to appeal to readers.

- **A range of hard and soft news stories**, often including a lot of celebrity news and human interest articles.

- **Page Three**: The *Sun* no longer features topless models, but still includes images of scantily clad females on this page.

- **Editorial** column, 'Sun Says': This comments on stories it considers important and communicates key messages about the newspaper's views and values.

- **Regular columns** by celebrities such as Jeremy Clarkson and Lorraine Kelly.

- **Sports pages**: The back pages are filled with sport, a common convention of newspapers. Football tends to dominate the coverage.

- **Advertising**: Many high street brands advertise in the *Sun*, reflecting the audience **demographic**. Some advertisements relate to *Sun* promotions, such as travel offers.

- **Entertainment**: 'Bizarre' column and television listings, for example. There are many of these features to appeal to the audience.

- **Different feature sections** on each day of the week, for example a health section on a Tuesday. There are also regular pull-out sections, for example on motoring. These features offer familiarity to regular readers.

- **Regular features**: Puzzles, horoscopes, 'Dear Deidre' advice column and letters. These provide continuity and offer opportunities for readers to interact with the paper.

The website reinforces many of the features of the print edition and is an example of the *Sun* using convergence to appeal to a range of audiences:

- The **house style** is consistent across the print newspaper and website, creating an identifiable brand.

- The homepage is regularly updated and readers can access additional features such as video clips.

- Readers are able to comment on articles and see other users' comments. This extends the experience of the newspaper (where friends or family might discuss the articles for example) and is a form of wider social interaction.

- Many of the pages relate to sections in the newspaper such as 'TV and Showbiz' and 'Money'. These are therefore familiar to the print audience and offer content additional to that in the paper.

 Quickfire 3.40

Who do you think is the target audience for the *Sun*?

 Top Tip

Make detailed notes on the key features of the set edition that you study. Think about what these reveal about the industry and audience.

Key Terms

Column
A regular short article in a newspaper, where a writer – often a celebrity – offers their opinions. Some are specific to a topic, for example a television review column, while others are more general and discuss a range of issues.

Demographic
The profile of an audience based on factors such as their age, gender and socio-economic group.

The *Sun*'s website follows the house style of its print newspaper.

- The advertising features many of the same brands as the print edition.
- Readers can sign up to features such as 'Sun Savers', which requires them to collect codes from the print newspaper to receive 'cash back'.

Activity 3.15

Study the pages from the set print edition of the *Sun* and the webpages chosen by your teacher.

Note down details of all the advertisements that you see.

- What types of product are advertised in the *Sun*?
- What does the advertising suggest about the target audience for the *Sun*?
- Do the same products or services appear in print and on the website?
- Identify three specific examples of convergence between the print edition and the website.
- Note down any references to other News UK products (examples of synergy).
- Identify three key articles in the print edition and three key features of the website and consider how these appeal to different audiences.

Stretch and Challenge 3.35

Conduct a survey of your friends and family to find out who consumes print and online newspapers, and why.

Audiences

Why do people still read newspapers?

Online sources of news have become very popular, but print newspapers do still attract a very large audience. Data published by the National Readership Survey in June 2017 revealed that 61 per cent of British adults aged over 15 consume a print newspaper. (nrs.co.uk/latest-results/facts-and-figures/newspapers-factsandfigures/) Professor Neil Thurman of City University and LMU Munich said, 'For younger readers… newspapers' print editions provide an experience they invest time in, compared to how they snack on and scan news online.' (pressgazette.co.uk)

The experience of reading a newspaper is very different from consuming news online, and offers particular pleasures and gratifications such as:

- The newspaper is a familiar form and audiences recognise the conventions.
- Content is organised in a clear structure: for example the main stories appear at the beginning, the sports pages are positioned at the back. (The website requires the reader to navigate and some stories or content may be missed.)
- Some people prefer, or require, a media product that they can carry with them and that does not require them to connect to the internet. Many readers prefer a print text to an online version.
- Newspapers fit into many readers' daily routines: they might read the newspaper as they eat breakfast or travel to work.
- An audience might value the in-depth coverage of events and issues in newspapers.

Audience data is collected by two main organisations in the UK:

- **Circulation** data: the Audit Bureau of Circulation (ABC)
- **Readership** data: the National Readership Survey (NRS).

The audience for the *Sun*

David Dinsmore, Chief Operating Officer of News UK, describes the *Sun*: 'The *Sun* is more than a newspaper. It is an instigator, an entertainer, a cultural reference point, a finger on the pulse, a daily relationship.' (newscommercial.co.uk/brands/the-sun)

The *Sun* is the biggest daily print newspaper in the UK in terms of both circulation and readership. The *Sun*'s average circulation for October 2017 was 1 517 314 (ABC statistics). The daily readership of the paper in June 2017 was over 3.4 million (NRS figures), while the number of daily browsers on the *Sun*'s website is more than 5.5 million (ABC statistics).

The next bestselling publication is the *Daily Mail* with a circulation of around 1.4 million. This newspaper's website, however, is the most popular of all national newspapers.

Demographic information for the print edition of the *Sun*

- Approximately one-third of *Sun* readers are in the ABC1 socio-economic group, and two-thirds are in groups C2 to E. Only one-tenth are in the top AB groups.
- Around 25 per cent of readers are aged 15 to 35, and 75 per cent are aged 35 and over.
- Nearly 60 per cent of readers are male (so just over 40 per cent are female).
- The majority of the audience for the *Sun* print newspaper, therefore, is made up of males, aged 35 and over, and in the lower socio-economic groups. (Information based on statistics from July 2016 to June 2017 from newsworks.org.uk.)

Defining the *Sun* audience using VALs (values, attitudes and lifestyles)

The audience for the *Sun* might share the newspaper's values and attitudes: for example they might support the Conservative Party and believe that there should be immigration limits.

The *Sun* includes many different sections on news, entertainment, business, motoring, and sport and so has wide appeal to audiences with a range of interests, and fulfils many uses and gratifications. For example:

- the news stories provide information about the world
- celebrity and entertainment features offer gossip and escapism
- human-interest stories might allow audiences to identify with the people and situations involved
- the focus on saving money resonates with people who have a limited income
- the website allows users to comment on stories, offering opportunities to interact socially.

You will need to consider how the *Sun* specifically targets and appeals to its audience through the different elements it uses in the print newspaper and on its website.

Quickfire 3.41

How does David Dinsmore's quotation suggest that the *Sun* appeals to readers? What gratifications does it provide?

Quickfire 3.42

How does the *Sun* appeal to its main demographic groups?

Top Tip

Study the edition of the set product chosen by your teacher and make detailed notes on the specific ways it appeals to the audience.

Top Tip

Check the most up-to-date circulation and readership statistics for the set product.

Stretch and Challenge 3.36

How would you categorise the audience for the *Sun* in terms of values, attitudes and lifestyle? Give examples.

Stretch and Challenge 3.37

Research the online audience for the *Sun* at newsworks.org.uk/The-Sun. What differences are there between the audience for the print and online editions?

How does the *Sun*, Saturday 25 June 2016, appeal to readers?

This special wrap-around cover was published following the result of the referendum in which Britain voted to leave the EU.

It assumes that the audience shares its strong patriotic values and believes that it is right for Britain to leave the EU. It suggests that belonging to the EU has been negative for Britain and that independence will benefit the country.

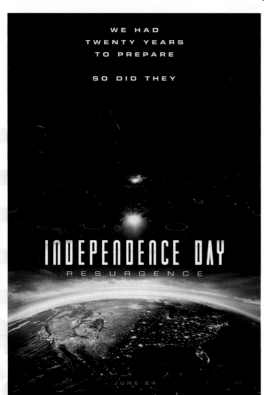

The use of images is very striking to appeal to readers who voted to leave the EU:

- The bright sun signifies positivity and a bright future.
- The union flag over Britain reinforces patriotism and national identify.
- Britain appears to be rising up away from Europe and there is a broken chain to emphasise that Britain is 'free'.
- Hyperbolic language codes anchor these images: 'rising from the shackles'. 'ADIEU', with some irony uses the French word for 'Goodbye' (with connotations of finality, in contrast to 'Au revoir').

Intertextuality: previous *Sun* front pages are included on the back cover. This is a conclusion to a long-running narrative that loyal readers will be familiar with. There are intertextual visual references to the film *Independence Day,* and 'So long, farewell…' is a song from *The Sound of Music*. These cultural references help to communicate the messages clearly and will be recognised by many people.

The trail in the bottom-right corner advertises several additional pages of 'brilliant Brexit coverage' in a similar way to a souvenir issue that commemorates a major celebration.

Theoretical perspectives: How might readers respond to the *Sun*?

Different audiences will respond in different ways to the same media product. The main target audience for the *Sun* might respond positively to the messages on the cover, but other audiences could take a different view due to factors such as their age, ethnicity, beliefs and life experiences.

Someone with a **preferred reading** of this cover would agree with the messages that Britain has a bright future as an independent country, separate from Europe. A person who was very certain that Britain should leave the EU would respond in this way.

Someone who has a **negotiated reading** of this cover might agree that it is probably the right decision to leave the EU but feel that the future is uncertain, and might reject the very optimistic message. A person who was undecided about how to vote, or who voted to leave but with some reservations, might respond in this way.

Someone with an **oppositional reading** would disagree with the message that the referendum result is positive. They would believe that it would be better for Britain to be part of a united Europe and might feel that the future is bleak. A person who was very certain that Britain should remain in the EU could respond in this way.

Top Tip

Identify possible preferred, negotiated and oppositional readings to the front page article in the edition chosen by your teacher.

Key Terms

Podcast
An audio programme made to be downloaded to a PC, tablet or smartphone, or listened to 'on demand' rather than being broadcast.

Public service broadcaster
A TV and/or radio provider that aims to serve the public rather than make a profit. (The BBC is publicly funded by the licence fee. It is required to be impartial and reflect the cultural diversity of the UK.)

Radio

You will study radio in relation to the set product, *The Archers*, broadcast on BBC Radio 4. This topic will allow you to explore industry and audience issues by studying specific examples from the set product chosen by your teacher:

- One full episode of *The Archers*
- Selected pages from the website for *The Archers*.

You will consider the development of the programme over time and its significance as a contemporary media product.

Overview of the radio industry

Radio is a media form that has seen many developments in recent years due to digital technologies. Radio streaming services are available on the internet and **podcasts** are created specifically for an audience to download. In Britain, radio stations fall broadly into three categories:

- BBC radio
- commercial stations
- community stations.

The BBC is a **public service broadcaster** that operates several national stations including: Radio 1, Radio 2, Radio 3, Radio 4, 5 Live, 6 Music, Asian Network, Radio Scotland, Radio Cymru and many local radio stations such as Radio Merseyside. Each of these stations has a distinct identity and targets a particular audience. Radio 1's intended audience, for example, is 15- to 29-year-olds interested in pop music.

Britain also has many not-for-profit **community radio stations**. These usually cover a relatively small area, such as Chorley FM based in the Lancashire town. Some community stations serve the interests of a particular social group, for example ethnic or religious. They can be funded from a variety of sources such as grants, advertising, dedicated fundraising and sponsorship.

Commercial radio stations are funded by advertising. There are currently over 30 national commercial stations in Britain. The two biggest commercial radio organisations in Britain are Global and Bauer who reach more than 30 million listeners every week, over half the adult population. Global Radio's stations include Heart, Gold and Capital, while Bauer Radio owns Kiss, Magic and Absolute. Both of these companies also operate TV channels for some of their radio stations, for example Magic TV. This is an example of convergence, which allows audiences to access the brand on different platforms. Bauer is also a major magazine publisher whose brands include *Grazia*, the film magazine *Empire* and the music magazine *Q*.

Radio technology

Digital (DAB) radios are now widely used in Britain. They have a better quality of sound and provide access to a much wider range of radio stations. Virgin Radio and BBC 1Xtra, 4 Extra, 5 Live Sports Extra and Asian Network are digital-only stations. Digital technologies allow media organisations to offer audiences many ways to experience a programme in addition to listening on a radio, for example:

- streaming a programme live online on a computer, tablet or smartphone
- listening again via catch-up services such as the BBC iPlayer or downloading a podcast
- consuming content on social media platforms, for example a radio station's official Facebook page or YouTube channel.

Podcasts are now regularly produced by radio broadcasters, offering audiences the opportunity to download a programme to listen when they choose. Many offer additional content to, or edited highlights from, the original programme, for example *Kermode and Mayo's Film Review*, which is an extended version of their weekly programme on BBC Radio 5 Live. Increasingly, podcasts are also produced independently of a radio broadcaster. These could be drama or comedy series or factual podcasts, about politics, for example.

Radio audiences

Radio is still very popular. **RAJAR** statistics released in October 2017 showed that 89 per cent of adults (people over 15) in the UK listened to the radio every week and that, on average, each listener consumed 21 hours of radio per week. (Statistics from: RAJAR/Ipsos MORI/RSMB.)

Radio fulfils a range of uses and gratifications for audiences. There are different pleasures associated with different genres of radio, such as speech or music programmes, but some of the main appeals are:

- companionship and background sound
- relaxation, entertainment and escapism
- information and education.

Radio is also convenient. It can fit into people's lives, and can be listened to in the car, for example, or while doing other things, as it doesn't always require someone's full attention.

Industry of the set product: the BBC

The BBC is funded by a **licence fee** that is paid by the public in Britain. The licence fee pays for a wide range of services including:

- nine BBC television channels (plus BBC Three, which has been online-only since 2016).
- ten national radio stations, the BBC World Service, which broadcasts overseas, and over 40 local radio stations
- dedicated television and radio services for Wales, Scotland and Northern Ireland
- BBC online, an extensive website.

The BBC also receives income from BBC Worldwide, the commercial arm of the organisation, which sells BBC programmes and develops the BBC brand in other countries. The BBC was established by a **Royal Charter** in 1922 and has a remit to inform, educate and entertain.

The BBC, like other broadcasters, is regulated by Ofcom and is required to follow the Broadcasting Code. This code covers areas such as impartiality and accuracy and protecting children and avoiding offensive language.

Radio 4 is a mostly speech-based radio station that includes many news, **current affairs** and factual programmes as well as a range of drama and comedy series. The BBC website states that Radio 4 'should appeal to listeners seeking intelligent programmes in many genres which inform, educate and entertain.' (bbc.co.uk)

According to the 'BBC Radio 4 44 Minute Drama' press pack, the target audience for Radio 4 is 35- to 54-year-olds in the ABC1 demographic. Individual programmes, however, have specific target audiences, and these might extend beyond the main audience for the station.

Key Terms

Licence fee
The charge for everyone in Britain who watches television programmes or accesses them through the iPlayer (on television or other devices). As of April 2018 the annual TV licence is £147.

Royal Charter
A legal document awarded by the King or Queen to create a company or organisation. The BBC's charter outlines the purpose of the organisation and guarantees its independence.

Current affairs
Programmes, or other media, that explore topical issues or events in detail.

Stretch and Challenge 3.38

Look up the categories of the Broadcasting Code on Ofcom's website. Identify the elements that are similar to the BBFC classification guidelines for film and the IPSO Editors' Code for newspapers.

Activity 3.17

Look at the Radio 4 schedule for one day.
- Create a table of the different types and genres of programme.
- Which of these aim to educate, inform or entertain?
- Select three programmes:
  - Find out a little more information about their content.
  - Who do you think is the target audience for each programme?

Broadcasting House, London headquarters of the BBC.

The Archers genre: soap opera

The Archers is the world's longest-running radio soap opera. You do not need to textually analyse the set product, but it will be helpful to have some knowledge of the genre to understand how it appeals to audiences.

Soap operas originated in America in the 1930s and were sponsored by companies who produced soap (and other domestic products). This gave the genre its name.

The traditional target audience for soap operas is females and soaps often feature strong female characters or **matriarchs.**

A key convention of the soap opera genre is a **multi-stranded narrative**, with ongoing storylines to reflect real life. The storylines usually revolve around relationships: family, friendships and work relationships. They are set in a specific location and scenes are often based in spaces where characters come together such as a pub, café or workplace.

Soap operas tend to feature more dialogue than action. The drama arises out of conflict between characters, so the genre works well as a radio format.

Contexts and *The Archers*

The Archers has been broadcast since 1951. One of the original intentions for the programme was to communicate information about modern farming methods to increase food production after the Second World War, as food was still being rationed in the early 1950s.

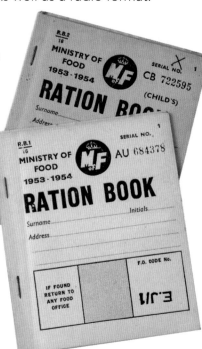

> Britain still had ration books several years after the Second World War. The newly launched *Archers* intended to help with farming.

The programme no longer has this aim, but it is still very carefully researched and is informative about many issues to do with farming and the countryside. *The Archers* also features plots that reflect wider contemporary social issues.
A recent storyline involved domestic abuse.
A character called Helen was put on trial for the attempted murder of her husband, Rob, who had been behaving in a controlling and abusive way for a long period of time. The verdict was announced in an hour-long 'special', featuring well-known actors who do not normally appear in *The Archers*, such as Rakhee Thakrar and Catherine Tate.

The verdict prompted a significant reaction on social media as *Archers* fans, celebrities and even politicians shared their responses. A 'Helen Titchener Fund' was set up by an *Archers* fan to raise money for Refuge, a domestic violence support charity, which had raised over £160 000 by November 2017. Refuge stated that they have used the *Archers* storyline and the Helen Titchener Fund to 'raise unprecedented levels of awareness of domestic violence' and support victims who are in the same situation as the character. (refuge.org.uk)

Stretch and Challenge 3.39

Listen to an episode of *The Archers* and make notes on the different storylines included. How might these appeal to different audiences?

Top Tip

Make notes about the genre conventions used in the episode of *The Archers* you study.

Key Terms

Matriarch
A strong female who has a lot of power and control, usually within a family.

Multi-stranded narrative
A narrative that contains several different stories or plots running alongside each other.

Quickfire 3.46

How does the original intention for *The Archers* fulfil the BBC's remit?

Quickfire 3.47

How does the response to the Helen and Rob storyline show that *The Archers* has an active audience?

A 2018 storyline about the sudden death of Nic Grundy was shocking for listeners and gained considerable attention in the wider media. This young female character accidentally cut her arm, then became unwell and died from sepsis a few days later. As a result, awareness was raised about the symptoms of this condition. Many listeners actively responded to this story, sharing their feelings of sadness and, in some cases, their own experiences of sepsis, on social media.

These are clear examples of the BBC fulfilling the public service remit and it demonstrates the way in which a fictional media product can reflect and possibly influence reality.

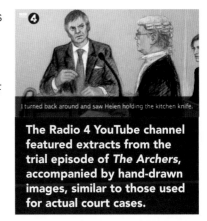

I turned back around and saw Helen holding the kitchen knife.

The Radio 4 YouTube channel featured extracts from the trial episode of _The Archers_, accompanied by hand-drawn images, similar to those used for actual court cases.

Production and broadcasting of _The Archers_

The programme is produced at the BBC's studios at the Mailbox in Birmingham.

The studio has separate areas for recording different types of scene, for example scenes set in a stable or a kitchen. This ensures that the sound is correct for the type of setting.

The programme often refers to actual events that are happening in the real world and if an unexpected event occurs, scripts are sometimes rewritten to include them.

Top Tip

Read the FAQs on the _Archers_ website. Summarise the planning and production process of the programme.

Scheduling

The Archers is broadcast in a regular timeslot: 7pm Sunday to Friday (six episodes a week of approximately 13 minutes each), and an **omnibus** on a Sunday morning at 10am. Each episode is repeated at 2pm on the afternoon after the original broadcast.

The regularity allows audiences to tune in at the same time every day and to fit the programme into their own daily lives. Offering the opportunity to listen in the afternoon or evening, or to catch up with all episodes on a Sunday, potentially allows the programme to reach a wider audience.

Key Term

Omnibus
A broadcast of a programme that usually includes all episodes from a particular week. This allows the audience to 'catch up' on a week's viewing or listening at once.

Each episode of _The Archers_ is also available for 30 days after broadcast on the BBC iPlayer. There is a weekly podcast of the omnibus edition, and episodes are also available to download from sites such as iTunes. This offers the audience even more flexibility to listen at a time that suits them, for example to catch up if they have missed an episode or to 'binge' on a number of episodes at once. The iPlayer Radio app also allows audiences in other countries to hear the show.

Activity 3.18

Select one story from the episode of _The Archers_ that you study, ideally linked to a social or environmental issue:

- Research how this story has been represented on the website, for example extra features or votes, and on social media such as the official Facebook page.
- Can you find links to further information about the issue on the _Archers_ website?
- Note examples of audience responses to this story, such as posts on the _Archers_ Twitter or Facebook pages. Identify the uses and gratifications that the story has fulfilled for these listeners.
- Try to find examples of the story being discussed in the wider media, perhaps in a newspaper or on television news (the issue of sepsis was discussed on Radio 4's _Today_ programme).
- How does the issue show the impact of social or cultural contexts? How is the issue relevant in contemporary society?

Quickfire 3.48

What is the current voting topic on the *Archers* website? How does this involve the audience?

Activity 3.19

Study the website for *The Archers* and select three specific features. Describe each feature in detail:

- How does it reflect content of *The Archers* radio programme?
- What pleasures does it offer to audiences?
- What opportunities does it offer audiences to interact?

Key Term

Opinion leader
A well-known, respected person who has the potential to influence people's opinions about a topic.

Stretch and Challenge 3.40

Look at some of the character profiles on the *Archers* website. How do these show a range of social groups? (Consider age, gender, ethnicity and socio-economic group.)

The BBC iPlayer homepage for *The Archers*.

The importance of convergence to industry and audiences: the *Archers* website

The website extends the world of *The Archers* to allow listeners to engage with the programme in different ways. It includes a regular blog, information about characters and links to *The Archers* social media sites. There are images of the characters to make the programme more visual, and features that explore the storylines, characters and themes to offer a range of pleasures. There are also regular polls where listeners can vote on a particular topic.

Information is provided for new listeners, including an invitation to listen to the Sunday omnibus and join fans around the world by commenting on Twitter. In this way, the producers engage an active audience who participate in sharing opinions about the programme as part of an online community.

In November 2017 there was a storyline about a 'hit and run' in which the character Matt Crawford was nearly killed. The website included a feature about the suspects in the case and commented how 'anonymous tip-offs from the public via Facebook and Twitter are leading the investigation in new and surprising directions'. The page then included examples of listeners' posts on social media suggesting possible suspects.

This is an example of an overlap between fiction and reality, where producers have involved audiences in the extended narrative of the *The Archers*. Some listeners care deeply about the storylines and characters. Websites and social media allow contemporary audiences to interact with the programme and become active participants by contributing their views.

Who listens to *The Archers*?

Professor Lyn Thomas from the University of Sussex conducted research into *The Archers* audiences, which she discussed in the *Guardian* in 2016. She found that online listeners who engaged in her research were mainly female, white British and aged between 40 and 59. (theguardian.com/higher-education-network/2016/feb/16/how-social-media-made-the-archers-cool)

This profile fits many elements of the Radio 4 target audience. *The Archers* does, however, appeal to wider audience groups:

- The characters are from different social backgrounds and there are also several younger characters, such as Phoebe Aldridge and Josh Archer, who might interest younger listeners.

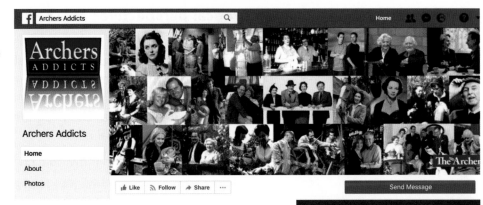

The 'Archers Addicts' Facebook page.

- The show explores topics such as financial problems and contemporary socio-political issues including Brexit.
- Many storylines involve relationships, which have wide appeal, as well as more dramatic events such as the recent 'hit and run' incident.

The website includes many articles that relate to the issues in the programme. Two young farmers, for example, provided advice about working in farming, linked to a storyline about Jonny's future career. Such features might appeal to young people in a similar situation.

The Archers also has many celebrity fans, and there is an introduction to the programme by Stephen Fry on the official website. He might act as an **opinion leader** and appeal to new audiences who then tune in to the show.

How do audiences respond to *The Archers*?

The Archers has a large audience and many listeners are actively involved in online communities related to the programme. Audiences can engage in many different ways, for example through the 'Read along with Lynda' feature on the website.

There are many fan forums and blogs about *The Archers*, including 'The Ambridge Observer' blog, 'Peet's Mustardland' fan forum and 'Archers Addicts' on Facebook. This demonstrates that some Archers fans are extremely active in sharing views and, in some cases, creating new content. 'Shambridge', for example, is a **pastiche** of *The Archers* created by a fan of the programme. All of this audience interaction demonstrates the popularity of the programme and how it has become an important part of British popular culture.

The Helen and Rob storyline led to some remarkable audience responses:

- As noted on page 98, thousands of pounds were raised for the Helen Titchener Fund.
- In September 2016 the 'Solidari-tea' campaign was launched, where people shared a cup of tea and a message of support for Helen and real-life victims of domestic abuse using the 'FreeHelen' hashtag. The campaign received 35 000 tweets in the weeks surrounding the trial and was nominated for the Best Socially Responsible Initiative at the 2017 'Social Buzz' Awards.

Key Term

Pastiche
A work of art or fiction that imitates the original product, possibly in a humorous way. A pastiche is usually a complimentary work, not designed to mock the original.

Top Tip

Look out for audience responses to the current storylines in *The Archers*, for example in newspaper articles or on the official website.

Stretch and Challenge 3.41

Interview a family member or friend who is an *Archers* fan. Find out how long they have been listening, why they listen, and whether they engage in social interaction relating to the show.

Top Tip

Make notes on the way in which listeners might identify with the characters and situations in the *Archers* episode you have studied.

Key Term

Turnover
A business term for the amount of money a company takes from sales of products.

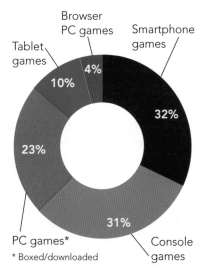

Browser PC games
Smartphone games
Tablet games
4%
10%
32%
23%
31%
PC games*
* Boxed/downloaded
Console games

A graphic from Newzoo showing the proportions of worldwide revenue generated by different formats of video gaming in 2017.

Quickfire 3.49

Why do you think smartphones have become a popular way for people to play video games?

Theoretical perspectives on *The Archers* audiences: Uses and Gratifications

Audiences might find pleasure in the familiarity of *The Archers*, for example if they have grown up with the programme. It can offer escapism and entertainment, especially as the soap opera genre constructs a 'parallel world' that runs alongside 'real' life. The programme also offers information and an insight into farming and rural issues.

Listeners might identify with individual characters and situations.

Many *Archers* listeners are active audience members who engage in social interaction on Twitter, Facebook and fan forums.

Video Games

You will study the set product, *Pokémon Go,* in relation to audience and industry issues by exploring pages from the *Pokémon* website, chosen by your teacher. Extracts from the game might be considered to explore relevant aspects of industry and audience.

Video gaming is a very significant media industry and has had a higher **turnover** than the Hollywood film industry in recent years. This is an interesting area to explore in terms of audience, as video games are very popular and offer ways for audiences to interact with the products to determine the outcome of a game or narrative. There has also been considerable debate about the possible negative effects of video games.

Video games and the importance of new technologies

Video games have traditionally been played on a desktop computer or on a games console, but tablets and smartphones are now very popular platforms for playing games. Mobile gaming is a fast-growing part of the industry, as it has the potential to reach a wider audience than more-conventional gaming. In 2017 more income was generated from smartphone games than any other individual type of game.

New and developing technologies are vitally important to video gaming and have driven developments in the industry. **Augmented reality**, used in *Pokémon Go,* is an example of an evolving technology. It allows producers to make advances in the types of games and experiences that they can create.

Pokémon Go is considered to be groundbreaking in its use of technology and the game has been extremely successful. Kat Brewster's review in the *Guardian* described the impact of the game and its possible future influence: 'It's not just another mobile game and it's not another Pokémon game – it's an entirely separate beast on the cusp of something vast; a glimpse into the future of widely accessible augmented reality.' (https://www.theguardian.com/technology/2016/jul/12/pokemon-go-review-it-may-not-be-a-good-game-but-its-a-great-experience)

Augmented reality technologies are still developing and are likely to feature in many future video games. In November 2017 it was announced that *Pokémon Go* producers Niantic are creating an augmented reality game called *Harry Potter: Wizards Unite*. This shows that the success of a product such as *Pokémon Go* can inspire other products and potentially increase market share and profits for a media organisation.

Overview of the Pokémon franchise

Pokémon Go is part of the Pokémon franchise that was launched in 1995 in Japan. It is a very well established and successful brand. The Pokémon Company was set up by three Japanese organisations:

- Nintendo: a major video games company that produces gaming consoles (such as the Nintendo DS) and games, including the Pokémon and Mario franchises.
- Game Freak: a video games developer that creates games for Nintendo, including many Pokémon games.
- Creatures: a video game development company that has also created toys and trading cards for Pokémon.

Pokémon is an entertainment brand with a wide global reach, backed by the very well-known Nintendo company. The first games were released in 1998 for the Nintendo Gameboy and many new games have been released in successive years. In 2017 *Pokémon Ultra Moon* and *Pokémon Ultra Sun* were the latest games to be released for the Nintendo 3DS. The Pokémon franchise also includes children's entertainment products such as animated television programmes and films, toys and trading cards. This allows the franchise to reach audiences through different platforms and offers users many opportunities to engage with Pokémon products.

Pokémon are small, brightly coloured creatures that appeal to children. The games are not particularly violent (the Pokémon do not die, for example) and are designed to promote values of friendship and teamwork. This reflects the young primary target audience and will appeal to parents who do not wish their children to be exposed to violent video games.

Stretch and Challenge 3.42

Research the *Harry Potter: Wizards Unite* augmented reality game in more detail. Identify how it is similar to *Pokémon Go*.

Key Term

Augmented reality
A form of technology that allows pictures of virtual objects to be overlaid onto images of the real world, for example on a mobile phone screen.

 Quickfire 3.50

Why is it important for media organisations to use a range of platforms to reach audiences?

A Pokémon store at Narita Airport in Tokyo.

The basis of the games is explained on the Pokémon website: 'In most games, the player takes on the role of a young Trainer whose journey involves traveling from place to place, catching and training Pokémon, and battling against other Trainers' Pokémon on a quest to become the Pokémon League Champion.' (pokemon.com/us/parents-guide) This provides audiences with a familiar concept across the different games and is a simple, accessible idea that players of all ages can understand.

The set product: *Pokémon Go*

The *Pokémon Go* game was created by Niantic, an American software development company. Niantic had previously produced a game called *Ingress*, a 'real world' science fiction mobile app. The influence of *Ingress* on *Pokémon Go* shows how technology inspires the development of different products.

Pokémon Go was launched in the summer of 2016 and became an enormously successful cultural phenomenon. Key points about the game include:

- It is an augmented reality mobile game available on iPhone and Android platforms.

- The game uses the player's mobile phone camera, GPS system and clock to create a 'real world' environment. Images of Pokémon are overlaid onto the phone's camera, so it looks as though they are actually in the player's local area, for example in their home or nearby streets.

- Players can see and catch the Pokémon using pokéballs. They can also take photos to share. The game allows users to create their own 'trainer' character and gain points as they capture the Pokémon.

- There are key places that players can visit in the game, such as pokéstops where players can get extra pokéballs, and gyms where battles take place: these are real buildings in the player's local area.

- The game can be played as a single player or multiplayer, as players have the opportunity to join a team and work together in battles against other teams. There are various challenges and levels that players can work through.

The game is free to download and play, but it makes money for the producers through:

- **in-app purchases** where users can buy pokécoins to exchange for power-ups and other items

- partnership deals with other companies, such as Starbucks, which became a partner and made thousands of stores in America into pokéstops and gyms for the game as well as creating a *Pokémon Go* drink

- the *Pokémon Go* Plus, a Bluetooth-enabled wristband that allows users to play the game simply and without looking down at their smartphone screen, so they can be aware of surroundings. It uses LED and vibration functions to notify players that a Pokémon is nearby.

A Pokémon on the California coast.

Key Term

In-app purchases
Additional content or facilities to buy from within a mobile phone app. They might enhance the experience or allow gamers to access extra features.

Quickfire 3.51

What elements of the earlier Pokémon games are used in *Pokémon Go*? What is new and different?

Stretch and Challenge 3.43

Research the different levels and challenges in the game. How might these appeal to both new and experienced gamers?

Quickfire 3.52

Why do you think this game was so successful?

A player wears the *Pokémon Go* Plus.

The launch and success of *Pokémon Go*: how did it reach its audience?

Pokémon Go did not rely on a major advertising campaign as the existing brand was already familiar to a wide range of audiences. A trailer was released in September 2015 and announcements were made on Niantic and Pokémon's social media feeds in the run up to the launch. Marketing was mainly viral 'word of mouth' as players joined in and shared experiences on social media.

A social intelligence company called Brandwatch that analyses conversations on social media sites found that, in its first week of release, *Pokémon Go* gained 4.5 million mentions and that the #PokémonGo hashtag 'made 5 982 616 734 impressions'. This has the effect of endorsing and raising the appeal of the product. It encourages more people to take part as many people are influenced by friends and family. As a product becomes successful, more and more people want to join the 'latest craze'.

A Pokémon in a Thailand supermarket.

The game was launched in July 2016, initially in Australia, New Zealand and the USA. This tied in with the summer holidays, when children have time to play and parents are keen to occupy them. The interest in the game led to huge numbers of people downloading it at once, and the launch in some countries, including the UK, had to be delayed. By the end of 2016 the game had also been released in Asia, Africa and the Middle East.

The *Guardian* reported that the game was downloaded 100 million times in the first month. *Pokémon Go* also reportedly earned $10 million per day at the height of its popularity, causing Nintendo's share price to rise. The success of a game can have a very positive effect on a media organisation.

The game was extremely popular in its first summer. Player numbers have dropped significantly since then, but it is still played by many people. There have been regular updates to the game and Niantic is still adding features to maintain interest and engage users:

- The *Pokémon Go* Travel Global Catch Challenge in November 2017 encouraged gamers to join a quest to find 3 billion Pokémon in seven days.

- An update on 8 December 2017 was announced on the website and social media. The Facebook page announced that Pokémon from the Hoenn region had been spotted all over the world. The post had received over 16 000 likes, 2000 shares and 1000 comments by 13 December. This demonstrates the active nature of the gaming audience and how the producers harnessed the potential for the audience itself to spread the word about the product.

Quickfire 3.53

How do new updates and special challenges appeal to game audiences?

Top Tip

Find out about the latest update from the Pokémon website. Make notes about how these offer audiences new features.

Pokémon GO team

The *Pokémon Go* website homepage updated for Halloween.

Studying the Pokémon website: industry and audience

The Pokémon website, and linked social media, is an important way for the brand to reach its audience. The website announces information about the game, and *Pokémon Go* has its own section of the website. There is also an official *Pokémon Go* YouTube channel where audiences can watch videos that provide playing tips and information about the latest developments. *Pokémon Go* also regularly updates its Twitter, Facebook and Instagram pages.

The *Pokémon Go* pages of the website encourage audiences to engage with the product. For example:

- The slogan on the website 'Get up and go' is an imperative and works on two levels; encouraging the audience to play the game and also be active. The use of 'go' reinforces the name of the game.
- The website includes a feature about *Pokémon Go* Plus, encouraging the audience to purchase it by announcing 'A Pokémon is nearby!', as *Pokémon Go* Plus alerts players to Pokémon. The group of three phrases 'Get going. Get alerts. Get Pokémon' is another persuasive technique.
- The website also features links to other Pokémon products in the menu bar – games, apps, a shop – to reinforce the brand and develop the potential for audiences to buy other products in the franchise, increasing the potential for commercial success.

How are video games regulated?

Video games are classified in Europe using PEGI (Pan European Game Information) ratings. The Video Standards Council Rating Board is responsible for rating video games and apps in the UK, using the PEGI system. The PEGI ratings work in a similar way to BBFC age certificates. For example, a game with a PEGI rating of 7 is suitable for children aged seven and over. The ratings are determined by factors such as levels of violence, bad language and how frightening the games are.

Most Pokémon video games have been rated PEGI 7 for mild fantasy violence. However, *Pokémon Go* was given a wide range of ratings. The Google Play Store rated the game as a PEGI 3, while the Apple iTunes app store rated it 9+. Common Sense Media, an American organisation that informs parents about safe use of technology, rated the game as 13+.

This highlights some of the issues raised by the internet and mobile technologies, which can be very difficult to regulate. Even though *Pokémon Go* does not feature a great deal of violence or bad language, there was still considerable debate about its suitability for children.

Concerns were expressed at the game's use of GPS tracking and the need for players to submit information such as an email address. This raises issues of children's privacy and safety, especially as players can interact with other people who might be complete strangers.

Many organisations, such as the NSPCC, issued guidance about playing the game, to inform parents about potential risks to their children.

Activity 3.20

Study the homepage of the Pokémon website.

- What are the main features?
- What Pokémon products are shown?
- How are audiences able to interact?
- What examples of synergy can you find, where one Pokémon product links to another?
- How does Pokémon reach a global audience?

Different certification boards have given *Pokémon Go* different minimum-age ratings, from 7 to 13.

The Pokémon audience

Tsunekazu Ishihara, president of the Pokémon Company, has described the universal appeal of the Pokémon concept. Even though the technology might change, 'Nothing brings us more pleasure than if we can let people experience the memories and excitement of something like bug collecting, which everyone has experienced as children.' (pokemon.co.jp/corporate/en/interview) This idea connects to a simple human pleasure of seeking and collecting 'treasure' and appeals to people of different ages and from different countries. This is one reason why the game had such wide audience appeal.

Research by Forbes (forbes.com/video/5050970867001/) found the audience demographic breakdown was:

- Gender: 37 per cent male, 63 per cent female.
- Age: 13 to 17: 22 per cent; 18 to 29: 46 per cent; 30 to 50: 25 per cent; 51 and over: 6 per cent.

The game also successfully reached a global audience. The diagram below, from Brandwatch, shows the worldwide mentions on social media. This is particularly interesting as the statistics relate to the first week of the game's release, when it had only launched in the USA, Australia and New Zealand.

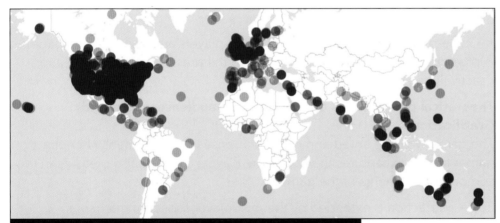

Geo-tagged mentions of *Pokémon Go* across the world, 4 to 10 July 2016. (Social data and image from Brandwatch.)

The fact that *Pokémon Go* was being discussed on social media before it had been released in many countries shows how the game was capturing people's attention and there was a 'buzz' around the product.

How did *Pokémon Go* appeal to such a wide audience?

The game captured the interest of several different audience groups, many of whom were not necessarily serious or committed video gamers, for example:

- fans of the Pokémon franchise who would want to be involved in the latest Pokémon product
- adult users who remember the original Pokémon games from the 1990s and might have a sense of nostalgia for the brand; these **'millennials'** might have plenty of disposable income to spend on the game
- younger players who have grown up with Pokémon and enjoy the familiarity as well as the new features of this game

Quickfire 3.54

Why do you think *Pokémon Go* had such a variety of age ratings?

Quickfire 3.55

What does the concern about the safety of *Pokémon Go* suggest about its current social and cultural context?

Quickfire 3.56

Who do you think is the primary target audience for *Pokémon Go*?

Stretch and Challenge 3.44

Do you think this audience (from Quickfire 3.56) is typical of video game users? Try to find out the audience demographics for other Pokémon games and compare them with *Pokémon Go*.

Quickfire 3.57

Where was *Pokémon Go* being talked about most?

Key Term

Millennials
An audience demographic group that describes people who were born from 1980 up to around the year 2000. They are the first group of people to reach adulthood in the new millennium.

- fans of technology in general keen to experience how the game makes use of the new technology
- more casual gamers who enjoy the latest popular product and were interested to test it out
- people who do not normally play video games, encouraged to play by their friends or family.

In addition:

- The significant media attention and word-of-mouth communication might also have inspired people to try the game if they wanted to be part of the cultural phenomenon.
- The fact that it can easily be played on a mobile phone and does not require a specific console, or even a computer, extended the possible audience.
- Also, because it is free to download it would be attractive to people unwilling to pay, again extending the audience reach beyond serious and committed gamers.
- The game also appeals to audiences through the augmented reality nature of the game which is personalised to the player's own location and environment.
- It can be played at any time and anywhere so is convenient and can fit in to people's lives.
- Game-playing is extremely interactive as players are required to engage physically with the game, responding to the presence of Pokémon and actively seeking them out.

Theoretical perspectives on *Pokémon Go* audiences: Uses and Gratifications

The game provides entertainment and a sense of achievement when the gamer finds and captures the Pokémon. Players can take also pleasure in the competitive elements of the game.

Social interaction is extended by the multiplayer aspect of the game.

The game was discussed at length in the media and so became a **watercooler topic** that players wanted to share. The game was also talked about extensively on social media, as detailed above.

Audience responses to *Pokémon Go*

Many people posted responses in the form of user reviews on the Apple or Google websites and comments on social media. Some people made negative remarks about technological problems at first, but much of the feedback was very positive.

The success of the game generated a very large amount of media coverage and it became a news story in its own right. In Britain, for example, the *Daily Telegraph* ran an article about the game and how to play it.

Some fans have created their own **user-generated content**, such as walk-throughs and training videos that they post online. This helps to maintain awareness and interest in the game and enhances other gamers' experiences of the product.

The impact of *Pokémon Go*

The game made a significant impact on popular culture. In addition to the large audience response, the effects of the game have been studied by university academics. The Department of Physics and Astronomy at Leicester University, for example, carried out a study to see how long it would take to track down every Pokémon in existence.

There is some evidence to suggest that *Pokémon Go* has had a positive impact on society. It can prompt people to become more social. Players need to be active to play, so it could be argued that the game encourages people to take exercise. Some medical research has suggested that playing the game could help people who suffer with conditions such as Type 2 diabetes, but they would have to continue playing over a long period of time for the game to have a lasting impact.

On the other hand, there have been concerns about negative aspects of the game. There are potential privacy and safety issues, particularly in relation to younger players, as identified above in the section on regulation. There have also been reports of people becoming so engrossed in the game that they take risks, such as:

- walking or running while concentrating at their phone instead of looking where they are going
- going out in the middle of the night to play
- going to dangerous places to track down Pokémon
- playing when cycling or driving (there were reports of car accidents near buildings that were pokéstops).

Some *Pokémon Go* players have even played while driving.

This type of behaviour would seem to support the argument that video games can have a negative effect on the audience. The immersive nature of video games potentially influencing user behaviour has been a hotly debated topic for many years. Some commentators argue, for example, that a person who plays violent video games might be more likely to commit violent acts. The concern with *Pokémon Go* relates to people's risky behaviour when they play the game, rather than danger from replicating the content of the game. Nonetheless, the combination of elements such as 'treasure hunting', the augmented reality technology, the competition and the ability to play the game on an 'everyday' smartphone resulted in many people becoming quite fanatical about *Pokémon Go*.

Quickfire 3.59

Which audience theory applies to the idea that video games might have a negative influence on people's behaviour?

Assessment of Component 1: Exploring the Media

Quickfire 4.1

Why is it important to use specific terminology?

Top Tip

Revise the theories you have studied with the aim of applying them in your responses.

Quickfire 4.2

How many set products will you need to analyse in Section A of the exam?

Top Tip

Make sure you analyse a selection of different products in the forms you have studied in Section A. This will help you to approach the unseen resource in the exam.

How Will I Be Assessed?

The Component 1 examination assesses media language, representations, media industries, audiences and media contexts.

- The examination is 1 hour 30 minutes.
- It counts for 40 per cent of the qualification.
- It is split into two sections, as detailed below.

You will be assessed on your use of appropriate subject-specific terminology and relevant theories or theoretical perspectives.

There is further information and advice to help you to prepare for the exam in Chapter 9 of this book.

Section A: Exploring Media Language and Representation

Any of the following media forms could be assessed:

- Advertising
- Marketing (film posters)
- Magazines
- Newspapers.

Section A will assess media language, representations and contexts. You will be required to analyse an **unseen media product** in this section. There will be two questions:

- **Question 1** will focus on media language and you will be asked to analyse one of the set products you have studied. You will be able to refer to a clean copy of the set product in the exam.
- **Question 2** will assess context and representation in relation to a different form from that in Question 1.

Part a will focus on knowledge and understanding of context in one set product.

Part b will ask you to compare a set product with an unseen product in the same form. This question will require an **extended response** and you will need to make judgements and draw conclusions.

Section B: Exploring Media Industries and Audiences

Any of the following forms could be assessed:

* Film
* Radio
* Newspapers
* Video games.

Section B will assess media industries and audiences. There will be two questions:

* **Question 3** will be a **stepped question** that will focus on knowledge and understanding of media industries in relation to one of the forms you have studied.

* **Question 4** will also be a stepped question, assessing your knowledge and understanding of audiences in relation to a different media form from that in Question 3.

Quickfire 4.3

In which area of the theoretical framework will you study film?

Top Tip

Plan your time carefully in the exam to ensure that you can complete all the questions.

Key Terms

Unseen media product
A media product that you have not studied in class. This will be provided in the exam and you will need to compare it with one of the set products.

Extended response
A longer exam answer where you will need to make judgements and draw conclusions.

Stepped question
A question that is broken down into a number of 'steps' that require shorter answers.

Component 2: Understanding Media Forms and Products

OVERVIEW

Component 2 aims to:

- build on the introduction to the theoretical framework in Component 1
- deepen your knowledge and understanding of media language and representation and media industries and audiences
- develop your ability to analyse audio-visual media products in depth
- consider how contexts, such as social and historical, can influence media products
- deepen your understanding of the theoretical perspectives of media studies
- extend your ability to use subject-specific terminology.

You will study three media forms in depth in Component 2:

- Television in Section A
- Music Video and Online Media in Section B.

Introduction to Analysing Audio-Visual Products

You will analyse many print products in Component 1 and some of these skills will also apply to the products from Component 2, for example decoding meanings and connotations. You will also need to develop an understanding of audio-visual forms of media: television and music videos. Each of these forms has specific codes and conventions, but there are some common elements to audio-visual products, as detailed below.

Technical Codes

The technical codes in an audio-visual product relate to camera techniques and editing.

Camera

Camera shots

In addition to the camera techniques outlined in Chapter 1 (page 18), you should consider the following types of shot:

- **Establishing shot**: This identifies the setting or location in a media product. It can convey information very quickly to help the audience to understand where the action takes place, as well as communicating information about the type or genre of product.

Sponsored by
MITSUBISHI MOTORS

This shot from the opening of Channel 4's *24 Hours in A&E* depicts the London skyline in the background, where the hospital is located. The inclusion of the field in the foreground connotes that people who are living their 'normal' lives will find themselves in A&E during the episode.

- **Point of view**: The camera is placed in the position of a particular character to show what they can see. This is often used to place the audience with the character, to show their perspective. It can also limit the audience's view, as they can only see what the character sees.

- **Canted angle** (sometimes called a **Dutch tilt**): Here the camera is at an angle, so the shot is not straight and it appears that the objects in the frame are slanted. This is often used to suggest that something bad has happened or that the narrative has been disrupted, for example in a television thriller.

This canted-angle shot connotes potential danger behind the fencing and barbed wire.

Camera movements

When you analyse audio-visual products, such as music videos and television programmes, you will also need to analyse camera movement. The main types of movement are:

- **Pan**: The camera moves across the view from one side to the other, usually from left to right as this is the way that we read text. This can be used to reveal information or establish setting, as it appears to the audience that they are looking around.

- **Tilt**: The camera moves up or down to reveal information or details within the frame, for example tilting up a character's body to reveal their face.

- **Tracking**: Here the camera moves backwards, forwards or alongside the action, which helps the audience to feel involved. The camera usually follows a particular character or part of the action. This type of shot can be achieved using a **dolly**, **crane** or **handheld camera**.

A camera on a dolly and track.

Key Terms

Dolly
A platform with wheels that usually runs along a track. The camera is mounted onto the platform and can be wheeled smoothly along the track to capture the action.

Crane
A camera mount that can move upwards to give a high-angled view of a location. This type of movement might be used at the end of a scene to move the action from one location to another.

Handheld camera
A camera not mounted on a tripod or dolly, but held by the camera operator. Handheld camera shots tend to be shakier but can create a sense of realism, immersing the audience in the action. Some documentaries use handheld camera shots.

Key Terms

Post-production
The stage after filming has been completed. Post-production includes editing images and sound and possibly adding particular effects to shape and 'polish' the product.

Continuity editing
Putting shots together so that the cutting seems 'invisible' and the sequence looks natural to the viewer.

Shot-reverse-shot
A filming technique often used for conversations. The first shot shows one character's point of view, looking at the other; then the action is edited to show a shot from the other character's perspective, and so on.

Editing

Editing takes place at the **post-production** stage of creating a media product, after the footage has been filmed. The editing of an audio-visual product is the process of selecting shots and putting them into a particular order or structure. Most products feature a large number of different shots, usually in different locations, that are edited or 'cut' to enable the audience to understand the narrative, themes and ideas.

Television programmes and music videos use particular editing codes and conventions, and you should become familiar with the following:

- **Continuity editing:** Many narratives, for example a television sequence, use **continuity editing** to structure the action in a logical way that the audience can understand. A continuity sequence will usually begin with an establishing shot, then move closer in to the action. Long shots, then medium shots might be used to introduce characters and then medium close-ups and close-ups, especially in sequences of dialogue. This method helps the audience to make sense of the scene and brings them closer to the action and the characters.

Here are some of the techniques used in continuity editing:

- **Shot-reverse-shot**: In this sequence from *Humans* (Channel 4, 2016) there is an example of **shot-reverse-shots** as Anita approaches Ed to tell him how she feels about him. This draws the audience into the action and shows the characters' emotions. In shot 1 Ed is looking down the steps. Shot 2 reveals Anita, the person Ed has been looking at. This is also a point-of-view shot. Shot 3 is a reverse shot of Ed as Anita approaches up the steps. Shot 4 is another reverse shot.

Top Tip

Look out for continuity sequences when you are watching television programmes. Make a note of the techniques used.

- **Eye-line match**: A character is shown looking off-screen; the action cuts to show what the character is looking at.
- **Match on action**: A technique where the edit is 'hidden' in the action. For example if a character walks through a door into a room we might see them from behind, approaching the door; then, as the character goes through the door, the action cuts to a front view of the door as the character comes into the room.
- **Parallel editing**, or **cross-cutting**: Where the editing cuts between two sequences of action that are happening at the same time. For example, if two characters are about to meet, the editing might cut between shots of each of them getting ready and travelling to the meeting point. This technique might be used to:

- give the audience insight into two different viewpoints
- make the action more interesting to watch
- build tension, for example if the action is building towards a moment of **climax.**
- **Montage editing**: In some products, such as trailers or title sequences, **montage editing** might be used to communicate the themes or ideas in the product. The trailer for *Educating Greater Manchester* (Channel 4, 2017) edits images from different parts of the programme in a montage to create an idea of what the school is like. The two images are placed together as the characters are dancing. Even though there is no obvious link between the scenes, both images suggest that the school is an uplifting place to be.

Music videos might use continuity editing in narrative sequences, but there are also likely to be elements of montage as they are short texts that need to communicate ideas quickly. Performance footage is usually included and this incorporates specific conventions that will be explored in Section B.

The **pace** of editing is also important. Slow-paced editing often builds tension gradually or establishes characters and their relationships. Fast editing is often a feature of music videos and is used in television action sequences and to build a scene to a climax.

Audio codes

Sound is extremely important in audio-visual products. Music videos primarily feature the music track or song, although some videos also include other elements of sound. Television programmes use a variety of sound including **dialogue**, music and sound effects. Some of the sound will be recorded at the same time as the action, but other elements of sound, such as music or narration, will be added at the post-production stage.

Diegetic and non-diegetic sound

Diegetic sound is part of the 'world' of the text. If the characters in the scene would be able to hear the sound it is diegetic. Any sounds and music that are added, for example to create atmosphere or tension for the audience, and that the characters would not be able to hear, are **non-diegetic**.

Activity 5.1

Which of these types of sound are diegetic and which are non-diegetic?
- Music playing on the radio in the room where the scene is taking place.
- Voiceover of a character's inner thoughts.
- Dialogue between two characters in a scene.
- A fire alarm sounding in a building where the action is happening.
- Orchestral music adding a dramatic effect.
- A heartbeat sound effect to connote that tension is building.
- The sound of breaking glass as a character drops a vase on the floor.
- A laughter track in a sitcom (where we hear the audience laughing at the action).

Key Terms

Climax
A point of high tension or action, for example a confrontation between the hero and villain. A narrative will usually build to a climax over a period of time and the outcome will often provide a resolution, for example the hero defeats the villain.

Montage editing
A technique where different types of image are put together. These are usually linked in some way to make the montage meaningful. Images might be linked by a theme or a character.

Pace
The speed of edit effects: fast-paced editing has many cuts between very short shots (or 'takes'), whereas slow-paced editing features fewer cuts between longer takes.

Dialogue
The words spoken by characters in a scene, usually a conversation between two or more characters.

Sound and semiotics

Sound can also be used to suggest deeper meanings in a media product. The sound of a ticking clock, for example might connote that time is running out or a deadline is approaching. The meanings created might depend on the genre of the product, and the audience will have certain expectations of the type of sound that might be used. A mystery drama might use slow-paced, classical music to build tension, while a romantic comedy is more likely to use more upbeat, pop music.

A **sound bridge** is an editing technique used to link scenes together. At the end of a scene in a television drama, for example, we might hear music from the next scene to link into what is coming next and provide continuity of meaning.

Dialogue and spoken language

The vocabulary and style of language used in a television programme communicates information about the genre, narrative and characters. Some products, for example news programmes and documentaries, will use mainly factual and informative language. Fictional programmes feature scripted dialogue that is used to construct the character, so factors such as their age, social background and where they come from will affect the way they speak. Some characters might use a particular **dialect**, for example. Dialogue can also be used to provide information about a character's professional role. Luther and his colleagues, for example, use specialist lexis (vocabulary or language tools) relating to their police work.

Music

Non-diegetic music is used in many different types of television programme and in a variety of ways. Producers often use music to construct meaning. For example, romantic music playing as two characters meet is a signal that they might fall in love. Music can also underscore the action and create atmosphere. Nature documentaries, for example often use music to connote danger as one animal preys on another. Images of sharks might be accompanied by threatening, dramatic music to signal the danger for their weaker prey. This often creates a sense that the stronger animals are the 'villains' and positions the audience to feel sympathy with the prey.

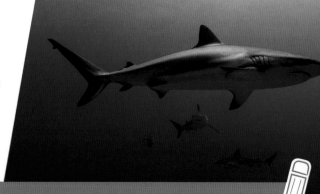

Quickfire 5.1

What might the following sounds connote?

- A heartbeat
- Thunder
- A nursery rhyme
- A siren or alarm
- A creaking door

Top Tip

Listen out for the lexis used in the set products. Make a note of the words and phrases that communicate information about the workplace in the product.

Key Term

Dialect
Language specific to a particular part of the country. A dialect will include words and phrases that are not generally used in 'mainstream' English.

Quickfire 5.2

Which element of narrative is used if a programme shows villains versus victims?

Activity 5.2

The IT Crowd and *Luther* have very different theme tunes. The *IT Crowd* theme tune was composed by Neil Hannon of The Divine Comedy. *Luther*'s theme song is a version of 'Paradise Circus' by Massive Attack.

Listen to the theme tune for each programme.

- How does the music signify the genre. How can you tell that one programme is a sitcom and the other a crime drama?
- What messages does the music (and lyrics) communicate about the themes in each programme?

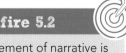

Sound effects

Sound effects can add to the realism of a scene, such as the sound of a bee buzzing on a summer day. These sound effects can also be enhanced, or made more noticeable: the sound of a bee buzzing might be louder than it would be in real life. This might connote that there is a threat; that something bad is going to happen.

The sound effect of a bee buzzing used on a soundtrack is usually louder than it would be in real life.

Section A: Television

Overview

You will study one television genre, chosen by your teacher, from the following options:

Options	1: Crime Drama	2: Sitcom
Set products	*Luther*, Series 1, Episode 1 (2010) *The Sweeney*, Series 1, Episode 1 (1975)	*The IT Crowd*, Season 4, Episode 2: 'The Final Countdown' (2010) *Friends*, Season 1 , Episode 1 (1994)
What will I study?	The complete episode of *Luther* plus a ten-minute extract from *The Sweeney*	The complete episode of *The IT Crowd* plus a ten-minute extract from *Friends*.

You will analyse and compare the products in relation to all areas of the theoretical framework:

- **Media language**, including:
  - the codes and conventions of media language used in television products
  - genres; how they change over time, principles of repetition and variation
  - narrative
- **Representations**, including:
  - gender, ethnicity and age
  - messages and values; themes and issues
  - stereotypes
- **Media industries**, including:
  - funding, ownership and control
  - the importance of the chosen genre to the TV industry
- **Audiences**, including:
  - the appeals of these genres to audiences
  - audience targeting, consumption and response
- **Contexts**: how the sitcoms or crime dramas reflect the society and culture in which they were made.

Analysing the Set Products

Studying the full episode of the contemporary product will allow you to analyse the narrative throughout the episode and explore a range of genre codes and representations.

Comparing the contemporary text with the ten-minute extract from the older product will enable you to consider:

- how genres change over time
- how the products reflect the contexts in which they were made in relation to:
  - the use of media language, including technology
  - representations of gender, ethnicity and age
  - themes and issues explored
  - the messages and values communicated
- key aspects of industry, including contemporary developments in broadcasting
- audience issues, including how audience interpretations of media products change over time.

Key Term

Event television
A 'must-see' programme that attracts a very large audience and generates a lot of discussion in the media. These programmes are usually marketed heavily to generate a 'buzz' before broadcast.

Overview of the Television Industry

Television has changed dramatically in recent years. Developments in technology have allowed audiences to access many digital channels, and online streaming services have become extremely popular, so audiences can now watch television when and where they like on any number of devices. This is very different from the experience of watching television in the past, when there were a limited number of channels and audiences had to watch at a particular time – when the programme was broadcast.

Some contemporary programmes achieve the status of **event television** and gain very large audiences on their first broadcast. The BBC series *Blue Planet II*, for example, had an audience of 14 million.

Digital technology has changed how media organisations now produce and circulate television programmes too, and how audiences consume media products. Programme producers can target different specific groups and some products are aimed at more specialised audiences.

The very wide range of channels available means that audiences are spread much more thinly across more programmes than in the past. *EastEnders*, for example, achieved viewing figures of up to 20 million in 1998, but currently has an audience of between 6.5 and 7 million for each episode. (Television viewing figures are published by BARB, the Broadcasters' Audience Research Board, which researches television audiences' viewing habits.)

The red-carpet launch of a new series of *Strictly Come Dancing* always causes considerable media and social media activity.

Timeline of key television developments in the UK

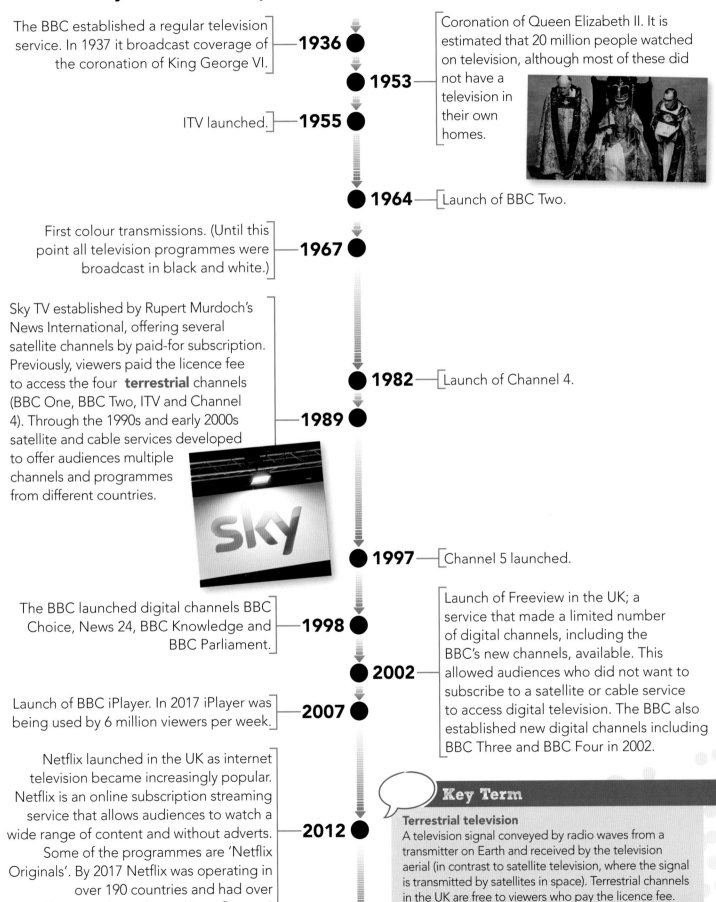

The BBC established a regular television service. In 1937 it broadcast coverage of the coronation of King George VI.

1936

Coronation of Queen Elizabeth II. It is estimated that 20 million people watched on television, although most of these did not have a television in their own homes.

1953

ITV launched. — **1955**

1964 — Launch of BBC Two.

First colour transmissions. (Until this point all television programmes were broadcast in black and white.)

1967

Sky TV established by Rupert Murdoch's News International, offering several satellite channels by paid-for subscription. Previously, viewers paid the licence fee to access the four **terrestrial** channels (BBC One, BBC Two, ITV and Channel 4). Through the 1990s and early 2000s satellite and cable services developed to offer audiences multiple channels and programmes from different countries.

1982 — Launch of Channel 4.

1989

1997 — Channel 5 launched.

The BBC launched digital channels BBC Choice, News 24, BBC Knowledge and BBC Parliament.

1998

Launch of Freeview in the UK; a service that made a limited number of digital channels, including the BBC's new channels, available. This allowed audiences who did not want to subscribe to a satellite or cable service to access digital television. The BBC also established new digital channels including BBC Three and BBC Four in 2002.

2002

Launch of BBC iPlayer. In 2017 iPlayer was being used by 6 million viewers per week.

2007

Netflix launched in the UK as internet television became increasingly popular. Netflix is an online subscription streaming service that allows audiences to watch a wide range of content and without adverts. Some of the programmes are 'Netflix Originals'. By 2017 Netflix was operating in over 190 countries and had over 100 million members. (https://ir.netflix.com)

2012

Key Term

Terrestrial television
A television signal conveyed by radio waves from a transmitter on Earth and received by the television aerial (in contrast to satellite television, where the signal is transmitted by satellites in space). Terrestrial channels in the UK are free to viewers who pay the licence fee.

Public service broadcasting

Ofcom has defined public service broadcasting as, 'high-quality content, made for as wide a range of audiences as possible, and for public benefit rather than purely commercial ends'. (ofcom.org.uk/__data/assets/pdf_file/0029/57638/psb_concise_summary.pdf)

The BBC is a public broadcaster, funded by the licence fee. Channel 4, ITV and Channel 5 are commercial public broadcasters. Most of their funding comes from advertising. These channels are available to all viewers who pay the licence fee and they have to meet public-service requirements, for example to produce a wide range of programmes and reflect the cultural diversity of the UK.

Ofcom regulates the television industry, including on-demand catch-up services. There is a broadcasting code that organisations must follow, including standards in relation to programme content to protect audiences from potentially offensive material. Ofcom also responds to complaints about television programmes.

Television viewers now have more choice than ever, but, Ofcom has reported, the main public service broadcasters in the UK (BBC, ITV, Channel 4 and Channel 5) accounted for 70 per cent of television viewing in 2016.

Quickfire 5.3

Why do you think the public service broadcasters have such a large percentage of the television audience?

The BBC

There is some introductory information about the BBC in Chapter 3 (page 97).

The BBC's Royal Charter was renewed in 2016 and the licence fee was guaranteed to continue for at least 11 years. As many viewers now pay for subscription services, however, it is not clear how much longer the licence fee will continue into the future. The BBC is the UK's longest-standing broadcaster and is known for producing high-quality products such as period dramas, news and nature programmes that can also be sold worldwide.

The BBC has developed many innovations over time to ensure that it provides a public service and that audiences continue to consume its products. It has introduced many interactive features, as its website states: 'Audiences wanted more interactivity with their favourite programmes and the BBC reacted by creating content for the Red Button on digital TV and fielding audience comments and reactions on message boards, chat rooms and online forums.' (downloads.bbc.co.uk/historyofthebbc/2000s.pdf)

This suggests that the audience has an important role to play in informing the organisation's developments and that the BBC responds to its viewers.

The BBC has in-house production facilities, which means that many programmes, including *Luther*, are produced by the BBC itself. Some are made by independent production companies.

BBC Worldwide distributes BBC programmes around the globe.

BBC One broadcasts many drama programmes. Some of these are long-running serials such as *EastEnders* and *Holby City*, while others are shorter series of around six episodes across different genres.

Top Tip

Research the BBC website and identify some of the high-quality programmes that help the organisation to remain at the forefront of British broadcasting.

Stretch and Challenge 5.1

Look at the BBC website and identify opportunities for audiences to offer views and feedback.

Channel 4

Channel 4 launched in 1982 to broaden the range of terrestrial channels in the UK. The channel's website describes it as 'a publicly owned and commercially funded UK public service broadcaster, with a statutory remit to deliver high-quality, innovative, alternative content that challenges the status quo.' (channel4.com/corporate/about-4/who-we-are/what-is-channel-4)

Channel 4 is a not-for-profit organisation, so the money it makes goes back into producing programmes. The channel does not produce its own programmes in-house, but commissions content from other production companies in the UK. It broadcasts many programmes that are outside the mainstream and do not necessarily support dominant messages and values. It is known for broadcasting alternative comedy as well as dramas, documentaries and reality television shows.

Channel 4 also operates E4, More4, 4seven, Film4 and 4Music. It also has a catch-up service called All 4. Channel 4 Distribution licences programmes to other broadcasters in the UK and Ireland.

Television Audiences

In the past, before the arrival of catch-up services and online streaming, audiences could only watch a television programme at the time it was broadcast and would have to wait until the next episode to see how the narrative developed. This provided specific pleasures, as an episode might end on a cliff-hanger so the audience would be keen to tune in next time to find out what happened. Television played an important role in many people's lives. Families would often sit down together in an evening to enjoy their favourite programmes and the most popular shows would be discussed in workplaces the following day.

Modern audiences have much more choice and flexibility in their television consumption. Viewers can actively select programmes and watch them where and when they want. While television is still important in people's lives, families are likely to spend less time watching the same programmes together and individuals might be watching different programmes on different devices in the same house, or even in the same room. Discussions about popular television programmes still take place, but this social interaction tends to happen more online and often while the viewer is still watching the programme, using a **second screen**.

Marie-José Montpetit, a media academic, has argued that audiences are more powerful in the internet age but that this increased interaction also benefits media organisations, as viewers help to publicise television programmes: 'Social television is a consequence of the convergence of TV and internet. Twitter, Facebook, and a growing list of tablet applications, allow ratings, checking-in and instantaneous communication between viewers, actors and characters. Soon applications will allow the sharing of snippets of programming. These are all builders of brand and programme loyalty.' (theguardian.com/media-network/media-network-blog/2014/jun/10/internet-changing-definition-television)

> **Stretch and Challenge 5.2**
>
> Research the '4' channels and find out what kinds of programme they broadcast.

> **Key Term**
>
> **Second screen**
> Where a viewer watches a television programme on one screen and uses a second screen, such as a phone, to tweet or text a friend about the programme.

Key Terms

Binge-watching
Consuming multiple episodes of a television series at once.

Instant gratification
A pleasure that comes from having everything at once rather than delaying or extending the enjoyment by, for example, waiting for the next instalment.

Quickfire 5.4

Which audience theory includes 'social interaction'?

Key Term

Action genre
A genre that focuses on action (often fast paced) more than dialogue, usually featuring elements such as fights, stunts and chases.

Stretch and Challenge 5.3

Look at TV listings pages for a week. How many crime dramas can you identify? When and where are they broadcast?

Binge-watching is a recent trend that has developed with the availability of DVD box sets and online streaming services such as Netflix. Every episode of a series is available at the same time, so audiences do not have to wait to find out how the narrative develops. Pleasures of binge-watching include:

- escapism; it provides an immersive experience, perhaps more like watching a film than a traditional television programme
- becoming involved with the narrative, and following it more easily, perhaps picking up on more clues or enigmas and making links between episodes
- personal identification with the characters as the viewer engages with them and watches them develop.
- **instant gratification** rather than having to be patient and wait for a future episode.

There are concerns, however, that binge-watching can become addictive or overwhelming and that viewers can feel isolated and sad when they have finished watching a series.

Section A, Option 1: Introduction to the Crime Drama Genre

Crime is a popular subgenre of television drama. The central feature of this genre is a narrative based around solving a crime, and this can be approached in many different ways. There are several further subgenres of crime, such as police or detective dramas. Contemporary crime drama often includes elements of hybridity with other genres. The BBC drama *Peaky Blinders* is an example of a period crime and gangster hybrid.

Each of the set products fits into the police subgenre of crime, but *The Sweeney* features elements of the **action genre**, while *Luther* includes conventions of different genres such as thriller. The crime genre has become more focused on psychology over time, by exploring the motives for a particular crime and the personal lives of the detectives.

The 'Nordic Noir' genre has become very popular in recent years and many British crime dramas have been influenced by the darker themes and complex narratives of programmes such as *The Killing* and *The Bridge*. *Broadchurch* is an example of a recent crime drama that, as Nordic Noir often does, explores one major crime across an entire series rather than focusing on a different case in each episode.

An example of how the crime genre has changed over time: Sherlock Holmes

Sherlock Holmes stories are an example of the detective subgenre of crime. Stories based on the popular character, created in the 1880s by Arthur Conan Doyle, have been reproduced many times, both as films and television series.

Granada Television produced a series of *The Adventures of Sherlock Holmes*, broadcast on ITV between 1984 and 1994, set in the original Victorian era.

Peter Cushing 1913–1994
Film and television actor

A postage stamp celebrating Peter Cushing as a classic television interpretation of Sherlock Holmes.

The BBC produced a new series, *Sherlock,* beginning in 2010. It starred Benedict Cumberbatch as Sherlock and Martin Freeman as Watson. Set in modern-day London, it updated many aspects of the original stories while retaining some familiar elements.

The series made use of digital technologies to reveal elements of the narrative, for example giving an insight into Sherlock's thought processes as he makes deductions or plans his next move.

Jeremy Brett and David Burke in Granada Televison's *The Adventures of Sherlock Holmes.*

The BBC's contemporary *Sherlock.*

Quickfire 5.5

Which visual codes in the Granada *Sherlock Holmes* images connote Victorian times?

Crime drama: repertoire of elements

There are many established codes and conventions in the crime genre, which can be grouped into the categories: narrative, characters and technical/visual codes.

Narrative

Television drama series generally focus on one crime that will be resolved in each episode. Some storylines, however, will continue throughout the series. This means that audiences can watch one episode and understand the narrative, but there are added pleasures in watching the whole series and seeing these stories develop. There are certain narrative events that usually occur in crime dramas:

* Crime, for example a theft, murder or assault
* Investigation, which might cover many stages, such as planning the investigation, surveillance, looking for clues at the scene of crime, interviewing witnesses, discussing developments, forensic investigation, chases, arrests and interrogating suspects
* Trial, which might include presenting evidence in court, questioning suspects and witnesses, verdicts and sentencing.

Stretch and Challenge 5.4

Note down key differences between the contemporary and older versions of *Sherlock.*

Quickfire 5.6

What is the 'repertoire of elements' in a genre?

Sarah Lancashire in the BBC crime drama, *Happy Valley*.

There is always a crime that needs to be solved at the centre of the narrative. Crime dramas usually reflect elements of Todorov's narrative theory, where the crime is the disruption and solving the crime is the resolution. Nonetheless, there are different ways in which the narrative may be structured around the crime and investigation, and you will need to consider:

- When does the crime happen?
  - Has it already happened at the start of the narrative, in which case is it shown in a flashback?
  - Does it occur at the beginning of the narrative?
  - Does it happen during the narrative after a period of equilibrium?
- How is the crime investigated?
  - How much information is revealed and when? What clues are given to the possible solution?
- Is the crime resolved?
  - Is the criminal caught? Is there a trial? Is the criminal brought to justice?
  - Are any elements of the narrative left open, possibly to be solved in a later episode?

There might be a **restricted** narrative in a crime drama, where the audience is given limited information about the crime or the characters. Crime dramas usually feature multiple enigmas to keep the audience guessing.

A different approach is the **inverted** narrative. This is where the criminal is identified very early, so there is no enigma surrounding the solving of the crime. The narrative centres instead on how the detective is going to catch the criminal and bring them to justice. *Luther* features an inverted narrative.

Crime dramas also tend to include many **binary oppositions** in the narrative, such as:

- crime vs justice
- police vs criminals
- good vs evil
- work vs relationships/family.

The narrative of a crime drama provides particular **pleasures** for the audience. The investigation elements enable the audience to actively engage by picking up on the clues to try to solve the crime. The audience is normally positioned with the detective, or hero, on the side of what is 'right' or good. The **messages** within a crime drama usually reinforce the idea that crime is bad and does not pay, that criminals will be caught and punished, equilibrium will return and society will be safe.

Characters

There are familiar character roles that fit into the crime genre repertoire, including:

- **Detective**: usually the protagonist. Crime dramas often construct detectives that are successful, but have flaws or weaknesses. For example:
  - They are usually very committed to the job, which can lead to problems in their personal life and they might become emotionally isolated
  - They are often 'mavericks' who will bend, and sometimes break, the rules in order to achieve results.

- **Sidekick**: the detective's professional partner who may help to investigate and solve the crime. (Dialogue between the detective and sidekick also allows the audience to have an insight into the crime-solving process as they discuss developments and evidence.)
- **Boss**: authority figure who could be supportive of the detective or might challenge their methods
- **Experts**: such as forensics experts who might help to solve the crime
- **Villain**: usually the criminal. There might be one individual perpetrator (for example Alice Morgan in *Luther*) or a group of criminals, usually under the control of a gang leader or 'master' criminal (as in *The Sweeney*).
- **Victim/s** of the crime
- **Witnesses**: people who may have seen the crime or have information that helps to catch the criminal.

Technical and visual codes of crime drama

- Low-key lighting is often used to connote mystery and evil deeds.
- **Partial vision**, a term coined by Pascal Bonitzer, is a technique used in the thriller genre and gives the audiences a restricted view. This creates enigma and connotes the mystery of the crime.
- Close–up camera work focuses on characters and important objects or clues to solving the crime.
- Gritty 'realism' is reproduced, through, for example, location shooting.
- Typical iconography and mise-en-scène include:
  - a police station within the setting, while the crime could typically take place in an isolated or urban location
  - costumes of police uniforms and forensic body suits
  - props such as crime scene tape, guns or other weapons, blood.

Audio codes

Dialogue has great importance in police dramas. Characters will often talk through the crimes and evidence in detail and discuss possible solutions, which gives the audience insight into the narrative. Some of these discussions may include **red herrings** to keep the audience 'guessing' as to the actual solution to the crime. This often involves specialist lexis relating to crime and policing.

Some contemporary crime dramas often incorporate modern technology into the narrative to communicate messages to the audience. *Sherlock*, for example, uses graphics of text messages on screen to convey information that might have been communicated by dialogue in the past.

The musical soundtrack is often used to establish an atmosphere of mystery and suspense through, for example, tense, dramatic non-diegetic music.

Quickfire 5.8

How might Propp's theory be applied to the typical characters in a crime drama?

Key Terms

Partial vision
A technique where the camera frames the scene to show only part of the picture, such as filming the villain from behind so that their face is hidden.

Red herring
A misleading piece of information which suggests a particular solution that is actually incorrect.

Dixon of Dock Green.

Analysing the set product: *The Sweeney*

The Sweeney was groundbreaking in the 1970s as it introduced many new elements into the police/crime genre. Earlier crime dramas tended to be much less violent than *The Sweeney* and provided reassurance that society was safe, as law and order was being upheld. *Dixon of Dock Green*, a **police procedural** drama broadcast from 1955 to 1975, focused on a policeman who patrolled his 'beat' and usually dealt with more minor crimes.

The Sweeney includes elements of the police procedural subgenre, but also codes from the action genre to create a more dynamic and exciting experience for the audience. There is a focus on complex, violent and organised crime that is not easy to solve.

Key Term

Police procedural
A subgenre that focuses specifically on the way in which the police work to solve crimes.

Activity 5.3

Analyse the ten-minute extract of *The Sweeney* chosen by your teacher, using the list of technical and visual codes above. What messages are communicated?

Media language

The Sweeney was recorded on 16mm film. The cameras were more lightweight and mobile, so filming could take place outside a studio. Ted Childs, who produced the programme, commented in the 2005 documentary *Must See TV: The Sweeney*: 'that meant we were able to introduce cinematic production values, lots of action, lots of car chases, lots of stunts.'

Location filming adds to the sense of realism. Many scenes were filmed on London streets and some plots were based on real events.

Quickfire 5.9

What is the effect of the use of the static camera in chase sequences in *The Sweeney*?

Top Tip

Make a note of any non-diegetic music used in the ten-minute sequence you study. What is the purpose and effect of it?

Stretch and Challenge 5.8

Watch the extract from *The Sweeney*. Identify three key quotes and note how these construct the character representations.

Static cameras are also used in many interior and exterior scenes. This is a technique that developed in the filming of television plays and dramas in the 1960s, where a number of cameras would be positioned around the studio to film the action from different angles. The programme's chase sequences also use some static camera work, filming from different points to show the action moving towards the camera or characters running across the shot.

There is more camera movement in the fight sequences, including close-up shots of violence. This immerses the audience in the action more fully.

The dress codes and props establish the 1970s setting. The Ford Consul car became iconic in *The Sweeney* and a very similar Cortina was later used in *Life on Mars*.

The use of music also reflects the period and underscores the action, such as the jazz-influenced music as Regan leaves Jenny's flat in the opening sequence.

The language used in the dialogue helps to construct the characters, and some of the phrases became very popular, for example 'We're the Sweeney, son, and we haven't had any dinner.' This suggests that the 'Sweeney' or Flying Squad is well known and connotes a threat, reinforced by the following phrase: 'You've kept us waiting, so unless you want a kicking you tell us where those photographs are.'

Narrative

The narrative of this episode begins with the build-up to the crime (Brooker takes delivery of the guns), but the main crime does not occur until much later in the story. Much of the episode is instead spent trying to prevent the crime from taking place.

The narrative ends with closure: the crime is prevented, the main criminal is dead and Regan is able to relax with his girlfriend and a glass of whiskey.

Representation

The police force in *The Sweeney* is shown as a male-dominated organisation with a clear hierarchy. The officers call their bosses 'sir' and Regan (John Thaw) is reprimanded by a senior officer who says he should have known what was happening sooner.

The police officers are constructed as strong and tough males who are not afraid to use violence to get results. Jack Regan is a maverick who believes his methods are necessary. This is shown in the way he threatens suspects and challenges authority.

There are many examples of masculine stereotyping, including patriarchal attitudes, heavy drinking, objectification of women and violent behaviour. There is also an obvious loyalty between Regan and Carter (Dennis Waterman), and their relationship is that of a typical detective/hero and sidekick/helper.

London is represented as a potentially violent place. The 'gritty' urban locations suggest that crime is a problem in society that needs to be solved. There is no use of the 'tourist imagery' of London, such as the famous buildings in the city centre, that is featured in later examples of the genre, such as *Sherlock* and *Luther*.

Feminist perspectives on representation in *The Sweeney*

Women feature as girlfriends, wives and mothers: stereotypically passive roles. The female in the opening sequence, Jenny, is a passive object in the bed, whose identity is not established. Although she is independent (she has a job, her own home and a car), her position in the narrative is as Regan's girlfriend and she becomes a victim of threatened violence from Kemble's men, who also objectify her. She needs to be rescued and protected by Regan.

Industry and audience

The Sweeney was produced by Euston Films, the film production division of Thames Television. Thames produced many programmes and held the ITV broadcast licence for the London area in the 1970s and 1980s.

Euston Films produced a range of television dramas and series in the 1970s and 1980s. The company created a series of single drama programmes in the early 1970s and one of these, a 1974 drama called *Regan*, was developed into *The Sweeney*.

Quickfire 5.10

What message does the ending of *The Sweeney* communicate about crime in society?

Top Tip

Watch the ten-minute extract of *The Sweeney* and identify examples of masculine stereotypes.

Quickfire 5.11

Why do you think crime dramas are often set in urban locations such as London?

Quickfire 5.12

Which of Propp's character roles could be applied to Jenny?

Stretch and Challenge 5.9

Watch the full episode of *The Sweeney* and make notes on all the female characters. What roles do they have? Does this support feminist perspectives that women tend to be absent, under-represented or objectified?

Quickfire 5.13

What is the term used to describe companies, such as Thames Television, that produce, distribute and exhibit television programmes?

Stretch and Challenge 5.10

Can you identify any recent television dramas that are filmed mostly on location rather than in a studio?

Key Term

Watershed
The 9pm cut-off after which broadcasters are able to show programmes with more adult content, for example swearing and violence. Before 9pm programmes should be suitable for children.

Quickfire 5.14

What similarities can you identify between the original *Sweeney* and the movie remake?

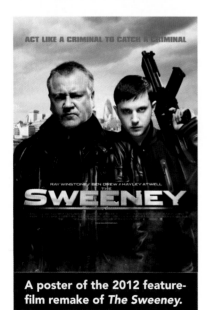

ACT LIKE A CRIMINAL TO CATCH A CRIMINAL

RAY WINSTONE / BEN DREW / HAYLEY ATWELL

SWEENEY

A poster of the 2012 feature-film remake of *The Sweeney*.

The Sweeney was filmed on location in parts of west London, which adds to the realism and intensity of the programme. The programme used new techniques which have influenced the way television dramas have since been produced, as cultural historian John Williams argues: 'Euston is important because it popularised a method of television production that was filmed entirely on location, with rapid turnaround times and no rehearsal, which has become the standard method by which television drama is now made.' (screenonline.org.uk/tv/id/1133069/)

The Sweeney was written by Ian Kennedy Martin. The series starred John Thaw, who later went on to play Inspector Morse, and Dennis Waterman, who also starred in *Minder* and more recently in *New Tricks*. These actors became associated with police crime drama, which indicates that *The Sweeney* was an important programme in the development of the genre.

Scheduling

The Sweeney ran between 1975 and 1978, broadcast at 9pm on weekday evenings on ITV. The set episode, 'Ringer', premiered on Thursday 2 January 1975. Video recorders were not available at this time, so audiences could only watch the programme as it was broadcast. As it was shown on a commercial channel, there were two breaks for adverts, so the narrative was structured into three sections.

The scheduling after the **watershed** shows that the programme was intended for an adult audience as some of the themes, language and violent action is not suitable for younger viewers.

The Sweeney was extremely successful and achieved audience ratings of up to 19 million (according to BFI Screenonline). This success led Euston to develop many more television dramas, including *Minder* and *Widows*. The positive response and high viewing figures also led to two spin-off films in the 1970s as well as a modern remake in 2012.

A 16-disc DVD box set of all episodes of *The Sweeney* was released in 2004 and was given a 15 certificate by the BBFC for 'frequent moderate violence'. The programme has far-reaching appeal to audiences who might remember the original series and feel nostalgia for *The Sweeney,* as well as to younger audiences viewing for the first time.

Re-runs of *The Sweeney* have been broadcast several times over the years. In November and December 2017, ITV4 broadcast all episodes with the opportunity to catch up on the ITV hub. In this way, digital technologies are enabling broadcasters to reach new and existing audiences for older television programmes. It also allows viewers to binge-watch if they choose, an option that was not available when the series were originally broadcast.

Audience responses

The original series of *The Sweeney* was very popular. One of the reasons for the positive response was the use of characters that the audience could relate to. The police officers were shown to be 'flawed' and human: they made mistakes, but still caught the criminals. This representation could also be seen as negative by, for example, the police force, as police officers were shown to be violent with little regard for appropriate policing methods.

Many contemporary audiences respond positively to the programme, perhaps for the 'retro' feel that people who remember the original series might feel nostalgic for. Phelim O'Neill commented in 2013, 'Jack and George, a pair of bleary-eyed, tough 70s coppers careering around in Ford Consuls and kipper ties, are a hard act to follow.' (theguardian.com/tv-and-radio/2013/feb/14/the-sweeney-box-set) This suggests that audiences have a lot of affection for *The Sweeney* as the characters and 'kitsch' iconography are so different from modern life.

Some viewers today, however, will have a more negative response. They might be disturbed by the violent way the police deal with suspects and offended by the patriarchal attitudes and misrepresentation of women.

The cultural influence of *The Sweeney*

The Sweeney can be seen to have influenced many other police dramas, including *The Professionals* and *Minder*. In 2006 the BBC created a new drama called *Life on Mars*, which intertextually referenced *The Sweeney* in many ways.

This influential effect points the way towards genres changing over time. Once the codes and conventions become established, producers might want to take a genre in a new direction and draw on elements such as hybridity and intertextuality. In *Life on Mars*, Sam (John Simm) is a 21st-century police detective who travels back to the 1970s, where society is very different. The iconography of the programme is very similar to *The Sweeney* and the themes are familiar: the police force is male-dominated, the senior detective is gruff and brusque and violence is used against suspects. The audience is positioned to experience the 1970s from Sam's perspective and are likely to be shocked at some of the approaches to policing. Viewers who remember *The Sweeney*, however, might be less shocked and enjoy the intertextual references.

Quickfire 5.15

How do the images above from *Life on Mars* show intertextuality with *The Sweeney*?

The station setting of *Life on Mars* uses familiar crime genre conventions:

- filing cabinets, paperwork, in-trays that connote busy investigative work
- low-key and dim lighting, with some light from windows
- window blinds that reference classic detective dramas and **film noir**
- medium shots of Sam help to show his thought processes, while wide shots of the detectives show the importance of the team in solving the crime
- hierarchy of characters – Sam and Gene (Philip Glenister) have higher status
- the team members are detectives, so do not wear uniform.

It also highlights iconography of the 1970s:

- the dress code of 'tank tops', wide collars and ties, and typical hairstyles
- the typewriter typical of technology at the time.

Key Term

Film noir
A genre that emerged during the 1940s and 50s in which narratives focus on crime and stylish visual conventions include low-key lighting. Character types include the world-weary detective and the **femme fatale**.

Historical context: the 1970s

The genders were less equal in the society of the 1970s and 1980s than today, and this was reflected in the structure of the police force. According to the Metropolitan Women Police Association, in 1980 there were 90 female detective constables in the Metropolitan Police Force and over 1400 males. There were very few high-ranking female officers. This is clearly reflected in *The Sweeney*, where the police force is extremely male dominated. A female police officer is featured in the set episode, but she is not involved in the investigation: she is sent to look after Regan's girlfriend Jenny, who has been threatened by Kemble's men.

Britain was becoming more racially diverse and multicultural in the 1970s, especially in cities such as London, but along with this was racial discrimination. The media did not fully reflect the multicultural nature of Britain, and minority ethnic groups were under-represented and, at times, misrepresented. In the set episode of *The Sweeney*, for example, there are no characters from minority ethnic groups.

The Sweeney was based on the real 'Flying Squad', a division of the Metropolitan Police that dealt with serious and violent crime. The Flying Squad achieved many successes but was involved in a corruption case in the 1970s and some high-ranking officers were jailed for taking bribes. There are hints in the set episode that officers might be open to corruption: Prosser, for example, suggests that Kemble could 'buy the police off' and Regan's boss expresses concerns about some of the methods he uses.

Socially and politically, the 1970s was a period of upheaval. Economic problems from the decline of manufacturing in Britain led to increased imports. The international oil crisis in 1973, coupled with miners' strikes, resulted in electricity shortages during which television broadcasting ended at 10.30 every night. There were also other strikes by, for example, refuse collectors, ambulance personnel and postal workers. Simon Heffer commented in the *Daily Telegraph* in 2015 that *The Sweeney* 'reflected the more turbulent, less ordered world of urban Britain in the Seventies'. (telegraph.co.uk/culture/tvandradio/11998344/The-Sweeney-gave-us-TVs-most-arresting-coppers.html)

Activity 5.4

Compare the stills from *Life on Mars* on page 129 with these stills from *Luther*. What similarities do you notice? What are the differences? Write a paragraph summarising your findings.

Analysing the Set Product: *Luther*

Luther was written by Neil Cross, who had previously been a scriptwriter on *Spooks*, and starred Idris Elba as the troubled Detective Inspector John Luther. The first episode was broadcast on 4 May 2010 on BBC One. There have been four series to date and a new series is planned for 2018. In 2017 John Luther was third in an international poll of viewers' favourite BBC characters.

Luther is one of many crime dramas that takes its title from the name of the protagonist. Other examples include *Inspector Morse*, *Taggart* and *Vera*. It implies that the main detective will be central to the narrative and also suggests that he or she is strong and independent.

Media language

Scriptwriter Neil Cross drew on different subgenres of crime when he developed *Luther*: the mystery/detective subgenre (texts such as Sherlock Holmes stories) and the psychological thriller. He discusses how elements from each genre informed the construction of Luther's character: 'It seemed to me that combining these properties – deductive brilliance and moral passion – in one man could make for a powerful and damaged, deeply heroic character.' (bbc.co.uk/blogs/tv/2010/04/introducing-luther-with-love-t.shtml)

Genre

Luther contains many familiar elements of crime drama, but it also shows developments in the genre when compared with *The Sweeney*.

The programme hybridises elements from other genres:

- There are many conventions of the thriller genre evident in the visual and audio codes, such as the low-key lighting, intense non-diegetic music and dramatic cross-cutting in the pre-title sequence. There is also some reference to film noir in the visual codes and the use of the **femme fatale** character.

- There are moments that reference the horror genre, for example the graphic shots of the dog and the blood at the Morgans' house, and there are 'jump scares', such as when Alice grabs Zoe outside her office.

- There are elements of the police procedural, but there is an increased focus on psychology, for example the analysis of why Alice committed the crime and Luther's conclusion that she is a narcissist. This psychological focus has been evident in many recent crime dramas and can be traced back to programmes such as *Cracker* in the 1990s.

The characters are more complex than those in *The Sweeney*. Luther's emotional life, for example, is explored through the narrative strand focusing on his failing marriage. Luther and Alice develop a relationship that extends beyond the police station and there is a suggestion of sexual tension between them. Female roles are much more developed and important within the narrative.

The programme reflects real developments in forensics. For example, Alice goes to extreme lengths to destroy any evidence of the gun and so make sure that she cannot be convicted.

> **Key Term**
>
> **Femme Fatale**
> A mysterious and dangerous female character who uses her sexuality to exert power over male characters.

Robbie Coltrane as Fitz in ITV's *Cracker*.

Quickfire 5.16

What familiar elements of the crime drama repertoire are evident in *Luther*?

Top Tip

Make detailed notes on the use of media language in the sequences from *Luther* that you analyse in class.

Stretch and Challenge 5.11

Watch one of the sequences between Alice and Luther and identify further examples of their 'psychological duel'.

Quickfire 5.17

What message does the ending of the narrative in *Luther* convey?

The filming style is very different from *The Sweeney*, partly a reflection of developments in technology. Shots are framed from multiple angles and much camera movement is used, including hand-held camerawork. This creates a sense of immediacy and immerses the audience by showing different viewpoints. The bird's-eye view of Alice grabbing Zoe outside the office, for example, positions the viewer at a distance and makes them feel powerless to help.

Narrative

Backstory: The pre-title sequence summarises the previous case and explains why Luther has been on 'gardening leave' – he was suspended for the violent way he dealt with the suspect, Henry Madsen. Madsen is still in a coma and is shown again at the end of the episode as Alice goes to the hospital. This is a continuing narrative **arc** that will be significant later in the series.

Inverted narrative: We know who the murderer is and that *Luther* will catch her, but we don't know how. Neil Cross discussed his decision to use this type of narrative to engage the audience: 'I thought it might be exciting to portray it as a kind of psychological duel between this driven, half-mad cop and the depraved criminals he hunts.' (bbc.co.uk/blogs/tv/2010/04/introducing-luther-with-love-t.shtml)

An example of this 'psychological duel' occurs in the set episode when Alice realises that Luther thinks she is the murderer. She tells him she did not kill her parents and Luther tells her to prove it. She says, 'I cannot prove a negative. It can't be done,' and goes on to tell Luther that it is his job to prove her guilt.

Crime: The murder of Alice's parents. Alice is implied to be involved as she is at the crime scene and has blood on her hands. John realises she is the killer very early on but finds it very difficult to prove her guilt. In the end, the evidence is inadmissible, so she will not be charged. There is no sense of justice in the usual way, no trial or conviction, but there is personal satisfaction for Luther.

Narrative strands: Neither solving the crime nor John's personal life and relationship with Zoe are neatly solved by the end, but there is some sense of resolution and equilibrium as Luther knows that Alice was the murderer and he makes peace with Zoe.

Visual codes: iconic signifiers

There are some iconic visual signifiers used in the set episode of *Luther*. The camerawork and editing are used to focus attention on these important narrative clues, for example the dog:

- A close up of the Morgans' dog covered in blood is shown when the police arrive to investigate the murder. This suggests that the dog is significant in the case.

- Midway through the narrative there is a short sequence showing the dog being cremated, which is enigmatic and adds to the sense of importance.

- Alice is holding the urn of the dog's ashes when she meets Luther near her flat. Luther realises that she hid the gun in the dog's body, which solves the narrative enigma of the missing murder weapon.

- The visual iconography of the blood and fire reinforces the extreme violence committed against an innocent animal and further constructs the representation of Alice Morgan as a cold and ruthless murderer.

Theoretical perspectives: Propp

We can apply many of Propp's narrative roles to the characters in *Luther*, but the characters are quite complex, so do not 'fit' precisely. John Luther himself, for example, demonstrates some qualities of the hero, but he is also 'flawed' and some of his qualities are not typically heroic. Consider, for example, his handling of the Henry Madsen case and his violent reaction when he realises that Zoe is seeing another man.

Activity 5.6

Try to fit the following characters from *Luther* into Propp's theory. Explain how they reflect the character type, and also ways in which they do not fit exactly into the theory.

Character	Propp's role	How the character fits the role	Ways in which the character does not fit the role
Rose (Luther's boss)			
Zoe (Luther's wife)			
Mark (Zoe's new partner)			
Justin (Luther's new police partner)			
Ian (Luther's colleague and friend)			
Alice			

Activity 5.5

Analyse the significance of Alice's hatpin and Luther's wedding ring in the narrative:

- Watch the episode and note down each time the prop is shown.
- How does the camerawork draw attention to the prop?
- What is the significance of the prop to the narrative?
- What does the prop reveal about the character?

Representation

The representations in Luther move beyond stereotypes, as the main characters are developed into complex individuals. This is likely to help the audience to engage with and understand the characters.

John Luther

Luther is an interesting representation of a black male in 21st-century Britain. He is a successful senior police detective who has a brilliant mind for solving crime. He also, however, uses questionable methods to get results, including violence and breaking into Alice's flat.

He is very committed to his job, almost to the point of obsession, and this affects his personal life as his marriage is breaking down. The producers construct a complicated character who experiences emotional anguish and passion and expresses this through anger and violence but also with pain and sadness.

The camera often frames Luther surrounded by a large amount of empty space to signify the emotional void in his life and a sense of isolation. This representation reflects contemporary notions of masculinity as Luther is not completely in control of his life and shows vulnerability. There are also some stereotypical elements of masculinity evident, however, such as the force he displays and the lack of emotion in his discussions with Ian, which suggest he is isolated and independent.

Stretch and Challenge 5.12

Can you identify any further visual signifiers that are important to the narrative in the set episode of *Luther*?

Alice and Luther: the alluring, dangerous femme fatale and the vulnerable, world-weary detective.

Female characters

There are several female characters who play significant roles in the narrative of this episode.

Alice is a complex character who demonstrates many traits of the femme fatale, a character type typical of film noir. Alice is the antagonist, a role more usually male in crime dramas, and her character has considerable power and agency as her actions drive the plot. She displays many traits stereotypically associated with masculinity: she is unemotional, highly intelligent, ruthless and violent. She subverts many female stereotypes, but she is attractive and uses her femininity to taunt and flirt with Luther.

Zoe is Luther's wife and is a humanitarian lawyer. She is shown as a professional in the workplace (unlike Regan's girlfriend in *The Sweeney*) but is also shown to be in need of protection. At one point Mark refuses to let Luther into the house, so Zoe is shown to have weaknesses and to depend on male characters.

Rose is a senior police officer and is Luther's boss. She shows strength of character by believing in Luther when others doubt him, and she works hard to try to ensure he follows the rules.

Quickfire 5.18

In what ways is Alice a femme fatale?

Stretch and Challenge 5.13

Look at the schedule for BBC One for a full day. What different types of programme are scheduled?

Top Tip

Watch the title sequence of the set episode of *Luther* and write down the names of the production team and actors. Research these to find out more about the roles and people involved with *Luther*.

Activity 5.7

Select three characters from *Luther* and watch at least three scenes in which they appear:

- How is media language (visual codes, technical codes and language) used to construct each representation?
- Does the representation uphold stereotypes, of gender for example?
- How does the representation subvert stereotypes?

Write a paragraph analysing the representation of each character.

Industry and audience

BBC One

BBC One is the corporation's primary channel. It offers a range of programme types and genres of programmes and aims to appeal to a very wide audience.

BBC One has a remit to create a high proportion of original programmes and to reflect the diversity of the UK. According to the BBC Trust service licence for 2016–17, BBC One programmes should 'exhibit some or all of the following characteristics: high quality, original, challenging, innovative and engaging, and it should nurture UK talent.'

Production

Luther is an original BBC production. The BBC has a commissioning department that accepts **pitches** of new ideas that may be developed into programmes. Piers Wenger, the controller of BBC Drama has said that the important features of BBC drama include:

- Talkability, drama that gets people talking
- Topicality and relevance to audiences
- Britishness, and reflecting the diversity of life in Britain.

The writer Neil Cross pitched the idea for *Luther* to the BBC who then commissioned the script. He had previously been a scriptwriter on *Spooks*, a BBC spy drama. Following the first series, Luther was re-commissioned and there have been four series to date. In 2017 the BBC announced that a new series would begin filming in early 2018.

In 2012 BBC America, a channel co-owned by BBC Worldwide and American broadcaster AMC, began to co-produce *Luther*, following the success of the first two series. Perry Simon, then General Manager of BBC Worldwide America said of Idris Elba: 'His iconic role as John Luther has quickly become one of the most powerful detective characters television audiences have ever seen. Luther has been integral in establishing our new Dramaville franchise, the home for groundbreaking British drama.' (bbc.co.uk/mediacentre/worldwide/270112luther)

Distribution and scheduling

The first series of *Luther* was aired on BBC One at 9pm on a Tuesday evening. Series 1, Episode 1 was broadcast on 4 May 2010. Crime dramas are often shown in this 'prime time' evening slot and audiences might be more likely to stay in and watch television early in the week. *Luther* was also available on the BBC's iPlayer catch-up service.

Key Term

Pitch
A summary of the key ideas for a new media product that a writer or producer presents to a media organisation for approval. The pitch is designed to 'sell' the idea to the organisation.

Quickfire 5.19

What elements of the set episode of *Luther* are likely to have been most talked about by audiences?

Idris Elba with his 2012 Golden Globe award for *Luther*.

Luther is also broadcast on BBC America, which broadcasts a mixture of American and British programmes. BBC America is part of BBC Worldwide, which is a commercial arm of the BBC, not funded by the UK licence fee. Crime drama brings in a large proportion of BBC Worldwide's revenue and *Luther* has been distributed to many parts of Europe including France, Germany and Denmark, as well as to countries in Africa and Asia. It is also available in many countries on Netflix and on DVD including a box set of the first four series.

The DVD of Series 1, Episode 1 was rated 15 by the BBFC for 'strong violence'. The scheduling of *Luther* after the 9pm watershed also reflects the violence and darker themes that are unsuitable for children. The clips on the BBC website also carry a warning that they contain adult themes.

How did the BBC reach a wide audience for *Luther*?

The marketing of the first series was important in reaching a range of audiences. A trailer was released on 16 April 2010 and published on the BBC's official YouTube site. A longer preview was shown at the end of April. Additional features and behind-the-scenes footage for each episode were released on the website, which replicates the DVD extras that viewers are used to accessing and gives an 'exclusive' insight into aspects of the production. An 'inside look' video was produced for BBC America when the programme was launched in the USA.

The global appeal of *Luther* can be linked to the star attraction of Idris Elba, who is known for roles in programmes such as *The Wire* as well as several Hollywood films. The BBC has a reputation for producing quality drama programmes and the setting in London, a centre of international business and a popular tourist destination, might also appeal to viewers in different countries.

Contemporary dramas can reach a wide audience through a variety of platforms and the *Luther* website allows viewers to engage with wider content related to the show and to connect via social media pages. The website includes interactive features such as:

- a 'Crime Board', which allowed users to create their own investigation board and upload it to their Facebook page
- 'Postcards from Alice': After the second series Alice went travelling and viewers were asked to create a postcard from a country where they thought Alice might have been and send it to Luther. Some of the viewers' postcards were shown in Luther's flat in episodes from the following series.

These features engage fans of the show and offer them opportunities to become active producers of content, some of which has been included in the programme. The further sharing of this user-generated content on fans' own social media helps to extend the programme's market further and potentially attract an even wider audience.

Luther has also won many awards, including Idris Elba's Golden Globe for his portrayal of Luther. This helps the BBC to market future series and strengthens the high status of the programme.

The programme itself appeals to a range of audiences in many ways including:

- **Genre**: Crime drama is popular and *Luther* includes familiar conventions along with interesting hybridisation and unexpected elements.
- **Star appeal**: Idris Elba is well known and popular, and this casting would appeal to audiences familiar with his previous work. He is an attractive and potentially aspirational persona with appeal for male and female viewers.
- **Narrative**: The Morgan murders and ongoing Henry Madsen case might engage an audience for the set episode and the remainder of the series. The use of a female killer is quite unusual and could appeal to audiences who enjoy thought-provoking and non-mainstream dramas.
- **Representations**: The range of complex male and female characters appeals to different audiences who may find a character that they are intrigued by or who they can identify with.

The set episode successfully attracted a large audience. According to BARB statistics, the first episode received 6.35 million viewers. Only *EastEnders* and *Doctor Who* achieved higher ratings on BBC One in the same week.

Audience responses

The first episode of *Luther* received mixed reviews, but there were many positive responses, such as this comment from Mark Pilkington on the Den of Geek website: 'The scene has been set, and if the rest of the series continues in the same tense, excellent tempo, then we are in for a treat.' (denofgeek.com/tv/luther/9772/luther-episode-1-review)

The complex features of the programme could generate both positive and negative responses. For example:

- Audiences might admire Luther's crime-solving skills but disapprove of the methods he uses and his violent responses to challenging situations.
- Viewers could respond positively to Alice and find her intelligence and resourcefulness appealing, but might respond negatively to the use of the 'femme fatale' conventions.
- An audience might agree that the ending reflects reality, as not all criminals are convicted, but viewers might be disappointed by the lack of closure and the fact that Alice gets away with the murder of her parents.

Contexts in *Luther*

Gender equality

The female representations in *Luther* reflect the fact that women now have more equality of opportunity and have gained power in the workplace. Zoe, Rose and Alice are all professional women in senior positions.

Rose, Luther's boss, is a detective superintendent. The programme shows that the police force now has a higher proportion of female officers in comparison with the 1970s when *The Sweeney* was made. According to a 2017 Home Office report, nearly 30 per cent of all police officers in England and Wales are now female and over 20 per cent of the more senior roles are occupied by women.

Stretch and Challenge 5.14

Research some of the other characters that Idris Elba has played. Can you identify any links with Luther?

Top Tip

Make notes on how you can apply the Uses and Gratifications theory to the set episode. Use the points above and your own analytical notes to help.

Quickfire 5.22

What factors might affect the way in which a viewer responds to *Luther*?

Cressida Dick, the first female Commissioner of the Metropolitan Police.

Racial equality

John Luther is a senior officer, a detective chief inspector, who is also black. His ethnicity is not a major focus of the programme, which in itself shows that there is now greater social equality in society. While black and minority ethnic groups only account for around six per cent of police officers in England and Wales, this percentage has been rising in recent years. The name 'Luther', however, is likely to have significance in relation to Martin Luther King, the American civil rights leader.

Cultural context: representation of London

There are many shots of central London in the episode, including establishing shots of modern buildings and skyscrapers, suggesting that it is a successful city. This reflects the contemporary context as London is a major financial centre for international business. It also implies that the series would target a global audience that would recognise the city and its iconic landmarks.

Section A, Option 2: Introduction to the Sitcom Genre

'Sitcom' is shorthand for 'situation comedy', a programme where humour is created through narrative situations that the characters experience. Sitcoms were originally broadcast on radio but became popular on television in the 1950s. In Britain, many successful sitcoms have been produced and broadcast on the BBC, ITV and Channel 4. American sitcoms are also popular in the UK and many of these are broadcast on Channel 4.

Traditionally, sitcoms are filmed in front of a live audience, so they gain an actual response, although some feature a 'canned laughter' track. The set products, *The IT Crowd* and *Friends*, were both filmed in front of studio audiences.

Products in this popular genre are filmed in series and each episode is usually just under half an hour in length. British sitcom series usually have six episodes. American sitcom series tend to be much longer, usually consisting of more than 20 episodes.

The setting is usually a home or workplace where characters are 'trapped' in a situation and cannot 'escape', as this provides many opportunities for humour. The characters are often exaggerations of recognisable types and the relationships between characters at the heart of the sitcom are important. The settings and characters become familiar to the audience as they see them in every episode.

The genre has developed over time. *The Royle Family*, for example, focused on dialogue and family relationships as the source of humour rather than situations, while *The Office* used documentary conventions to create a **mockumentary**. Many contemporary sitcoms retain familiar elements, however, as noted by critic Phil Wickham: 'Their subjects are individual disappointment and social failure and the courage of people in the face of their problems.' (screenonline.org.uk/tv/id/445368/)

Sitcom: repertoire of elements

The comedy in a sitcom might be based on verbal or visual humour, or a combination of both:

- Verbal humour relies on the words to make the audience laugh, through jokes, wordplay, satire or other techniques.
- Visual humour creates comedy through images, including body language, gestures and facial expressions. Some sitcoms use a lot of **slapstick** comedy: exaggerated visual humour.

Quickfire 5.23

Why do you think many American sitcoms are broadcast on Channel 4?

Stretch and Challenge 5.16

Look at TV listings pages for a week. How many sitcoms can you identify? When and where are they broadcast?

Key Terms

Mockumentary
A fictional, usually comedy, programme or film that is filmed in the style of a serious documentary, which creates satire and a sense of realism.

Slapstick
Visual humour created by over-exaggerated actions. Characters in slapstick comedy are often made to look foolish, awkward and clumsy.

Activity 5.8

Watch the set products and write down specific examples of verbal and visual comedy. Analyse how this use of humour communicates meanings, referring to the examples below:

Sitcom	Example	Analysis
Friends	**Verbal humour** Rachel says to the other characters, 'You all have jobs?'	Rachel seems surprised, which connotes that she has been financially dependent on her parents and did not expect to have a career. This allows her character to grow and develop.
The IT Crowd	**Visual humour** Roy rides the window-cleaner's bike; he wobbles as he tries to turn around when he sees Alastair and the ladder nearly knocks over a pedestrian.	This shows Roy's concern for status as he worries that Alastair will think he is a window cleaner. He feels inadequate in comparison with his old friend and wants to impress him. His failure creates humour and the audience might feel a sense of superiority or sympathy for him.

Roy suffers some slapstick humour springing from a believed misunderstanding.

Narrative

Many sitcoms begin with equilibrium before a situation takes the narrative in a new direction, for example a disruption, but the narrative ultimately returns to the starting point. This is called a **circular narrative**, as identified by theorists Neale and Krutnik, as there is no real character development or transformation. The equilibrium at the end is not a new equilibrium: it is the same as the beginning.

Sitcoms might also include an element of **linear narrative** in which situations continue throughout a series or across a number of series, for example the relationship between Rachel and Ross in *Friends*. The narrative closure at the end of each episode allows audiences to watch a single episode in isolation, while the continuing narratives encourage continued viewing and offer the pleasure of engaging with developing storylines.

The narrative **situations** that occur in sitcoms are often quite mundane but the humour is created through factors such as mistaken identity, misunderstandings or unlikely coincidences.

Many sitcoms explore similar **themes** and ideas relating to social class, identity or status, including:

- inadequacy: characters wanting to achieve higher status, a new identity or climb the social ladder
- escape: characters trying to break free from their current situation
- delusion: characters who believe they have higher status or try to persuade others that this is the case, or, for example, unrequited love
- failure: characters rarely achieve their objectives, for example those trying to raise their social status find their plans thwarted.

Messages and values

British sitcoms often focus on social class as a key theme, as this is an important aspect of British society. Many programmes construct characters who try to convince others that they have a higher social status, for example Roy in the set episode of *The IT Crowd*.

The themes featured in sitcoms can communicate messages and values, and reflect the context of production. Circular narratives, where characters fail to escape or achieve higher status, might suggest that people should not try to over-reach themselves, and it has been argued that sitcoms reinforce messages that the dominant people in society will always retain power.

Some programmes explore issues that are directly relevant to society at the time. *The Vicar of Dibley*, for example, featured a female vicar in a rural village shortly after the ordination of women priests was introduced. The series reflected some of the actual attitudes to female priests in the 1990s, as many of the characters were opposed to the appointment of a woman.

Residents of Dibley were unhappy at first about their new female vicar.

The main **appeals** of a sitcom lie in the entertainment value of comedy and the escapism that this offers. Viewers might also take pleasure in seeing characters struggle to achieve their aims and fail, as this can give a sense of superiority. The recurring settings, characters and situations provide familiarity and reassurance.

Characters

Sitcoms usually revolve around a small number of main characters who appear in every episode. There are also likely to be additional minor characters who appear less frequently as well as other characters specific to a situation or episode.

Sitcoms often rely on stereotypes to communicate messages quickly and clearly to an audience, and these are usually exaggerated for comedic effect. Particular character types that feature in sitcoms include:

- a domineering character, who tries to overpower other people, such as Basil in *Fawlty Towers*
- a joker, who is not very serious and makes jokes or 'wisecracks'
- a 'straight' character, the opposite to a joker, who reacts to situations rather that being the main cause of comedy
- an innocent or naïve, who does not always grasp what is happening in a situation
- a 'nerd' or 'geek', typically a male character who is interested in topics such as science fiction and is awkward in social situations
- the 'lad', who is interested in stereotypically male topics and might be a 'womaniser'.

Ellie Kemper as Kimmy who fits the role of the 'innocent' in *Unbreakable Kimmy Schmidt*.

Representations in context

Ethnicity

In the 1970s British society was becoming increasingly diverse and multicultural, as many people from countries such as the West Indies had emigrated to Britain from the 1950s onwards. People from black and minority ethnic groups were nonetheless under-represented in British television and, when they were included, were often constructed as extreme stereotypes, especially in sitcoms. Some programmes also featured characters with extremely racist views, such as Alf Garnet in *Till Death Us Do Part*. His opinions are offensive and would not be acceptable in today's society.

Adil Ray in *Citizen Khan*.

A wider range of representations have emerged since the 1970s that reflect developments in society and the fact that media production teams are also more diverse. In the 1980s the Channel 4 sitcom *Desmond's* was one of the first sitcoms to feature a majority of black characters. Critic Ali Jafaar commented that the show avoided racial stereotypes and that 'the protagonists are seen as upwardly mobile members of a multicultural Britain.' (screenonline.org.uk/tv/id/490845/index.html) This shows a positive development in the representation of ethnicity in the mainstream media.

More recently, British sitcoms such as *Citizen Khan* have been focused on specific ethnic groups, but there is still a limited range of non-white representations within the genre.

Jennifer Saunders and Joanna Lumley in *Absolutely Fabulous.*

Gender

In the past, sitcoms were criticised for the narrow range of stereotypical female roles, for example the domineering battleaxe wife. Sitcoms produced since the 1990s have featured a wider range of representations, influenced in part by the fact that more writers of sitcoms are now female, for example *Dinnerladies*, written by Victoria Wood, and *Absolutely Fabulous*, written by Jennifer Saunders. More recent examples include *Unbreakable Kimmy Schmidt*, co-written by Tina Fey.

Analysing the Set Product: *Friends*

Friends was produced by Warner Bros Television and Bright/Kauffman/Crane Productions. It was broadcast on NBC in the USA. In the UK, *Friends* was shown on Channel 4 from 1995 and also on Sky between 1996 and 2001. There were ten series in total, showing the popularity and longevity of the show and enabling audiences to engage with the characters' lives over many years.

Friends is often described as one of the world's most popular sitcoms. It was extremely successful and has influenced many other texts. *Friends* won many awards including Primetime Emmys, Golden Globes and a BAFTA in 1998.

Friends broke new ground, as one of the main settings was not a home or workplace but a coffee shop. There were also six regular main characters and the **ensemble cast** did not include a major star, which was unusual for an American sitcom.

Key Term

Ensemble cast
A group of actors who have an equal role in the production: there is no main protagonist or star.

The basis of the sitcom is a group of friends rather than a family. The series revolves around issues such as jobs, friendships and relationships, which many young adult viewers could relate to and identify with.

Media language

Friends is typically set in a limited number of locations, primarily the coffee shop and apartment, which are communal places where the characters meet.

There is a limited range of shots in the interior scenes, mostly long shots and medium shots filmed from specific points in the studio to show the interactions between the characters.

There are many examples of verbal and visual humour, such as Rachel entering in her wedding dress, which looks out of place in the coffee shop.

The mise-en-scène of the apartment in this scene:

- The combination of bright colours, contemporary artwork, throws on the sofa and clutter connotes a young, carefree lifestyle, reinforced by the cans of soft drinks on the table.
- Rachel has run away from her wedding, and lifelong commitment, and has arrived at the apartment, which offers a different lifestyle.
- The friends are watching and shouting at the television screen as Rachel tries to explain her decision on the phone. This undermines the seriousness of the situation and creates humour.

The **narrative** of the set episode establishes the characters and their lives. It seems to begin with equilibrium as they discuss their relationships, but there are several disruptions that have happened or happen, including:

* Ross's wife has left him
* Rachel walks out of her wedding
* Monica is misled by her date, 'Paul the wine guy'.

The friends at Central Perk.

The narrative shows characters failing in their aims: Monica's date does not develop into a relationship and Rachel fails to get a job. The narrative is circular, as all of the characters are still single at the end of the episode, although there is a hint that Ross and Rachel might get together in the future.

The set episode explores the themes of friendship and relationships, as two characters have just broken up from long-term partners and are trying to establish a new identity. Traditional values such as the importance of marriage are subverted as the messages in the text suggest that friendships and independence are more important.

There are some clear sitcom character types evident in *Friends*. Joey demonstrates traits of the 'lad' and the 'joker', while Monica is, or attempts to be, domineering.

Propp's theory of narrative is less applicable to *Friends*, partly due to the ensemble cast, as there is no clear 'hero' or 'villain'. Paul the wine guy could be seen as the false hero as he misleads Monica, and Rachel fulfils elements of the princess in her wedding dress and reliance on her father, but she is trying to break free from that role.

Representation

Age

Friends represents a group of characters from **'Generation X'** and targets this same demographic. The characters are young adults: they are no longer teenagers or students, but could be said to have not yet reached full adulthood. None of the characters is married (Ross's marriage has broken up and Rachel walks out of her wedding) and they do not have children. In *Friends*, family relationships are replaced by friendships.

The characters have little responsibility and appear quite carefree. It could be argued that they lack purpose in life and are trying to establish their identities as adults. The issue of independence is shown through Rachel as she relies on her father's credit cards while her new friends persuade her that she needs to find a job and earn her own money.

Gender: masculinity

Joey and Chandler demonstrate some stereotypically male attitudes and behaviours. Joey, for example, is clearly interested in the opposite sex and suggests that Ross should go to a strip club now that he is single.

Activity 5.9

Analyse the mise-en-scène of one of the other settings, for example the coffee shop. Make notes on the setting, props, colours and costumes. What messages do they communicate about the narrative, themes and characters?

Quickfire 5.25

Which sitcom types could be applied to the other characters in *Friends*?

Key Term

Generation X
The name given to people born in the 1970s and 1980s, after the 'baby boomers' and before the 'millennials'.

Top Tip

Note specific examples of how representations of age are constructed in the ten-minute extract that you study.

Matt Le Blanc as Joey. Much of the humour in this character comes from his stereotypical attitudes and behaviour.

Stretch and Challenge 5.18

Find three further specific examples of stereotypically masculine attitudes or behaviour in *Friends*.

NBC (National Broadcasting Company) broadcast *Friends* in the USA.

Key Term

Pilot
An initial episode of a television programme that is produced to 'test' whether the idea may be popular with an audience.

The focus on friendships and relationships, however, shows a development in male roles that reflects the social context of the 1990s and the idea of the 'new man' who is more open to discussing his emotions. Ross demonstrates these qualities in the set episode as he is upset following his marriage break-up. The male characters spend considerable time talking, which is a trait stereotypically associated with females. In the set episode, Joey and Chandler fail to build Ross's new furniture, which further subverts masculine stereotypes.

Ethnicity

America is a culturally diverse society and some American comedies have shown this, for example *The Fresh Prince of Bel Air* in the 1990s. In *Friends*, however, all the main characters are white and middle class, which does not reflect New York in the 1990s and reinforces the fact that people from minority ethnic groups have been under-represented in the mainstream media.

Industry

Friends was created by Kevin Bright, Marta Kauffman and David Crane, who pitched the idea initially to NBC and then produced a script for the **pilot** episode. NBC commissioned a series and the pilot became the first episode, 'The One Where Monica Gets a Roommate'.

Friends was filmed at the Warner Bros studios in California. Warner Bros Television produces original programmes for the American broadcast networks, including NBC, as well as for cable channels such as HBO and streaming services including Netflix. The company is part of Warner Bros Entertainment, which encompasses the film and television divisions and is owned by Time Warner, a very large media conglomerate. Warner Bros has produced many successful programmes and the size of the parent company allows it to create products with sizeable budgets and high production values.

Each episode is 22 minutes long, which allows 8 minutes for advertising content within a 30-minute slot in the television schedule. Season 1 has 24 episodes, which is quite typical of American sitcoms.

Each member of the cast was reportedly paid $22 500 per episode in the first series. This figure rose to $1 million per episode in the final series, which shows how the success of the programme resulted in a much higher budget and made stars of the actors. NBC paid Warner Bros a $10 million licence fee for each episode of the final series, and a 30-second advertising slot for the final show cost $2 million dollars (news.bbc.co.uk/1/hi/entertainment/3689029.stm). These extremely high costs demonstrate the popularity of the programme as companies were willing to invest high sums of money to be associated with the brand and reach their audience.

Distribution and scheduling

Friends was first broadcast in the USA in autumn 1994 and began screening in Britain on Channel 4 in April 1995. In Britain, 8.6 million people watched the final episode in 2004.

Friends was shown on Channel 4 in the UK from 1995 and then Sky won the rights to show the programme first, before it was broadcast on Channel 4, from 1996 to 2001. Channel 4 reportedly paid approximately £100 million for exclusive rights to show a number of Warner Bros programmes, including *Friends* and *ER*, from 2001 onwards. This was a large proportion of Channel 4's programming budget, so it shows the importance of *Friends* as it was a very popular programme. This deal was also significant as Channel 4 launched a digital channel, E4, in 2001, which specifically targets an audience of 16- to 34-year-olds. *Friends* became a core element of this new channel's programming.

By 1998 *Friends* was enormously popular, and Channel 4 agreed a deal with Wella (hair products) to sponsor *Friends*. Advertisers are likely to have been attracted by the young, affluent and predominantly female audience for *Friends*. In later years, companies including Nescafé and Jacob's Creek sponsored *Friends*. This shows the cultural significance of *Friends* and its importance in terms of attracting lucrative sponsorship to the television industry.

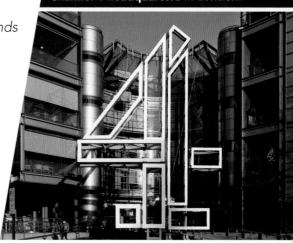
Channel 4 headquarters in London.

Friends was also repeated extensively on Channel 4 and E4 after the end of the original run and until 2011 when the rights were acquired by Comedy Central. *Friends* is still broadcast on Comedy Central, a channel available via cable or satellite in the UK. It is owned by the multimedia conglomerate Viacom and creates original programmes as well as showing syndicated content such as *Friends* and *Da Ali G Show*.

Friends has been available on Netflix in the USA since 2015 and has been broadcast in many countries worldwide. In the UK *Friends* is available to download on sites such as Amazon and iTunes, and all ten series are also available on DVD. Netflix began streaming *Friends* in the UK in January 2018. This wide distribution across different platforms has enabled *Friends* to continue to attract an audience more than ten years after the final series ended. It suggests that there is still a great demand for the show.

The BBFC rated Season 1, Episode 1 on DVD as a 12 for 'moderate sex references'. Most episodes are rated 12, although some are PG, which allows the programme to reach a wide family audience.

Audience

The primary audience for *Friends* was young adult females. Channel 4's sponsorship manager David Charlesworth described the programme's audience profile as 'ABC1 women aged 25 to 44'.

The series did, however, have broad appeal to audiences of both genders and of different age groups. The long-running popularity of the show means that *Friends* now has an even wider audience as some remember the original series while younger audiences are discovering it for the first time. Michelle Davies argues, 'Parents who loved the show in their 20s now sit down to watch the repeats with their teens, while students who were toddlers when it first aired proclaim their appreciation on Twitter as they become hooked on Ross and Rachel's will-they-won't-they storyline (even though they know the outcome).' (dailymail.co.uk/home/you/article-2465332)

This shows that television plays an important role in people's lives and reinforces the idea that viewing can be a sociable experience. A younger audience might be more likely to continue to watch the programme if they have watched it together as a family.

Quickfire 5.26

How do the products that were used to sponsor *Friends* link to the programme and its target audience?

Quickfire 5.27

Why do you think *Friends* is now shown on Comedy Central rather than Channel 4?

Top Tip

Identify specific examples from the set episode to support each of the four Uses and Gratifications.

There are many ways in which *Friends* appeals to its audiences. These can be linked to the Uses and Gratifications theory:

- Entertainment
- Escapism, especially the New York setting for a British audience
- Personal identity: Many viewers can identify with the relatable characters experiencing friendships, work and relationships in the late 20th and early 21st centuries. An older audience might feel as though they have grown up with the characters and have a sense of nostalgia for the show.
- Social interaction: The programme was very much a watercooler topic during its original run and still generates discussion. The release of all series on Netflix in the UK was covered in the British news media and gained responses on social media.

Contexts

Social context

The early series of *Friends* were made before the 9/11 attacks in the USA, during a period of relative stability. This is reflected in the characters' carefree lives and the focus on personal issues rather than wider social concerns.

It has been argued that the 1990s was a period in American society where young adults lived independently, free from their parents and without the responsibility of long-term relationships or children. Professor Elayne Rapping states, '*Friends* stands out as a sign that we are now living in a culture where youth rules, where the image of youth has become the dominant image of our culture.' (buffalo.edu/news/releases/2004/04/6680.html)

This society is particularly relevant to *Friends* as the Generation X characters have the freedom to explore life and they have not yet 'settled down'.

Cultural context

The characters regularly watch television in the programme, which reflects the important role that television plays in many people's lives. The way in which the characters 'interact' with television programmes, for example shouting, 'Push her down the stairs' in the set episode, possibly mirrors the relationship that the audience will have with *Friends* if they become engaged with the show.

Friends was not only extremely popular, it also had an influence on many areas of contemporary life:

- The 'Rachel' hairstyle became a fashion trend and many women adopted the style.
- Linguist Sali Tagliamonte studied *Friends* and co-wrote a study entitled 'So weird; so cool; so innovative: The use of intensifiers in the television series *Friends*'. She found that the characters used words such as 'so' a lot, to emphasise their speech and that this has influenced the way that people speak in real life: 'The data shows us that language changes in these very strong ways depending on what people think is cool or trendy.' (theparisreview.org/blog/2016/08/31/truly-trending-interview-intensifiers)
- Coffee-shop culture: The popularity of coffee shops has grown in the UK since the millennium and it has been argued that this trend is partly due to *Friends*.

Jennifer Aniston as Rachel.

Quickfire 5.28

What does Tagliamonte's point about language suggest about the influence of *Friends*?

Analysing the Set Product: *The IT Crowd*

The IT Crowd was produced by Talkback Thames for Channel 4 and first broadcast in the UK in February 2006. There have been four series of six episodes and a final one-off special broadcast in 2013. *The IT Crowd* was written by Graham Linehan, who had previously been involved with *Father Ted* and *Black Books* for Channel 4, and starred Richard Ayoade, Chris O'Dowd, Katherine Parkinson and Matt Berry.

The series won several high-profile awards, including a Best Sitcom BAFTA in 2009 and an International Emmy in 2008.

The IT Crowd is a work-based sitcom focused on three young adult characters who work in the IT department of a large company, Reynholm Industries. Jen is the head of department who manages Roy and Moss but, ironically, she has no understanding of IT. The boss of the company, Douglas Reynholm, appears in several episodes but most other characters are minor and only appear in one or two episodes, which is typical of the sitcom genre.

The set product is Episode 2 of Season 4, 'The Final Countdown', broadcast in 2010.

Katherine Parkinson, who plays the IT-illiterate IT manager, Jen.

Media language

Genre

The set episode of *The IT Crowd* includes many familiar elements of the sitcom repertoire, alongside some new features:

- The workplace setting is typical and the IT office is an enclosed environment that can be seen to 'trap' the characters.
- The narrative is circular, a key convention of the genre.
- The three main characters have aspirations linked to status:
  - Moss wants to appear on *Countdown* as he is a big fan of the show – and he earns higher status by winning several episodes and gaining entry to '8+'.
  - Roy is frustrated as he feels inadequate compared with Alistair, especially when he believes Alistair mistakes him for a window cleaner.
  - Jen wants to be accepted into the head-of-department meetings when she feels she is being left out.
  - All of these aspirations relate to the character's sense of identity rather than being linked to social class, so this is a development from earlier sitcoms such as *Fawlty Towers*.
- The structure is based on three different narrative strands, or storylines, one relating to each main character. This is similar to the set episode of *Friends* as the action cuts between the three different narrative strands (showing the males in Ross's new home, Rachel alone in the apartment and Monica's date).
- There are typical sitcom characters, and character types from other genres in the *Countdown* sequences. The inclusion of characters such as Prime from outside the world of the sitcom is less typical but, as it is a comedy, this is accepted as a 'version' of reality.

Fawlty Towers drew much of its humour from social class and aspiration in the 1970s.

Key Term

Surreal
Events or occurrences that are not realistic and do not seem to make sense; they have no logic. (Comedy programmes do not attempt to create fully realistic representations of the world, so surreal humour might be used to communicate a deeper message about society or culture.)

Quickfire 5.29

Which other events in the set episode of *The IT Crowd* are surreal?

Quickfire 5.30

What messages does the mise-en-scène communicate about the environment of the IT office?

Stretch and Challenge 5.19

Can you identify any similarities between the *IT Crowd* office and the apartment in *Friends*?

Quickfire 5.31

What are the connotations of 'street' in relation to 'Street Countdown'? How does this challenge our expectations of *Countdown*?

Stretch and Challenge 5.20

Watch an episode of *Countdown* and note all of the ways that the quiz show is referred to in *The IT Crowd*.

- The intertextual references to *Countdown* and other texts are less typical of the genre, although not completely new. Most episodes of *The Simpsons*, for example, directly reference different forms of popular culture.
- The use of **surreal** humour shows a development of the sitcom genre, although viewers of Graham Linehan's earlier work will find these elements familiar. The 'Street Countdown' sequence is an example of surreal humour as it is completely the opposite of what an audience expects from *Countdown*. This creates comedy and connotes that *Countdown* has an almost 'cult' following among its fans.

The **mise-en-scène** of the IT office is constructed through the following visual codes (not all visible in this image):

Roy and Jen in the *IT Crowd* office.

- mismatched furniture: desk, shelves, green sofa
- posters, postcards and stickers on the walls and desk, many of which relate to popular culture such as comics and video games
- props such as the toys and clutter on the desk, mugs, and books piled on shelves
- Roy's appearance: T-shirt, untidy hair.

Intertextuality is a major feature of the set episode of *The IT Crowd* as Moss takes part in *Countdown*, the long-running Channel 4 show, popular with students and older audiences as it is broadcast in the middle of the afternoon. Some contestants are very competitive and show dedication and skill in winning many episodes.

Countdown audiences will recognise Moss as a typical contestant as his intellect and attention to detail result in him winning more than eight episodes.

There are many intertextual references that fans of *Countdown* will recognise, for example the prize of the teapot and the picture of former presenter Richard Whitely on the wall at the 8+ Club.

There are further intertextual references, for example in Prime who resembles characters in the *Matrix* films. This is another example of surreal humour and connotes that *Countdown* champions have high status among fans.

The codes of sitcom are hybridised with the quiz-show sequence that uses the conventions of *Countdown*, for example the wide shots of the studio, close-ups on each contestant and the ticking clock.

The scenes in the 8+ Club use different conventions, such as low-key lighting and a low-angle moving camera to connote danger and excitement at the beginning of the 'Street Countdown' sequence. These elements are more familiar from the thriller and action genres and create a surreal atmosphere for comedic effect, especially as the actual 'street' game is not at all violent or dangerous.

Narrative

There are different narrative strands relating to each of the main characters:

- Moss appears on *Countdown*. He is successful and becomes a champion, which allows him to experience the 8+ Club and gain a new identity as an attractive and desirable young man.
- Roy is trying to start a new life but spends most of the episode trying to convince Alistair that he is not a window cleaner.
- Jen is trying to be accepted at the head-of-department meetings, especially when she sees her colleagues wearing bathrobes as they enter the room. She achieves her aim, but it is not what she expected.

The narrative subverts expectations and this creates much of the comedy. We do not expect *Countdown* champions, for example, to have a secret club and enact a 'street' version of the quiz, and we do not expect the head-of-department meeting to be an aerobics class, led by the company boss.

The characters 'escape' the IT office in the set episode, but they are back in it at the end and nothing has really changed. The episode ends in disappointment for Jen and Roy, while Moss has achieved his aims – and more besides – but there is little sense that this will have a lasting impact on his life. This is a **circular narrative**, typical of sitcom, which returns the characters to the original point prior to the next episode.

Propp's theory can be applied to some of the characterisation. Moss, for example, demonstrates many attributes of the hero as he wins *Countdown* and defeats Negative One, who challenges him and fulfils the role of the antagonist or villain. Prime can be seen as the donor as he gives Moss the invitation to the 8+ Club.

Chris O'Dowd, who plays Roy, has gone on to film and TV success in the USA.

Representation

The location of the IT office is in the basement, at the bottom of the building and below everyone else, which connotes that it is less important than other departments. This also constructs a stereotype that the IT staff are 'shut away' and do not interact with colleagues, and perhaps that they are socially awkward. The mis-en-scène of the office establishes the stereotype that IT workers are untidy, quite 'geeky' and interested in comics and science fiction. Roy's comment, 'Have you tried turning it off and on again' is stereotypical of an IT worker, implying that they have a lot of technical skill but that their colleagues do not try even simple solutions before calling the IT department.

Jen does not understand IT and is not required to attend the head-of-department meetings, which suggests that the IT team is not really valued within the organisation.

The representation of the department upholds many stereotypes, but the *Guardian* website published a blog in 2010 where three IT professionals discussed how some aspects of *The IT Crowd* were quite true to life.

There are many stereotypical character types in *The IT Crowd*:

• Moss is constructed as a 'geek' or 'nerd'. He is extremely intelligent and quite obsessive about things that interest him, such as *Countdown*. He is also quite a 'straight' character. Richard Ayoade is of mixed race, but Moss's ethnicity is not a focus of the programme. This in itself shows that there is now greater social equality in society.

• The other *Countdown* contestants are similarly stereotyped: many of them are dressed in unfashionable pullovers and the 8+ Club does not stock alcoholic drinks.

• Roy is a typical sitcom character trapped in a job that he does not particularly enjoy and feels jealous of his old college friend who has a successful career in gaming and an attractive girlfriend. He is trying to better himself by moving house but is thwarted in appearing this way as his old friend thinks he is a window cleaner.

• The representation of Negative One subverts stereotypes for comedic effect. He is constructed as a neat and tidy white male, but his dress codes, language and gestures are stereotypically those of a young black rap artist.

• Jen is one of the few female characters in *The IT Crowd*, which possibly reflects the fact that IT departments tend to be male dominated. She is Roy and Moss's manager, but is technically incompetent, so, in this sense it is not a particularly positive representation. In the set episode, she is unaware of what is happening at the heads-of-department meetings and shows an element of naivety.

Industry and audience

Production

The IT Crowd was produced by Talkback Thames for Channel 4. Talkback Thames was a production company owned by Fremantle Media, part of the RTL conglomerate. Talkback was established by Mel Smith and Griff Rhys Jones in the 1980s and it produced many comedy programmes including *Never Mind the Buzzcocks*. Talkback merged with Thames Television in 2003 but Fremantle split the brands again in 2011 and Talkback now specialises in comedy programmes while Thames focuses on entertainment.

Writer Graham Linehan's earlier programmes for Channel 4, *Father Ted* and *Black Books*, were successful series and suggest that his work appeals to Channel 4's audience. Fans of these shows will be familiar with the surreal style of humour and might find gratification in the 8+ Club scenes in *The IT Crowd*.

Some of the actors were well known when the show was released. This would attract an audience who had enjoyed their previous work. Richard Ayoade, for example, had appeared in *Garth Marenghi's Darkplace*, a Channel 4 comedy, and the BBC cult comedy *The Mighty Boosh* (along with Noel Fielding, who also appears in *The IT Crowd*). He has won a Television BAFTA for his performance in *The IT Crowd* and has gone on to direct the film *Submarine* and present *Gadget Man*, *Travel Man* and *The Crystal Maze* on Channel 4.

Graham Linehan has described the process of making the programme in front of a live audience: 'We start rehearsals on a Monday in order to film the show in front of an audience the following Friday (location material is shown on monitors in story order). Under the threat of such an unpredictable group of people, any line that doesn't get a laugh stands out like an old guy at a party. Because *The IT Crowd*, is, like *Father Ted* before it, just a device for generating laughter, this extra pressure is invaluable to me.' (theguardian.com/media/2007/nov/19/television.features1)

This type of production process is more likely to be used for comedy programmes as there is an immediate 'live' audience response to the humour. As Linehan comments, this adds pressure for the cast and producers, but potentially creates a more successful product.

Distribution and scheduling

Ofcom described Channel 4 in its 2017 'Channel 4 Corporation Remit' report: 'Channel 4 is recognised as the original brand, with an edgier, more risk-taking image than other PSBs, broadcasting content that can at times be challenging and controversial, but still enjoying fairly broad appeal.' (ofcom.org.uk)

The set episode was broadcast on Friday 2 July 2010. Comedy programmes are often scheduled on a Friday evening. According to BARB statistics, the first episode received 2.2 million viewers. Only *Big Brother* achieved higher ratings on Channel 4 that week. This demonstrates the popularity of *The IT Crowd*, which had developed a loyal audience.

The IT Crowd is also available on the Channel 4 catch-up service All 4 and on Netflix in the UK. It had a reasonably limited international release. It was shown on Comedy Central in Germany and the Netherlands, for example, and was available in the USA via online streaming. Each series has been released on DVD and an 'ultimate' box set was released in 2016. This included all four series and the 2013 'special'.

The set episode of the programme was awarded a 12 certificate by the BBFC when released on DVD.

How does *The IT Crowd* appeal to audiences?

Channel 4 tends to appeal to a younger demographic than BBC One, although it still aims to reach a broad audience, as stated by Ofcom. *The IT Crowd* targets a more specialised audience than *Friends* due to the particular setting and situations in the programme.

- The primary target audience might be young adult males, particularly those with an interest in technology.
- There are specific appeals for people who are IT literate due to some of the specialist lexis and 'in jokes'.
- The set episode might appeal specifically to fans of *Countdown* and its spin-off *8 Out of 10 Cats Does Countdown*.

The IT Crowd does, however, also target viewers who do not have a specific interest in IT, such as other office workers with an IT department. Appeals for a broader demographic include:

- storylines that have universal appeal, such as Roy's mistaken identity as a window cleaner

Richard Ayoade at the premier of the film *The Watch* in 2012.

Stretch and Challenge 5.23

Research the other main actors, producer and director to find out which other programmes they have been involved with.

Quickfire 5.36

What elements of the set episode of *The IT Crowd* might be seen as 'edgy' or 'risk-taking'?

Quickfire 5.37

Why do you think that *The IT Crowd* had quite a limited international release?

Quickfire 5.38

What does the 2016 release of a box set suggest about the audience for *The IT Crowd*?

Quickfire 5.39

How does the title sequence for *The IT Crowd* appeal to an audience that is interested in technology and video games?

- humour that is not specific to technology, such as the aerobics class
- the inclusion of characters such as Jen who do not understand IT.

Marketing

The *IT Crowd* page of the Channel 4 website includes links to the episodes, clips and 'extras' and character profiles, typical of many television programme websites. There are also some specific elements to appeal to *IT Crowd* fans:

- A game that invites the audience to 'Assist Jen, Moss and Roy in protecting Reynholm Industries from hordes of electronic nasties!' This encourages interactivity and further suggests that the programme is targeting an IT-literate audience.

- A range of *IT Crowd* wallpapers that can be downloaded by fans who wish to customise their desktop. This reinforces some of the ideas in the programme as Roy's desk is surrounded by memorabilia relating to popular culture, and this allows viewers to do the same.

Channel 4 ran an *IT Crowd Night* in December 2013. This was an evening of programming devoted to the show, featuring *The IT Crowd Manual* (a documentary about the making of the programme) and favourite episodes including one that was chosen by fans. This demonstrates the lasting appeal of the programme, even after the final episode had been screened. Channel 4 issued a **press release** for the event that used specialist lexis such as 'reboot' and 'decrypt' to appeal to the fans of the show.

This use of such language reinforces the branding in the title sequence of the programme and also the DVD cover. The series 1 DVD, for example is called 'Version 1.0' to reflect the IT context. These also reference video games and further appeal to the specialised audience.

Contexts

The characters are young adult 'millennials', in contrast to the Generation X characters that feature in *Friends*. Moss, Roy and Jen work for a large company and seem to have responsible jobs, although Roy in particular feels quite inadequate in this episode in comparison with his old friend Alistair. This relates to the contemporary social context where young adults have high student debts and many have to work in jobs for which they are overqualified. Roy's character demonstrates insecurities, which makes a link to modern concerns about anxiety and mental health issues.

The IT team shows greater cultural diversity than *Friends* as there are characters from different social and ethnic backgrounds, reflecting the context of contemporary London.

The *Countdown* sequences reflect the cultural context as that programme is extremely popular with particular audiences and is 'cult' viewing for many university students. The programme transports *Countdown* to a contemporary urban setting but then upholds the stereotypical view that the contestants are not actually radical. The transformation of Moss's image reflects the cult of celebrity in contemporary society where people who have appeared on television achieve fame and status and take on the trappings of celebrity.

Section B: Music Video and Online Media

Overview

In Section B, you will study three music videos:

- one contemporary music video by a female artist
- one contemporary music video by a male artist
- one older music video from the 1980s or early 1990s.

This chapter includes analysis of some different music videos by the same artists to illustrate the codes and conventions of the form and to contextualise the set products. You will need to analyse the set music videos chosen by your teacher in detail.

You will also explore online, social and participatory media products in relation to the two contemporary artists whose music videos you have analysed.

This chapter includes some illustrative examples from the artists' websites and social media accounts, but these types of media product are regularly updated and you will need to study appropriate current examples, chosen by your teacher, during your course.

Michael Jackson on the photoshoot of his *Bad* album, 1987.

Contemporary music videos	Music videos from the 1980s and 1990s	Online, social and participatory media
Two music videos from the following options: **Either** Katy Perry, 'Roar' (2013) **or** Taylor Swift, 'Bad Blood' (2014) **and either** Pharrell Williams, 'Freedom' (2015) **or** Mark Ronson and Bruno Mars, 'Uptown Funk' (2014)	**One** of the following music videos: **Either** Duran Duran, 'Rio' (1982) **or** Michael Jackson, 'Black or White' (1991)	**Either** katyperry.com **or** taylorswift.com **and either** pharrellwilliams.com **or** brunomars.com

You will analyse the music video from the 1980s or 1990s in relation to media language, representations and contexts. The contemporary products are studied in relation to all areas of the theoretical framework:

- **Media language**, including:
  - the relationship between technology and media products
  - the codes and conventions of media language and how these become established as 'styles'
  - intertextuality
- **Representations**, including:
  - representations of gender, ethnicity and age
  - viewpoints, messages, values and beliefs
  - stereotypes
- **Media industries**, including:
  - production, ownership and control; conglomerate ownership
  - the impact of convergence across different platforms
  - how music operates as a commercial industry in a global context

- **Audiences**, including:
  - interactivity via online platforms
  - audience targeting, consumption and response
- **Contexts**: how the music products reflect the society and culture in which they were made.

Analysing the Set Products

Studying the two contemporary music videos alongside the artists' websites and social media pages will allow you to consider the way in which record labels use convergence to:

- market the artists and their music
- establish a brand identity for the artist
- appeal to audiences.

In analysing an example of an older music video together with contemporary examples you will explore:

- how codes and conventions change over time
- how the products reflect the contexts in which they were made in relation to:
  - the use of media language, including technology
  - representations of gender and ethnicity
  - themes and issues explored
  - the messages and values communicated.

Overview of the Music Industry

Music is a very large global media industry. In Britain, the music industry contributes billions of pounds to the economy, and is the third largest market for recorded music in the world. The music industry has faced many challenges in recent years as record sales have been decreasing and the internet has changed the way audiences consume music.

Downloading and sharing music has been an issue for some time, although audiences can download music legally from sites such as Amazon and iTunes. **Online streaming services** such as Spotify and Deezer have become very popular and streaming now accounts for more than 50 per cent of music consumption in the UK according to the **BPI**.

These services allow users to access a wide range of music, and the record label receives a payment every time a track is streamed. The sites are funded by advertising (some allow users to listen for free if they accept advertising) and subscription fees (where listeners pay for an advert-free service and enhanced features such as the ability to listen offline). In addition, most artists also have their own YouTube and Vevo pages which generate income from advertising.

Key Terms

Online streaming services
Websites and apps that allow users to listen to music (or consume other digital content, such as television or film) via the internet. (Depending on the service and subscription level, listeners might be able to save their music to listen to offline.)

BPI
The British Phonographic Institute, a trade organisation that represents the British recorded music industry. The BPI organises the annual BRIT Awards and Mercury Prize.

Many people now listen to music through sites or apps like Spotify on a phone, tablet or computer.

A record shop in Iceland with shelves full of CDs.

The technological developments that once seemed to threaten the future of the industry have allowed it to generate profits in different ways. The availability of music online enables artists to extend their reach to audiences in different parts of the world.

Although CD sales are in decline as much of our music consumption has become digital, **vinyl records** are becoming more popular again. In 2017, more than 4 million vinyl albums were sold in the UK, which was almost one in ten physical record sales (BPI statistics), suggesting that this is an important trend in the industry. Some music fans prefer to own a physical copy of their favourite music and take pleasure in holding it and looking at the album artwork and sleeve notes. Nostalgia is also a possible factor here, as older music fans might enjoy the format they remember from their youth, while younger people might be attracted by the current trend for vinyl.

The music industry has to adapt to change and respond to audience demands, as Matt Ingham from independent label Cherry Red Records, commented, 'The combination of new and old technology means the industry can continue to rise to the challenge of providing the public with music to treasure forever.' (bpi.co.uk/news-analysis/ rising-uk-music-consumption-enjoys-fastest-growth-this-millennium)

Top Tip

Make a list of the streaming and download sites linked from your contemporary artists' websites.

Stretch and Challenge 5.24

Research the contemporary artists to find out if they have released any of their music on vinyl and consider why they might have done so.

Ownership and the music industry

Record labels are companies that make contracts with artists and release their music. Record companies usually fund the costs of producing, distributing and circulating music to audiences. The process of creating and releasing music includes:

- Artist and repertoire, the department of the record company that finds and nurtures new artists. An 'advance' is often paid to the artist before they have released any music. This allows them to pay their living costs while they are developing new material.
- Production: the recording and mixing of the music, and production of physical formats such as CDs.
- Distribution and circulation: marketing, press and promotion teams to advertise and publicise the music:
  - A single release from an album will usually be accompanied by a music video which becomes a major part of the marketing campaign.
  - Publicity for a new single or album will be generated through, for example, articles in newspapers and magazines and television appearances by the artist.
  - The promotion department will also arrange airplay on the radio and broadcast of the video on channels such as MTV.
  - Record labels usually have a dedicated online and social media department to ensure that the artists reach their audiences through digital platforms.
  - The sales division of a label will be involved in circulating the products to shops and online retail outlets.

Key Term

Horizontally integrated
The structure of a large media organisation which owns companies that produce the same type of media product.

Quickfire 5.41

What is the advantage for a major record company of owning many subsidiary labels?

There are currently three major record labels within the industry: Sony Music, Universal Music Group and Warner Music Group. These three companies are part of major conglomerates and are **horizontally integrated**: they have subsidiary record labels that operate under the main organisation. Some of these subsidiary labels have previously been independent and are associated with a particular genre. Island Records, for example, owned by Universal, was established in Jamaica and originally produced a lot of reggae music.

The major labels detailed below belong to large, powerful media organisations and are able to invest large amounts of money in artists that are, or are likely to be, commercially successful. There are high costs involved in producing music. Videos for major artists often have a budget of over a million dollars.

These organisations operate with high budgets on a global scale and are able to reach large audiences through high-profile marketing campaigns. They also have the potential to benefit from synergy with other companies in the conglomerate.

Record label	Conglomerate	Subsidiary labels
Sony Music	Sony Corporation. Sony also produces films, games consoles, smartphones and other electronic goods.	Columbia Epic RCA
Universal Music Group	Vivendi. Studio Canal is another Vivendi brand that produces film and television.	Capitol EMI Island
Warner Music Group	Access Industries. This industrial conglomerate has interests in many areas including media and communications, chemicals and technology.	Atlantic Asylum Parlophone

There are also many independent record labels, such as Big Machine and Warp Records, that are not linked to a major label. Some very high-profile artists with mainstream appeal, including Taylor Swift, are signed to independent labels, although these are often associated with more alternative acts. 'Indie' music was traditionally non-mainstream, but has become increasingly popular, with many Indie artists achieving commercial as well as critical success. Nonetheless, the industry is still dominated by the 'big three' companies above, especially as they are vertically integrated and also distribute the work of some artists from independent labels.

Some independent artists are not signed to a record label at all and use the internet to promote and distribute their work. It could be argued that this has made the industry more democratic as an artist does not necessarily need to be tied to a record deal. Many independent artists have their own websites and use social media and sites such as YouTube to reach an audience.

Regulation

The music industry is not regulated by a single organisation, but there are regulatory guidelines that apply to music products such as music videos in Britain.

The BPI runs the 'Parental Advisory Scheme', a voluntary system that uses the 'Parental Advisory' logo to notify audiences about content that might be offensive or unsuitable for children. The record company has the responsibility for assessing the product (for example, a song or a music video) and applying the logo where appropriate, using the BPI guidelines. The criteria include:

- strong language
- depictions of violence
- sexual behaviour
- discriminatory behaviour, for example racism
- dangerous or criminal behaviour, such as drug abuse.

The logo is applied as a sticker on a physical product such as a CD. It is also used online, for example next to the icon for a song or music video on a streaming service.

Quickfire 5.42

What type of synergy might a record company develop with another media organisation in the same conglomerate, for example a film company?

Stretch and Challenge 5.25

Research an independent artist who has achieved success by using the internet to reach an audience.

Quickfire 5.43

What are the similarities between the 'Parental Advisory' guidelines and the BBFC categories for classifying film? Why do you think these categories are alike?

Mark Ronson - Uptown Funk ft. Bruno Mars
2,967,755,783 views

10M 650K SHARE

MarkRonsonVEVO
Published on 19 Nov 2014

SUBSCRIBE 3.9M

Mark Ronson's official music video for 'Uptown Funk' ft. Bruno Mars. Click to listen to Mark Ronson on Spotify: http://smarturl.it/MarkRonsonSpotify?...

Partner rating   PG

SHOW MORE

Regulating music videos released on DVD

The Video Recordings Act of 1984 states that certain types of product released on DVD or Blu-ray do not need to be classified by the BBFC. Music videos are in this category. An amendment from 2014, however, requires all products to be classified if they contain material that 'could be potentially harmful or otherwise unsuitable for children'. (bbfc.co.uk/education-resources/student-guide/legislation/video-recordings-act) All music videos on DVD now need to be classified if they would achieve a 12 certificate or above.

Regulating music videos online

The internet presents many challenges to media regulators, as content can easily be created and shared online. Internet service providers are subject to regulation and the Internet Service Providers' Association works to promote online safety, especially for children.

Since 2014, the BBFC has been working with YouTube and Vevo to age-rate online music videos. This is an additional service to the Parental Advisory system. UK record companies are required to submit any video for classification if they feel it would gain at least a 12 certificate. 'Uptown Funk' received a PG rating, shown as 'Partner rating' under the video on Mark Ronson's YouTube channel. BBFC research indicates that 78 per cent of parents value this guidance.

Marketing: the star persona

The set products of music videos, online, social and participatory media are all examples of marketing that record labels use to try to reach a target audience in a global context. The image of an artist that we see in the media is a constructed representation, not simply the 'real' person. This is called the **star persona** and is established through many different elements, including:

- the music and lyrics
- the visual image of the artist shown on album artwork, in music videos and in publicity shots
- the design of the record artwork, website and merchandise
- the artist's social media posts.

This persona embodies particular values and beliefs and communicates messages to consumers. While music artists are real people, the image presented to the audience is often carefully constructed by the artist and the music producers to appeal to the target audience. An artist's persona is not fixed, however. It will change and develop over time as the artist gets older and possibly moves into different musical genres.

The Spice Girls each had an individual persona, such as 'Sporty Spice', which conveyed a message about the importance of individuality. Together, the group embodied values of 'girl power'.

Activity 5.13

Define the star persona of the contemporary artists that you are studying.

Refer to the website and social media pages that you have studied in class, including the images of the artist, such as album artwork and other photographs, clips from songs and music videos, merchandise, comments on social media etc.

Make notes on:

- visual and technical codes used to construct the star image, including dress codes, colour palettes and iconography
- messages and values communicated on the website, in the music and the social media posts.

Write a detailed paragraph explaining how the artist's persona has been constructed to appeal to the target audience.

Stretch and Challenge 5.27

Make notes on how the current star persona of your set contemporary artists compares with their image in the set music video.

Music Audiences

Music plays an important role in many people's lives and is often linked to their identity. It is particularly associated with youth culture, as many people develop a keen interest in music during their teenage years and become fans of particular genres. Rock and roll music became popular in the 1950s and 1960s in America and Britain, particularly as many young people had money to spend on leisure and consumer goods when the economy recovered after the Second World War.

Many genres have developed over time. Pop music, for example, is a very broad genre that originated in rock and roll but now covers a range of mainstream styles and targets a wide audience, while genres such as rap or country music have more specific conventions and appeal to a narrower audience.

Different musical genres, especially those that are less mainstream, often have a particular identity or image associated with them. Fans may respond positively to the music and then adopt the style of clothing and appearance linked to the genre. They might also share the particular values and beliefs that are communicated through the music and lyrics. The punk culture in the 1970s, for example, conveyed rebellious, **anti-establishment** beliefs that challenged **mainstream values**. This genre was considered to be a possible threat to society by some people at the time, showing that different audiences have varied responses to music.

Young people in particular can enjoy the experience of belonging to a group or 'culture' associated with a genre of music as they grow up and explore their identity. Friends might dress in similar clothes, listen to music and attend concerts together. In the digital age these interactions are less likely to occur in person than online as communities of fans around the world can meet in a virtual space and share their enjoyment of the music.

A poster advertising Bruno Mars' appearances at the Park Theater in Las Vegas.

Key Terms

Anti-establishment beliefs
Ideas that challenge authority or go against the accepted 'norms' in society.

Mainstream values
Ideas that the majority of people agree with, such as family values or a desire for material wealth.

Quickfire 5.45

What visual codes connote rebellion in the image of a punk?

Target audiences

The main target audience for popular music tends to be young people: teenagers and young adults. This is the age group that has time to enjoy and money to spend on music, and might be using popular culture to help establish their identity. It is also often assumed that music targets more males than females. Some music magazines target male readers and many music videos have tended to represent women in quite a sexual way, arguably to appeal to young men. The audience demographic for music, however, is actually very broad. The generation that first experienced rock and roll music in the 1950s has retired, and there are now more artists of both genders, different ages and ethnicities that appeal to a wide range of people. Particular genres will have more specific audience demographics and each artist within the industry will target a specific group or groups of listeners.

Fandom

Music offers many opportunities to actively engage in fandom, a particular pleasure or gratification for audiences who are really interested in a particular genre or artist. They might, for example:

- buy physical artefacts such as CDs and vinyl records, including limited editions and rare releases that could become valuable
- collect memorabilia such as concert tickets, posters and programmes
- purchase official merchandise such as T-shirts and bags
- dress in the style of a genre or artist
- attend concerts or festivals
- follow an artist on social media, and engage in activities such as competitions
- join an online fan community such as Katy Perry's 'Katy Cats', or even create their own fan site.

The internet, and social media in particular, allow audiences to feel that they 'know' the artists and have an insight into their lives, perhaps imagining that they are 'friends' with them if they interact on social media sites. This provides a particular kind of pleasure and also links to the idea of identity, as a fan can feel that they are part of the artist's world. The boundary between fantasy and reality can sometimes become blurred, especially in modern society where social media can make a star seem 'available' and 'real' rather than a constructed persona.

Some artists do engage with their followers, for example by 'liking' their tweets or even arranging to meet groups of fans, which offers additional gratifications to audiences.

Fandom also benefits the industry as audiences can play an important role in sharing information and promoting the artist to generate more sales.

Theoretical perspectives: active audiences

Audiences now have more choice of music than ever and can access bands and artists online that they might not have heard in the past. They can also listen to music when and where they wish on portable devices. Downloading sites offer audiences the ability to select and buy particular songs rather than purchasing an entire album, and, like streaming services, allow audiences to create personalised playlists. This suggests audiences are more active than in the past, when listeners bought an album of several tracks chosen and structured by the artist or media producers. Listeners today choose from what is available on these sites, which also generate suggestions of other music that they might like. This arguably suggests that, while listeners are more involved and have more choice, the industry is still in control of what the audience can listen to.

Audiences are important in driving developments in the industry. If, for example, a particular artist is popular, the record company is likely to release more of their music and might also develop similar products from other artists in the same genre. Record companies are able to use technology to gather data from record sales and from digital platforms to show which music is popular with which audiences, and this can inform what producers invest in.

The Contemporary Artists

The contemporary male and female artists that you study are mainstream solo artists who have achieved major success in terms of record sales and critical acclaim. Analysing them allows you to study all areas of the theoretical framework in relation to music videos and online media. Each artist has a clear star persona, although this is fluid and develops over time, and each could also be considered to be a 'brand' that can be marketed and 'sold' to audiences.

Katy Perry

Katy Perry is an extremely successful singer who has won several American Music Association Awards and is currently a judge on the television show, *American Idol*. She is signed to Capitol Records, part of Universal Music Group.

Top Tip

Note specific examples of fan behaviour that you identify on the set artists' websites and social media.

Stretch and Challenge 5.29

Make a list of all the ways in which a music audience can be actively involved in their choice of music and of the ways in which the industry controls music output. Write a paragraph explaining how far a contemporary audience can choose the music they consume.

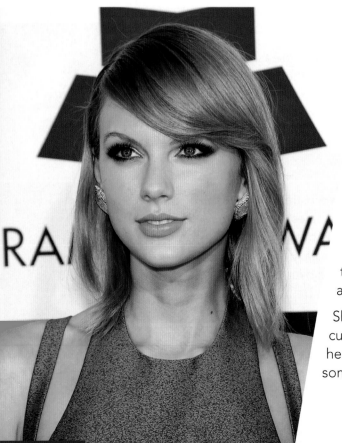

Quickfire 5.47

Why might an artist release additional products to tie in with an album release?

Key Term

Platinum record
A record that has sold more than 1 million copies.

Her most recent album, *Witness*, has not achieved the **platinum record** sales of her first three albums, but she is still a major commercial success. In June 2017 she was presented with Diamond Awards by the Recording Industry Association of America for three songs, including 'Roar', that have achieved over 10 million sales and streams in America. Katy Perry currently (early 2018) has more Twitter followers than anyone in the world, over 108 million.

Perry regularly makes significant changes to her image and her onstage persona is very theatrical with elaborate costumes, hair and make-up. Her recent persona is more androgynous than the feminine image constructed in her earlier work.

To tie-in with the release of *Witness*, Perry created a video called 'Will You Be My Witness', recorded when she went into a 'live streaming' house for four days. The video is available to buy and has similarities with the release of the 'making of' video released alongside Michael Jackson's 'Thriller' in the 1980s.

Taylor Swift

Taylor Swift is a Grammy award-winning American singer-songwriter who has released six albums and achieved extremely high record, sales. She has over 85 million followers on Twitter, placing her fifth in the world in January 2018.

Swift is signed to the independent label Big Machine Records, which is part of the Big Machine Label Group based in Nashville, USA. The label mainly specialises in country music, although Taylor Swift is now a much more mainstream pop artist. Big Machine's music is distributed through Universal Music Group, one of the three major record labels, which ensures that her music reaches a wide audience.

Swift's persona has developed over time and her website was completely rebranded to tie in with the release of her latest album, *Reputation*, in 2017. Her early persona was youthful and created a sense of the 'girl next door' that young female fans could relate to. This image is evident in the video for 'Love Story'. As Swift has grown older, however, her image has changed and her fans will be able to identify with the more mature persona that has developed. 'Bad Blood' shows an independent and more sexualised persona for example. *Reputation* demonstrates a further development as Swift looks more grown up and 'stripped back', and the branding uses starker, black and white imagery in contrast to the more colourful tones on her previous albums. The themes at this time seem to reflect on her relationship with the media and the 'reputation' that she has developed.

She has recently launched 'The Swift Life' app which offers customers exclusive insights and the chance to connect with her. It has received very positive responses from her fans, sometimes known as 'Swifties'.

Bruno Mars

Bruno Mars is a very successful Grammy award-winning artist who has appeared at the Superbowl and was named on the Forbes '30 Under 30 List' in 2014. He is signed to Atlantic Records, which is part of Warner Music Group. Mars has also been a producer, plays several instruments and voiced a role in the film *Rio II* in 2014. His music covers many different styles including pop, R&B and dance and he has been influenced by artists such as Michael Jackson and Prince.

Pharrell Williams

Pharrell Williams is signed to Columbia Records, part of Sony. He works in a range of media forms, produces music for other artists and was a producer for the film *Hidden Figures* in 2016. He can be considered a mainstream artist, perhaps best known for his very successful single 'Happy', which was included on the *Despicable Me 2* soundtrack and won the Academy Award for Best Original Song. Pharrell has the potential to appeal to a wide range of people, beyond a traditional pop music audience. For example, his website includes an article about his residency at New York University's Tisch School of the Arts, which might appeal to academics and artists.

Analysing Music Videos

A music video is a 'clip' that usually fits the length of the song, although some have a narrative that begins before the song. It is a commercial product, designed to promote the music, and coincides with the release of the song as a single. It is important that the video captures the key elements of the song, along with the artist's persona, to engage the audience. Many music videos have very large budgets and demonstrate high production values to help sell the product. Exotic settings and special effects are often used to create an aspirational 'fantasy' world.

As a form of advertisement, music videos may be seen as 'disposable' and not intended to last, but they are also media products in their own right, and many are highly creative and artistic. They often use codes and conventions of film and some film directors, such as Michel Gondry, Anton Corbijn and Spike Jonze, began their film careers by directing music videos. There are specific award categories, for example at the Grammys and the MTV Awards, that recognise the artistic achievement of music videos.

Taylor Swift at the 2014 MTV Video Music Awards in Los Angeles.

The video for Queen's 'Bohemian Rhapsody' in 1975 is considered to be one of the first genuine music videos and used groundbreaking technologies such as a prism camera lens, shown in this still, to create strong visual images.

Quickfire 5.48

What message might the video for 'Take On Me' communicate about the relationship between fans and music artists?

Key Term

Lip-synching
Mouthing or miming lyrics exactly in time to the recorded song in a music video or other performance.

A brief history of the music video

The music video became established as a form in the 1970s, as record companies began to release a visual accompaniment to help promote a new song. Music videos were shown on television programmes such as *Top of the Pops* and became an important part of the marketing and promotion of singles. MTV was launched as a specialist music video channel in 1981, allowing music videos to reach a much wider audience. Now, music videos can reach an even bigger global audience online, through platforms such as YouTube.

Music videos often use cutting-edge technology to create products that look very contemporary at the time they are made, although as time passes these effects can appear 'dated' and old-fashioned. The use of technology adds to the 'aspirational' value of the video as a promotional tool. For example, A-ha combined animation and live-action footage in the video for 'Take On Me'. This video explores the boundaries between fantasy and reality as the female character imagines that the lead singer comes to life from a cartoon strip.

The 1985 video for A-ha's 'Take On Me'.

Codes and conventions of music videos

Performance

Most music videos, especially mainstream artists' videos, will include an element of performance:

- The singer will usually be filmed **lip-synching** the lyrics; band members might be shown playing instruments.
- The performance might be at a live concert, in a rehearsal room or filmed on location.
- There might also be choreographed dancing, depending on the genre of the music.

This helps to sell the music and establish a connection with the audience.

Mark Ronson and Bruno Mars on a location set in the video for 'Uptown Funk'.

Narrative

Many music videos also have an element of narrative, usually interwoven with performance footage. It is unlikely that a music video will contain a complete narrative due to its length, but there might be elements of narrative or images that communicate stories, themes and messages.

Most music videos show a clear link to the words and ideas in the song in interpretation of the lyrics. Sometimes there will be a literal link between the lyrics and visual images, but it is more usual that the links are metaphorical. In the video for 'Human' by The Killers, for example, the phrase 'cut the cord' is matched to a visual image of an eagle hovering over the desert, connoting a sense of freedom linked to the lyrics.

In the Killers' 'Human', the eagle image fits with the setting, and the feathers on Brandon Flowers' jacket also link his persona to the majestic bird of prey.

The video usually reinforces the star persona, the image of the artist designed to appeal to the target audience and promote the artist and their music.

- The artist might appear as a performer (on stage, in the rehearsal room) and/or as a character within the narrative.
- The artist often directly addresses the audience, creating the impression that they are singing directly to the viewer.
- In some music videos the artist or band does not appear. This tends to be the case in independent or alternative videos, where there is less of an emphasis on the star persona.

Technical codes

- There are particular filming conventions in music videos:
- A range of shots is usually used, including multiple close-ups of the artist.
- The video is usually edited to the beat of the music; often fast paced.
- Narrative sequences might use techniques of continuity editing.
- Intertextuality:
  - Artists are often influenced by other musical genres or bands, as well as by other forms of popular culture such as television and film.
  - As music videos are very short products, intertextual references can provide a 'shortcut' to communicate a message quickly and clearly.
  - Music video is also a relatively new media form, so videos often 'borrow' ideas from film or other texts and use them to create something new. Madonna's video for 'Material Girl' in 1985, for example, directly references the film *Gentlemen Prefer Blondes* from 1953, starring Marilyn Monroe. An audience familiar with Monroe would recognise the physical similarity to Madonna, and those who had seen the film would appreciate the links between 'Material Girl' and the iconic scene where Monroe sings 'Diamonds are a Girl's Best Friend'. There is a consumerist message in both songs, relating to the value of material possessions, which also reflects the context of each product: the 1950s and 1980s were periods of economic success.

Top Tip

Use this list of codes and conventions when you analyse the set products.

Quickfire 5.49

How does 'Material Girl' intertextually reference *Gentlemen Prefer Blondes*?

Analysing an example: 'Love Story' by Taylor Swift, 2008

'Love Story' is a song about a relationship between a young male and female and references the Shakespeare play, *Romeo and Juliet*, in the lyrics.

The video constructs a 'love story' between two young students and Taylor Swift plays the role of the female character. It juxtaposes a contemporary college setting with a fantasy element set in a castle and garden.

The music video uses expected conventions:

- Swift sings/lip-synchs the lyrics in many sections of the video. She performs from an arch in the castle, part of the 'world' of the narrative, and is dressed in period costume.

- The narrative depicts a recognisable story of two young people falling in love. The setting connotes a sense of the 'fairy tale' romance. We can apply theoretical perspectives on narrative:

  - The reference to the 'prince and princess' in the lyrics is reinforced by the dress codes and behaviour of the characters, and links to Propp's character types of the hero and princess.

  - There is a sense of disruption as the female's father disapproves: an obstacle to be overcome. We do not see any conflict, but the female is alone for much of the video before she is 'rescued' by the man and there is a classic happy ending.

  - There are some binary oppositions, for example the present versus the past, and the young people versus the father. The ending reinforces a message that problems can be resolved and love can conquer all.

  - The narrative shows the young female's point of view and the audience is positioned with her character. The lyrics refer to the man 'saving' her from loneliness and proposing marriage, which conforms to stereotypical representations of gender and reinforces the view that women 'need' men. The video upholds traditional values relating to relationships and marriage.

  - The lyrics are interpreted quite closely throughout the video and the narrative is very easy to follow. In some cases the lyrics are matched exactly to the image, which communicates the story very clearly and literally. Other images are more metaphorical, for example the close-up shot of Swift picking the fruit, which has connotations of eating forbidden fruit, referencing Eve in the Garden of Eden and suggesting that there is a sexual attraction between the characters.

Top Tip

Always apply theoretical perspectives on narrative when you analyse the set products. Consider the messages that are communicated through the narrative.

Stretch and Challenge 5.30

How might you apply feminist theoretical perspectives to 'Love Story'?

This image is edited to appear just after Swift sings about going into the garden in 'Love Story'.

- Taylor Swift's persona is constructed as a relatable 'girl next door' college student at the beginning of the video, which allows her primary target audience of young females to identify with her. The construction of the 'princess character' is more aspirational and creates an image of Swift as a star persona:
  - The framing of her in the arch, backlit by sunlight, connotes that she is an almost angelic presence, and it shows her high status.
  - The hairstyle and dress construct an image of a princess familiar from fairy tales and products such as Disney films.
  - The light colour palette, blonde hair and use of sunlight contribute to the sense of innocence and romance, but the off-the-shoulder dress with laced-up bodice connote a slightly more daring, passionate persona that is reinforced by some of the lyrics. This suggests that Swift is a mature young woman and some of her fans may relate to this more 'grown up' persona.

 Quickfire 5.50

Which element of continuity editing is evident in these two shots from 'Love Story'?

- Technical codes:
  - There are multiple close-ups of Swift to reinforce her star image. There is direct address to the audience to establish a relationship with the viewer.
  - Some of the shots frame Swift through arches, inviting the audience to look closer.
  - The video is edited in time to the beat. The sequence where 'Romeo' and 'Juliet' run towards each other uses continuity editing to cut between the two characters and increases in pace in time to the music to show their excitement.
- Intertextuality:
  - *Romeo and Juliet* is a very familiar story that has universal appeal.
  - The period costumes, settings and choreography reference the play.
  - The narrative is closely linked as two young lovers are separated by the disapproval of the father, although this version ends happily.
  - The play has influenced many other media products, including the films *West Side Story* and *Warm Bodies*, so the references are very recognisable to a range of audiences.

Taylor Swift as Catastrophe in 'Bad **Blood**'.

Quickfire 5.51

How has Taylor Swift's star persona developed from 'Love Story' to 'Bad Blood'?

Exploring Music Videos from the 1980s and 1990s

You will analyse either 'Rio' by Duran Duran or 'Black or White' by Michael Jackson.

Context

The 1980s began with a period of economic instability in Britain and there was high unemployment. From the mid to late 1980s, however, the economy grew and this is often seen as a period of 'excess'. The **yuppie** lifestyle, characterised by wealthy young people with disposable income to spend on luxury goods, became an aspiration. The fashion trends for bright colours, bold patterns and shoulder pads reflected this sense of optimism and confidence.

Key Term

Yuppie
'Young urban professional' or 'young upwardly mobile professional', a term used in the 1980s to describe a young middle-class person who had achieved financial success and was enjoying material wealth.

167

The feminist movement was developing in society, and women were gaining more power in the workplace, but much of the mainstream media was still creating traditional and stereotypical representations of gender. One of the early Duran Duran videos, 'Girls on Film' from 1981, caused controversy for the sexualised images of women that it featured.

There was also social unrest in Britain the early 1980s, including miners' strikes and riots in Brixton and Toxteth due to the level of racial inequality at the time. In America there was also racial tension. While progress had been made towards equality during the civil rights movement of the 1960s, in the 1980s people from minority ethnic groups tended to have low levels of income and a poorer quality of life, showing that society was not yet integrated.

Stretch and Challenge 5.31

Research the clothing fashions of the 1980s and note how these are evident in the video for 'Rio'.

The set product: 'Rio' by Duran Duran

Duran Duran is a British band who had many big hits in the 1980s, including 'Rio'. Their music had mainstream appeal during this period and can be categorised as the **synth-pop** characteristic of the 'New Romantic' bands. Their early career coincided with the launch of MTV, and music videos were extremely important to their success. Their videos were imaginative and, as their success grew, high budget, and included many techniques that have now become established as video conventions, including narrative sequences, intertextual film references, special effects and exotic locations.

Key Term

Synth-pop
A genre of music that became popular in the 1980s, where a synthesiser is a main instrument.

Analysing 'Hungry Like the Wolf' by Duran Duran

The video for this single from the *Rio* album was shot in Sri Lanka and released in 1982. It was directed by Russell Mulcahy, who created many videos for Duran Duran in the 1980s.

'Hungry Like the Wolf' is not the set product that you will need to study for the exam, but the following analysis will help you to understand the conventions used in Duran Duran's videos and the context of the set product, 'Rio'.

Media language
The mise-en-scène of the city, for example the dusty, busy streets, the market, the restaurant, is juxtaposed with the jungle to create an exotic world where the narrative takes place.

Quickfire 5.52

How do the page-turning and page-ripping effects in 'Hungy Like the Wolf' communicate messages to the audience?

The camera work, for example the hand-held camera and tracking shots, immerses the audience in the exciting world of the narrative.

The use of special effects, such as the page-turning and page-ripping effects, shows off the technology available at the time.

There are intertextual references to the Indiana Jones film *Raiders of the Lost Ark,* which was extremely successful at the time and would have been recognisable to the audience. This gives the music video an additional layer of meaning and appeal to 'sell' the music. Visual references include the hat and clothes Simon Le Bon wears and the protagonists having to overcome many challenges in a hostile environment.

This intertextual reference to Indiana Jones establishes Le Bon as a hero who is rewarded with the 'princess', according to Propp's theory.

The success and 'excess' of the 1980s context is evoked through some shots of the band in bright suits, drinking champagne surrounded by attractive females, connoting the glamour and luxury of the pop stars' celebrity lifestyle.

Theoretical perspectives: representation

The star persona of lead singer Simon Le Bon is constructed to be strong, active and desirable to a young female audience. He is shown swimming in the river through the jungle, connoting fearlessness and independence, stereotypically masculine traits. Other band members have longer hair and in some shots are shown wearing make-up, suggesting that they do not conform to stereotypically 'macho' representations. This reflects changes in society and a move towards less rigid definitions of masculinity and femininity that contemporary audiences will recognise.

Feminist theoretical approaches see that females in the video are mostly passive and often objectified. There are several shots of women's bare legs, for example. The title of the song connotes male desire and, while the female in the jungle shows some strength in fighting, she is ultimately 'captured' by the male who has been 'hunting' her.

The representation of the female character in the jungle is constructed to connote a sense of the 'exotic': she is wearing bright face paint and is framed behind foliage to suggest mystery. She is quite scantily clad, suggesting that she is an object of desire. She is also represented as 'prey', hunted by the male, implying that white men have dominance in society.

There are some further stereotypical representations of ethnicity, for example Sri Lankan children wearing rags running along dusty streets and a woman begging on the roadside, connoting poverty in a developing country. Other characters, however, in the restaurant and market appear to be wealthier, suggesting that the society is socially diverse.

These representations reflect the context of the 1980s where there was less equality in society and therefore gender and ethnic stereotypes were more evident.

'Rio'

The video was also directed by Russell Mulcahy. It was filmed in Antigua and also released in 1982.

The video is typically set in an exotic location and creates a 'fantasy' world where the carefree band members enjoy a luxury lifestyle. It uses many technologies that were cutting edge at the time, including split-screens, filters and overlays. The video is structured as a series of 'moments' of the characters engaging in various activities by the sea, and there is limited sense of a linear narrative.

'Hungry Like the Wolf' intertextually references *Raiders of the Lost Ark*, released in 1981.

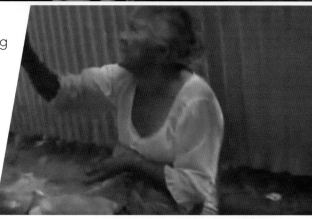

Quickfire 5.53

Where else in the media might you see representations of poorer people in developing countries?

Activity 5.15

Watch 'Rio', pausing to make notes. Then answer these questions, with examples:

- Describe the mise-en-scène in detail. What do the visual codes say about the world of the video?

- How does the mise-en-scène reflect the context of the 1980s and an 'excessive' celebrity lifestyle?

- What impact do the special effects have?

- Identify intertextual references to Bond films. Why are these used?

- Outline the narrative. Can you identify any of Propp's character types?

- How are representations of males and females constructed? Are stereotypes upheld or subverted?

- Consider whether the female is viewed more as a passive object or active subject in the narrative. Is she sexually objectified?

- How did you respond to the representations? How might an audience in the 1980s have responded differently?

The video intertextually references James Bond films and represents males as successful and fun-loving with a keen interest in women. The main female is beautiful, exotic and rarely fully clothed. She is clearly an object of desire, but she is not completely passive within the narrative and the males are not completely in control.

The set product: 'Black or White' by Michael Jackson

Michael Jackson was a pop superstar who had a significant influence on music and popular culture. He died in 2009.

He began performing as a child with his brothers in the Jackson Five, before becoming a solo artist. He achieved major critical and commercial success, winning many Grammy awards, and his 1982 album *Thriller* is still the best-selling album in the world, selling over 65 million copies.

His videos were innovative and groundbreaking. Jackson was also a very influential artist in a social context. *Thriller* was important in 'establishing him as a black star who appealed to audiences of all backgrounds and paving the way for future African-American stars'. (telegraph.co.uk/music/artists/michael-jacksons-thriller-pioneering-album-broke-racial-barriers/)

Analysing 'Thriller' by Michael Jackson

'Thriller' is not the set product that you will need to study for the exam, but the following analysis will help you to understand more about Michael Jackson's persona and use of groundbreaking techniques.

The video was directed by John Landis, who had directed the horror film *An American Werewolf in London*, and was released in 1983. It is a 13-minute film that extends beyond the length of the song and uses many techniques from film, which has since become a convention of music videos. 'Thriller' has been copied, parodied and used as a reference many times in media culture and was described by Phil Hebblethwaite in the *Guardian* as 'less a promo clip than a cultural phenomenon'. (theguardian.com/music/2013/nov/21/michael-jackson-thriller-changed-music-videos)

The video was played extensively on MTV and was premiered in the UK on Channel 4. The video had a very high budget and the producers filmed a documentary about the making of 'Thriller' which was released for fans to buy, contributing to the financial success of the project.

Media language

The horror genre was extremely popular in the 1980s and audiences would have recognised familiar codes from films such as *The Fog* and *An American Werewolf in London*. This links to the cultural context and how Jackson was reflecting popular cinema culture of the time.

David Naughton and Griffin Dunne in *An American Werewolf in London*.

The horror genre is clearly established through the use of conventions:

- The settings and locations such as the forest, graveyard and isolated haunted house are typical, and recognisable as places of danger.
- Visual codes such as the full moon in the night sky, low-key lighting, shadows and smoke/fog effects, create mystery and menace.
- There are typical horror characters, such as zombies and the werecat, but also the young couple and the 'innocent' **final girl**.
- Special effects from the horror genre are used, such as the werecat transformation.
- Tense and dramatic music is used in the narrative sections not accompanied by the 'Thriller' track.
- Vincent Price, a famous horror actor, narrates the section in the middle of the song.

Narrative

There are different narratives within the video, all featuring Michael Jackson:

- The young couple at the start whose car has broken down are characters in a 1950s-style film. The couple watch the film and then encounter the zombies rising from the grave. The girl wakes up from a dream at the end.
- It is not clear which situation is 'real'. There are narratives within narratives, which creates enigma and blurs the boundary between reality and fiction.
- At key points of tension the narrative cuts to a 'safer' place to reassure the audience.
- In relation to Propp's characters, the female is in need of rescue so could fulfil the princess role, while Jackson is the protagonist, a protective boyfriend, or hero. However, he also transforms into a werecat and a zombie, which suggests the role of the antagonist, or villain.
- There are stylised, choreographed dance sequences, which have become a typical convention of music videos.

The costumes reflect 1980s fashions, especially the young woman's bright blue jumpsuit and Jackson's iconic red leather jacket.

Representation

Michael Jackson's star persona is emphasised.

- He was very well-known for his dancing skill (his 'moonwalk' became particularly famous) and this video showcases his abilities.
- Jackson is usually central in the frame and there are multiple close-ups and low-angle shots to reinforce his star image and appeal to the audience.
- He plays different roles in the narrative: the 1950s college student, the modern-day boyfriend, the werecat and the star performer. This creates a complex persona: the 'boyfriend' is stereotypically strong and protective, while the werecat is dangerous. The zombie/werecat occurs in the 'fantasy' or 'dream' world of the video and the pop-star persona returns at the end, with something of a twist.

The female roles fulfil many stereotypes: sweet, passive, frightened and dependent on males, which reflects the social context at a time when women were still fighting for equality in society.

Key Term

Final girl
A central female character in a horror film who is 'good' – hardworking, responsible, innocent – and survives at the end.

The central characters are black, which shows a positive development in representations of ethnicity in mainstream media products. Michael Jackson was breaking boundaries in the 1980s, especially as his videos became a permanent feature on MTV.

'Black or White'

The video for 'Black and White' was also directed by John Landis and had an extremely large budget of approximately $4 million. It premiered on Fox Television in the USA, scheduled after an episode of *The Simpsons*, on 14 November 1991. It was also shown on the same day on cable networks MTV, BET (Black Entertainment Television) and VH1 (Video Hits 1) as well as on *Top of the Pops* in the UK. The premiere of the video was a major cultural event, viewed by an estimated audience of 500 million people worldwide.

The video begins with a short narrative sequence starring the young actor Macaulay Culkin, famous at the time for his role in the film *Home Alone*. This has similarities with the beginning of 'Thriller' and reflects Landis's background in film directing.

The main body of the video is constructed as a montage of sequences where Michael Jackson appears in various locations with dancers from different ethnic groups, communicating a message about racial equality.

Activity 5.16

Watch 'Black or White', pausing in key places, for example in each different location, to make notes. Then answer these questions, giving examples:

- Describe the mise-en-scène in detail. How do the visual codes communicate meanings about the different worlds of the video?
- What impact do the special effects have?
- Outline the structure of the video. Can you identify elements of narrative such as disruptions or oppositions?
- What is Michael Jackson's star persona and how is it established?
- How are representations of different ethnic groups constructed through visual and technical codes? Are stereotypes upheld or subverted?
- What messages are communicated? How do they reflect the social context of the early 1990s?
- How did you respond to the video? How might an audience in the 1990s have responded?

The video uses many special effects, most notably the 'morphing' technique where one person transforms into another at the end of the video. This technology was relatively new at the time, having been used in the film *Willow* in 1988.

The video originally included a controversial dance sequence after the end of the song where Jackson transformed into a panther. It received negative reviews and audience responses when it aired on American television and the final four-minute sequence was cut from future broadcasts.

Representation in Music Videos

Gender representation: females

Music videos often feature quite stereotypical representations of gender, and some genres, such as rap, have been criticised for constructing sexually objectified images of females. The focus on constructing a star persona results in many close-up camera shots on the artist's, and other actors', faces, and other parts of their bodies, to create an image that will 'sell' the music. Saul Austerlitz argues in his book *Money for Nothing* (Bloomsbury/Continuum, 2006) that women are usually represented as fantasy objects: 'Music videos, for the most part, are intended for men's eyes, providing them with endless opportunities to delectate in the spectacle of beautiful women performing for their pleasure.' Music artists have large fan bases and are potentially influential as role models, so it is important to consider the messages and values communicated through the representations in their music videos.

Applying feminist theoretical perspectives

Laura Mulvey's Male Gaze theory argues that, in film, the female is represented as a passive object of desire, to be looked at by a male character or spectator. This can also apply to music videos. The male gaze can be shown through the use of the camera, for example by using a male point of view or close-up shots of women's bodies. Dress codes can also suggest that a female is objectified. Revealing or tight-fitting clothing might 'sexualise' a character.

Quickfire 5.54

How does this image from 'Rio' fit with the Male Gaze theory?

The Male Gaze theory can be applied to the music video for 'Rio'. Many shots objectify the female by showing fragments of her body in a sexualised way to construct her as a fantasy object of desire for a male audience. She does have considerable power in the video, however, and is shown to outwit and make fun of the males, as she, for example, catches one band member in a fishing net. This possibly reflects the fact that women were gaining more power in society in the 1980s.

The video for 'Uptown Funk' also upholds many gender stereotypes. The video begins, with similar images to 'Rio', with a tracking shot of bare female legs. The male performers, especially Bruno Mars, are constructed as dominant, high-status stars and the females in the video are seen through their eyes. At the beginning of the video a woman in high heels and low-cut short dress walks across the frame, objectified by Mars' gaze in the background. She plays no role in the narrative.

There is also a sequence where Mars and Mark Ronson appear next to an older female in a hair salon. They wear curlers and use stylised feminine gestures. This suggests that they are either making fun of women or do not take their star personas too seriously, which might reflect the breaking down of gender barriers in recent years.

Bruno Mars demonstrates an exaggerated feminine 'pout' in this close-up.

173

The set products by contemporary female artists, 'Bad Blood' and 'Roar', are interesting because both construct representations of strong, independent females, demonstrating the fact that these are two very successful female stars with strong personalities. Swift and Perry are shown to be in control of the narrative and do not rely on men, which subverts many female stereotypes. The artists are arguably also objectified, however, which reinforces feminist perspectives that gender equality is not fully established within the mainstream media.

Activity 5.17

Watch 'Bad Blood' or 'Roar'. In 'Bad Blood', Taylor Swift plays many different roles that resemble characters from action films. In 'Roar', Katy Perry plays one character that develops as the narrative progresses.

Use the images below as a starting point and complete the following tasks.

Make detailed notes on the following visual codes:

- Costume, hair and make-up
- Gestures and facial expressions
- Colour and lighting
- How are these elements used to construct the representation of the star persona?
- Note examples of the following types of camera shot:
- Close-ups on the artist's face
- Shots of different parts of the female's body.

Does the combination of visual and technical codes suggest that the female is sexually objectified? How?

Write a detailed paragraph about the representation of the female star, applying feminist perspectives.

Representation of ethnicity

Popular music is created by artists from different ethnic backgrounds and many black artists, for example, achieved great success in the industry throughout the 20th century. In the early 1980s, however, MTV attracted criticism for playing very few videos by black artists. This reflected the under-representation of people from black and minority ethnic groups in many media industries at the time. It has been argued that Michael Jackson brought about a change when videos such as 'Billie Jean' and 'Thriller' were regularly played on MTV. Later in the 1980s, videos by black rap and hip-hop artists became a popular feature of the channel and a wider range of representations has been in evidence since.

The video for 'Black or White' presents the issue of racial discrimination and promotes a positive message about equality, reflecting the lyrics. The sequences of Jackson appearing with different ethnic groups, such as Native American, Russian and Thai dancers, suggest that music and dance can break down barriers and unite people. The lyric 'I'm not gonna spend my life being a colour' reinforces the point of view that skin colour should not define a person and this message is further supported at the end of the video when a wide range of people are featured 'morphing' into each other, connoting that we are all the same, regardless of our ethnicity.

Contemporary music videos encompass a diverse range of ethnicities and there are some interesting representations to explore in the set products. White ethnicity, for example, is constructed in 'Roar' through the patriarchal male who fails to survive in the jungle and the resourceful female who succeeds in taming the wild animals, but there is an absence of people from other ethnic groups. 'Bad Blood' juxtaposes the representation of Swift as a blonde-haired white female star with Kendrick Lamar as the black rapper, dressed in black with dark glasses and baseball cap. There are perhaps some stereotypical representations of ethnic minorities, for example in Arsyn, played by Selina Gomez, as the antagonist.

In 'Uptown Funk', the male performers, who are from different ethnic backgrounds, demonstrate a clear sexual interest in females, which upholds a masculine stereotype, particularly of Latin and African American men. Bruno Mars is an American artist whose father is Puerto Rican. *Latina* magazine recently stated that Mars is 'embracing the Latin Lover archetype' (*Latina*, February 2017). The video is set in an urban location and many of the characters are from ethnic minorities, although the shoe-shine men are older white males in a very low-status role, which subverts expectations and stereotypes.

Quickfire 5.55

Watch 'Black or White'. What is the connotation of the image at the end of the video of the black and white babies sitting together on the Earth?

Quickfire 5.56

How might the representations of Taylor Swift and Kendrick Lamar in 'Bad Blood' appeal to different audiences?

Quickfire 5.57

How do the technical and visual codes in this image from 'Uptown Funk' construct the male representations?

The video for Pharrell Williams' 'Freedom' represents many different situations, social groups and creatures in the wild to communicate a message that everyone has a right to freedom. Many of the images show ethnic minorities in positive situations, and Williams is a strong and empowering presence throughout the video.

Other scenes, however, show minority groups being oppressed in order to convey the key messages and values of the song. The sequence where black males are breaking stones shows what people still face in some countries and has connotations of the historical slave trade and 'chain gangs' for example, while the factory scene references contemporary 'sweat shops'.

Quickfire 5.58

What polysemic meanings can you identify in these images from the 'Freedom' video?

Stretch and Challenge 5.32

Can you identify any influences from older music videos on the contemporary products?

Analysing the Contemporary Set Music Videos

You will need to analyse the media language and representations in the set music videos that you are studying and consider how these may appeal to audiences. You can use the list of codes and conventions on pages 164–165 to structure your analysis. When analysing contemporary videos, compare them with the older example you study, identifying similarities and differences in:

- the codes and conventions of music videos, for example:
  - use of the camera and editing
  - performance and/or narrative
  - intertextuality
- the use of technology
- representations of gender, ethnicity or issues
- the way in which the video reflects its contexts.

You will also need to study industry and audience in relation to the contemporary music videos by, for example, considering how the videos target an audience and how audiences respond to them.

Contemporary contexts

Consider the ways in which the products by the contemporary artists you study reflect the context in which they were made.

Social contexts

Society is now more equal than it was in the past. There are laws in Britain, for example, to prevent discrimination against people in relation to their age, ethnicity or gender. However, there are areas where progress still needs to be made. In some industries, women do not yet receive the same level of pay as men.

The issue of gender equality in the Hollywood film industry has recently been the subject of attention, not only in relation to equal career opportunities and pay for women, but also from the accusations that some powerful men in the industry have sexually assaulted women. This highlights that some areas of society are still male dominated, and that some individuals might abuse the power they have, although there is a hope that the film industry will become a more equal one as a result of these revelations.

There are also issues relating to racial equality in society. For example:

- A report published in 2016 by the Equality and Human Rights Commission showed that, while progress had been made, there was still racial inequality in Britain and that people from ethnic minorities were more likely to live in poverty and less likely to achieve a position of power within the workplace.
- There is a concern that Brexit might result in further racial discrimination in Britain. Immigration had been a focus for much of the referendum campaign and there was an increase in cases of racial abuse being reported following the referendum.
- In the USA, and to a lesser degree in the UK, the Black Lives Matter movement has developed to campaign against police brutality towards black people.

Social inequality is a global issue, as many people worldwide live in poverty. In Britain, issues such as zero-hours contracts and changes to the welfare system in recent years have impacted on people's quality of life. The use of 'sweat shops' in countries such as China and India, where factory workers work very long hours for extremely low pay, concerns many people. These countries supply low-priced products such as clothing and electronic goods to overseas markets, so this is a global economic issue.

An anti-racism rally in London in 2016.

Cultural contexts

There is increased hybridity in many areas of popular culture, such as film and music, and many older, 'retro' styles have influenced contemporary artists in recent years. This is also evident in fashion, as versions of clothing trends from the 1970s and 1980s have become popular again.

Popular culture also reflects social change. Mainstream films, for example, are now more likely to feature a female action hero than in the past.

Technology contributes to the cultural framework of media products such as music:

- Although audiences can stream and download music legally, there is still a potential threat to the music industry through illegal downloading, which many artists are working to prevent.
- Modern media makes stars seem much more accessible than used to be the case. 'Gossip' magazines have always featured stories about artists' lives, but this is added to by aspects of modern living, such as stars including personal posts on social media. These make audiences feel closer to these artists, as though they 'know' them.

Top Tip

Make notes on the way in which the contemporary products you study reflect their social context. Not all of the social issues listed relate to every product, but think about which ones apply.

Top Tip

Make notes on how the contemporary music videos you study use hybridity and/or 'retro' influences.

'Roar' by Katy Perry

The video for 'Roar' makes use of CGI technology and intertextually references films such as *Tarzan* and *The Jungle Book*. The linear narrative conveys a clear message about female empowerment as Perry's character leaves behind a domineering male and takes control of her destiny. Lyrics such as 'I am a champion' are illustrated with images of Perry taming wild animals, and humour is created through visual codes such as the 'Katy Purry' tag. It has been suggested that the video is partly autobiographical as Perry had recently split from her husband, a story much covered in the media.

The video was extremely popular and had over 2.3 billion views on YouTube by January 2018; the eleventh most viewed on the site.

Top Tip

Make detailed notes on the ways in which each music video targets and appeals to the artist's audience.

'Bad Blood' by Taylor Swift

The song features hip-hop artist Kendrick Lamar, showing how music genres can be hybridised and how artists broaden their audience by working with different performers. The collaboration with Lamar, who works in a very different genre from Swift's earlier country-influenced pop music, arguably widens each artist's appeal and is mutually beneficial. Directed by Joseph Kahn, the video has had over 1 billion views on YouTube and won the best music video Grammy in 2015.

The video stars some very high-profile female performers, such as Jessica Alba and Ellie Goulding. This reinforces Swift's elite persona as she can attract such stars to her project. This will also appeal to fans of the other stars and potentially introduce Swift to new audiences.

The video has very high production values and is constructed as a mini-film with captions that mirror film credits. There is a clear narrative, interspersed with performance, and Swift fulfils the role of action heroine assisted by a range of character types. There are many intertextual references to comic-book action films, in particular *Sin City*, which offer gratifications to fans of this genre.

'Uptown Funk' by Mark Ronson, featuring Bruno Mars

Mark Ronson on stage at the Dcode music festival in Madrid.

The song was released as a single featuring Bruno Mars by Mark Ronson, a DJ and record producer who is known for collaborations with artists such as Amy Winehouse. Ronson is signed to Columbia Records, a subsidiary of Sony Music, and so the song was released on this label. It also appeared on his album *Uptown Special*. Sony described the song as having a 'fresh new retro sound', influenced by funk and R&B artists of the 1980s.

The video was released in 2014 and stars Bruno Mars, Mark Ronson and Mars' backing band, The Hooligans. 'Uptown Funk' is a performance-based video filmed in a city location and the stylish choreographed dance sequences reference artists such as the Jackson Five. The video has high production values and the mise-en-scène also creates a 'retro' feel through the costumes, settings and props. This combination of factors potentially attracts an audience of fans of both Mars and Ronson, as well as people who enjoy the older styles that are intertextually referenced.

Top Tip

Note down examples of how elements of media language construct the 'retro' world of the 'Uptown Funk' video.

Examples of audience responses

The song and video were phenomenally successful and gained positive critical responses:

- The song became the fifth best-selling single of all time in Britain in 2015 and achieved a Diamond Award from the Recording Industry Association of America for over 10 million sales and streams. 'Uptown Funk' also won Record of the Year at the 2016 Grammy Awards and Best British Single of the year at the 2015 Brit Awards.
- The video won the MTV Video Music Award for Video of the year and has had over 2.8 billion views on YouTube as of January 2018. It is the fifth most viewed video on the site.

The video for 'Uptown Funk' was released on YouTube in November 2014 and it was widely reported that the record was due for release in January 2015. However, a performance of the song by a contestant on *The X Factor* in early December gained an extremely positive response and this version of the song went to number one in the iTunes chart. The record release was then brought forward and Ronson and Mars topped the charts. As both Simon Cowell's record label Syco and Mark Ronson's label Columbia are part of Sony, this can be seen as a commercial success for the organisation and an example of the benefits of horizontal integration.

Audience responses to the song included model and actress Cara Delevigne posting a video on Instagram of friends performing the track at Thanksgiving, which received over 270 000 likes. This type of post can act like a celebrity endorsement and allow the product to reach a wider audience.

The song was also received positively by other musicians. Chilly Gonzales, for example, said, 'We have a mix of the old, the new, the modern and the classic. And that's why I love "Uptown Funk".' (bbc.co.uk/newsbeat/article/30900427/why-does-everyone-love-mark-ronsons-uptown-funk) This also adds to the status of a product and might encourage more people to buy it.

There were many online responses from fans too, including cover versions of the song and video that were posted on YouTube. Mark Ronson clearly sees this as a positive response to his music and commented, 'That's when you know that something has resonated with people.' (youtube.com/watch?v=C2THq4UG_Eg) He later collaborated with six of these YouTubers to create his own cover version of the song, which shows how audiences can become active participants and create media products themselves.

'Freedom' by Pharrell Williams

The song 'Freedom' features on the soundtrack for *Despicable Me 3* (Williams composed other songs, including 'Happy', for *Despicable Me 2*). The video for 'Freedom' was released on Apple Music on 30 June 2015 and launched on YouTube some weeks later. It was directed by Paul Hunter, who has also directed music videos for artists such as Jennifer Lopez, Christina Aguilera and Justin Timberlake.

The video is a montage of images that all relate to the central message of the song: freedom. There are many shots of animals and birds in the wild to connote a free life, juxtaposed with footage of humans freely expressing themselves, for example in church. There are also many references to slavery and a lack of freedom which act as a binary opposition. Williams features throughout the video as a star presence, but he is dressed simply in jeans and a shirt and performs the song in a heartfelt manner to convey the seriousness of the issue. This contrasts with previous videos such as 'Happy', where he dances and is dressed stylishly and colourfully to reflect the different mood of the song.

Top Tip

Find other examples of audience responses to 'Uptown Funk'.

Quickfire 5.59

What are the benefits to audiences and industries from this type of collaboration between an artist and their audience?

A scene of free expression from the video 'Freedom'.

Quickfire 5.60

What are the benefits of a song being used on a film soundtrack?

Online Media: Analysing Websites

A website is an important platform in the contemporary music industry. Each of the contemporary set artists has a website that reinforces their star persona, or brand image, and ensures that they can reach a wide global audience. The record company is able to use an artist's website to promote the latest single or album and associated products such as merchandise and tour tickets. This is extremely important as the industry is competitive and artists' work needs to generate a profit. Most websites are regularly updated and rebranded to reflect the current image of the star and their music.

Websites use convergence to bring together the different aspects of an artist's work, for example the music and the videos, as well as other projects such as films or charity work that the star may be involved with. This also potentially offers opportunities for synergy with other parts of the media conglomerate.

The website is likely to offer interactive features and links to download or streaming sites where audiences can listen to and/or purchase the music, increasing the potential for audience contact and commercial success.

The importance of social media

Websites will also include links to the artist's social media sites, such as Twitter, Facebook and Instagram, offering audiences the opportunity to respond and interact by following their favourite artists. The artists' social media accounts are usually carefully managed by the record company. Katy Perry, for example, releases tweets on most days.

Social media has become increasingly important in recent years, as artists can connect with listeners, and fans can receive frequent updates from the stars they admire. This symbiotic relationship benefits the industry and the audience: the record company can

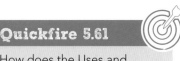

Katy Perry's Twitter page from 2013.

gain greater brand loyalty, promote the artist's music and potentially attract new listeners through audience 'likes' and 'shares'; while audiences feel part of a community, identify with the artist and interact with other fans. Kate Franklin of Brandwatch has summarised the benefits of social media for music audiences: 'Social media is where music audiences naturally congregate, forming their own communities and sharing their experiences of bands and artists.' (brandwatch.com/blog/social-media-the-music-industry/)

Artists' websites and social media accounts also reflect the social and cultural contexts in which they are produced. Current clothing trends might be shown, for example, or artists might reference other creative products such as films that influence or interest them. Many artists are involved with charities, so stories or comments about this work can reveal issues in society at the time. The website might refer to contextual issues in the music industry, for example by encouraging fans to download music legally.

Codes and conventions of music websites

The homepage usually has a menu that links to other pages, including:

- News
- Biographical information
- Music and videos
- Tour details
- Store/merchandise. Some artists also have a range of their own products, for example Katy Perry's cosmetics collections.

The layout and design of the website usually includes:

- a clear 'house style' with consistent use of colour palette, font and so on
- branding of the latest single or album release, with images and information about the music and promotional performances.

In January 2018 Bruno Mars' website constructed a house style through a colour palette of black, white and gold, connoting high production values. The new single, 'Finesse', was promoted through a looped extract from the video and audiences were invited to 'Watch Finesse. Download or Stream. Buy 24K Magic. See Bruno on Tour'.

Typically, an artist's star persona is clearly established online through:

- images of the star
- videos, including personal posts that give fans 'exclusive insights'
- quotes from the star or blog entries
- news items, for example showing the star winning an award or undertaking charity work

The 'Photos' page of Katy Perry's website includes a range of images to portray different aspects of her identity such as:

- her glamorous onstage persona that fans admire and might aspire to.
- Perry as an 'ordinary' person away from the music that fans can identify with.

The website usually promotes the music and encourages interactivity and purchases, for example:

- Images and the music video for the latest release of the music
- Opportunities to listen to clips from songs and links to streaming and/or downloading sites where listeners can make a purchase
- A store page selling CDs and official merchandise such as clothing and other collectible items
- Links to a ticket agency where fans can buy tour tickets
- Links to the artist's social media pages.

Pharrell Williams' website includes a link to his separate 'I am Other' site. This reinforces his persona as an acclaimed and versatile artist who works in different forms and collaborates with other artists.

An example of how Katy Perry uses social media to engage audiences

Perry's Twitter page of January 2018 is branded to match her latest album and tour and her image is quite androgynous. Her short hair and bright, stylised make-up create a striking image reminiscent of 1980s popular culture. The tour is currently the main selling point, as the album was released in 2017.

The pinned tweet from May 2017 reinforces the branding and shows how this has been extended over a long period of time:

- '*Witness* The album! The Tour! It's all Happening!': the latest album is the main focus, showing a commercial imperative to sell the product.

- The use of the eye, the logo for the album, links to the idea of being a witness and seeing what is happening in the world.

- Exclamation marks create an engaging sense of immediacy. Perry is constructed as a current, dynamic artist who is making things happen.

- The link to the website and the hashtag invite fans to engage further.

- The pinned tweet includes an embedded trailer for the tour featuring live footage from previous concerts, including theatrical performances of her most famous hits such as 'Roar' and 'Firework' to appeal to long-standing fans. The image at the beginning and end references the current album and the trailer ends with a clip from 'Chained to the Rhythm' from her latest album. This creates a strong sense of branding for the new work and might appeal to new audiences as well as existing fans.

The 'Holidays are over' tweet from 13 January 2018 includes an embedded video clip of Katy Perry visiting charitable organisations that she supports, such as the Boys and Girls Club of America:

- The clip includes footage of Perry dancing with the children and a young fan explaining why 'Firework' inspired her.
- This demonstrates the charitable work that many major stars undertake and gives a social context.
- It also creates a very positive representation of the artist as a 'real' person away from her music.
- The end of the video offers audiences the opportunity to interact further by watching the full video, while the inclusion of the charities' Twitter handles encourages users to find out more about the organisations.
- Fans have also commented, shared and 'liked' the Tweet, which potentially increases the reach of Katy Perry to a wider audience.

Quickfire 5.62

How might Katy Perry's Twitter account generate different audience responses? For example, how might a fan respond compared with someone who is not familiar with the music?

An example of a social media marketing campaign: Taylor Swift

In 2017 Taylor Swift released *Reputation*, and her image was rebranded. The slogan posted on her new website and social media sites was, 'The old Taylor Swift can't come to the phone right now.' This communicates a clear message that the star persona has been reinvented and that she has left behind her 'old' image.

Taylor Swift removed all posts from her social media pages in August 2017, resulting in speculation in the media that she was about to release a new album. She then began to post again, including three short videos of snake imagery on her Instagram and Twitter accounts. This created an enigma and generated a great deal of discussion on social media and in the news. The *Daily Telegraph*, for example, ran an article speculating about the meaning of the videos. This shows that music artists use similar viral techniques to film companies to create interest in a product: in this case a 'buzz' was created around the upcoming release of her new album.

Taylor Swift's Twitter page in 2014.

Swift's social media pages became a marketing vehicle for the new album. Her Instagram account featured:

- video clips of the new songs
- branding for the new album including a UPS delivery truck featuring *Reputation* artwork (UPS was the official delivery partner for the album)
- the front cover of *Vogue* magazine featuring Swift
- reviews of the album and statistics about sales
- some personal videos, such as Swift with her cat, but mainly posts relating to the new music.

Quickfire 5.63

How does Taylor Swift's new Twitter page differ from the old version, and what message does this communicate?

Quickfire 5.64

Why do artists include personal posts on social media?

Taylor Swift is known for her online and in-person interactions with audiences. The 'Secret Sessions' footage posted on her Instagram page, for example, shows her playing her new album to fans from around the world before it was released. This 'exclusive insight' and opportunity to meet Swift generated a very positive response from her fans, who are shown to be excited and share enthusiastic comments about the new music. This type of activity encourages loyalty to an artist and helps to promote the music as the fans 'spread the word' among their friends and on social media.

The marketing campaign was clearly successful: *Reputation* became the biggest-selling album of the year in America in just its first week of release.

An example of how an audience plays an active role: Pharrell Williams

Pharrell Williams' website – as of April 2018 – is quite unconventional as there is a loading page before the main homepage. This almost-empty page features a small image of Williams and the instruction, 'Discover Pharrell's world through his fans'. This offers audiences a different experience from most websites, which are constructed by media producers to prioritise the latest commercial products: album, tour, merchandise and so on.

The design of the homepage features a montage of images, or 'cards', written and selected by fans relating to different areas with which Pharrell is involved, such as 'Music', 'TV & Film' and 'Social Good'. Audiences can select the areas they wish to explore and are able to create their own cards for the website if they wish. This engages audiences in an interactive experience and they can also become active participants and creators of media content. The pages do include many of the expected features of a website, for example the 'Music' section, which includes a 'behind the scenes' video about the making of 'Freedom'.

In 2015 Williams worked with the United Nations for the International Day of Happiness and audiences were invited to submit short video clips of themselves dancing to Williams' song 'Happy'. They also signed a 'Live Earth' petition to campaign for action on climate change. These videos are featured on the website and show how audiences have responded to Williams and supported the causes he is involved with. It also demonstrates his high status, as he worked with a major international organisation.

Although Williams is signed to a major label, his website is quite unconventional and does not simply promote his latest album release, which shows that he has been able to create a more personal, alternative product. The fans select the cards that appear on the website, but they are only able to choose from specific categories, so the media producers control the main content of the site.

Quickfire 5.65

How does Williams' involvement with the United Nations reflect the social context of his work?

Top Tip

Watch the 'behind the scenes' video about the making of 'Freedom' and make notes about the production process.

Quickfire 5.66

How might different audiences respond to Pharrell Williams' website?

6

Assessment of Component 2: Understanding Media Forms and Products

How Will I Be Assessed?

The Component 2 examination assesses media language, representations, media industries, audiences and media contexts.

- The examination is 1 hour 30 minutes.
- It counts for 30 per cent of the qualification.
- It is split into two sections, as detailed below.

You will be assessed on your use of appropriate subject-specific terminology and relevant theories or theoretical perspectives.

There is further information and advice to help you to prepare for the exam in Chapter 9 of this book.

Section A: Television

You will answer questions on the topic you have studied:

- crime drama   or   sitcom.

You will be required to analyse a short extract from one of the set products, either *Luther* (crime drama) or *The IT Crowd* (sitcom). The extract will be screened twice in the exam and you will have six minutes between each viewing to make notes. There will be two questions:

- **Question 1** will assess either media language or representations based on the extract from the set product that you have studied. Reference to context might be required.
  - In Part a you will analyse media products.
  - Part b will assess your ability to analyse, make judgements and draw conclusions.
- **Question 2** will focus on knowledge and understanding of media industries, audiences or contexts in relation to the set products.

Quickfire 6.1
Why is it important to use relevant theories or theoretical perspectives in the exam?

Top Tip
Revise the subject-specific terminology you have learned and use it in your exam responses.

Top Tip
During your revision, practise analysing extracts from the set products. This will help you to approach the extract screened in the examination.

Quickfire 6.2
What will you need to do in the exam in order to demonstrate your analytical skills?

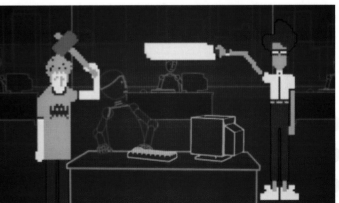

Section B: Music

Music videos and online media will be assessed in Section B. You might be required to answer questions on any of the set products you have studied:

- the music video from the 1980s or 1990s ('Rio' or 'Black or White').
- the contemporary music video by a female artist ('Bad Blood' or 'Roar').
- the contemporary music video by a male artist ('Uptown Funk' or 'Freedom').
- the online, social and participatory media in relation to the two contemporary artists whose videos you have studied (Taylor Swift or Katy Perry and either Bruno Mars or Pharrell Williams).
- **Question 3** will assess either media language or representations in the set products you have studied. Reference to context might be required.
  - This question will require an extended response and you will need to make judgements and draw conclusions.
  - Any of the set products could be assessed.
- **Question 4** will focus on knowledge and understanding of media industries, audiences or contexts in the set products.
  - Any of the set products could be assessed.
  - The music video from the 1980s or 1990s would only be assessed in relation to contexts here.

MTV, the original 'home' of music videos.

Component 3: Creating Media Products

7

OVERVIEW

In Component 3 you will:

- develop your practical media production skills
- respond to a brief set by Eduqas
- draw together the knowledge, understanding and skills you have gained
- apply the knowledge and understanding of the theoretical framework gained in Components 1 and 2 by:
  - using codes and conventions of media language
  - constructing representations
  - creating a production for a target audience.

Non-Exam Assessment

Component 3 is a non-exam assessment unit. You will create an individual media production in response to a **brief** set by Eduqas. You will complete this work in your centre over a period of approximately 12 weeks and it will be assessed by your teacher. A sample of the work from your centre will be sent to an Eduqas moderator who will check that the standard of marking is the same as in other centres across the country.

Component 3 is worth 30 per cent of the GCSE qualification.

You will create a media production in **one** of the following forms:

Form	Brief
Television	An audio-visual sequence from a new television programme **or** a website to promote a new television programme
Music marketing	A music video to promote a new artist or band **or** a website to promote a new artist or band
Film marketing	Print-based marketing material for a new film
Magazines	A new print **or** online magazine

Your teacher might set a particular option or offer you a choice of briefs. You will be able to develop your own ideas for your production, for example by planning the narrative or design and constructing representations.

Key Terms

Cover sheet
A document that must be submitted with your production to provide information to the moderator and confirm that this is your own, original work.

Original material
Work created yourself, such as footage you have filmed, photographs you have taken and text or dialogue that you have written.

Authentication statement
A signed declaration that the Statement of Aims and production are your own, original work. This is a formal requirement that every learner has to complete.

The Briefs

The briefs will be released by Eduqas each year and will set:

- the genre for your production
- the target audience for the product you create
- specific requirements, such as the length or quantity of work that you need to produce and key details about the content of the production.

It is essential that you complete all of the tasks set out in the brief, as you will be assessed on your ability to meet these requirements.

What Do I Need to Complete for the Non-Exam Assessment?

You will need to complete and submit the following:

- a **Statement of Aims** explaining how you will respond to the brief and apply your knowledge of media language and representation
- a **cover sheet**, which is available on the Eduqas website, to provide details about your production, the work that you have undertaken and the resources you have used
- the media production, which must be in one of the forms above and fulfil the requirements of the set brief for the year in which you are assessed.

Key points of meeting the brief

You must create an individual production for Component 3. You are able to have assistance from other people as long as they work under your direction. Family members, friends and fellow learners might appear in your work as performers or models, or help as crew members by operating lighting or sound equipment. It is really important that you give your cast and crew clear instructions about their roles to make sure that the finished product is your own work. You need to list the names on the cover sheet of any unassessed people who help with your production.

The work you complete and submit must be your own **original material.** All of the images, footage and text in your production should be created by you. You cannot use material from other sources, so it is important to make sure that you will be able to take photographs or film the footage for your planned production. The only material that you might take from another source is music, for example a song for a music video or a soundtrack for a television sequence. There are specific guidelines about the use of music in the sections below.

You will sign an **authentication statement** to confirm that the work you have submitted is all your own. Your teacher will monitor your production as it develops and will review your work at key stages to ensure that it has been produced by you.

You will need to use appropriate **equipment** and **software** to create your media production. If you are producing a website you can use web-design software or templates but you must design the webpages yourself and create all of the content such as images, text and audio-visual material. You must list the software packages that you use on the cover sheet, and provide a brief explanation of how these were used.

7 Component 3: Creating Media Products

Assessment of Component 3

The total number of marks available is **60**:

- **10** marks for the Statement of Aims
- **20** marks for creating a media product that meets the requirements of the set brief, including suitability for the specified form, genre and audience
- **30** marks for creating a media product that uses media language to communicate meanings and construct representations.

You will be assessed on your ability to:

- respond to the specific requirements of your set brief
- complete all of the tasks listed in the brief
- create a suitable media product for the form and genre
- appeal to and engage the intended audience, using an appropriate mode of address
- apply your knowledge and understanding of media language to communicate meanings
- create a suitable design or narrative for your production
- use media language to construct appropriate representations.

Research and Planning

When you have been given the brief you will need to research independently and plan your work carefully before you begin to construct the media production. The research and planning will not be assessed but will help you to complete your Statement of Aims and ensure that you meet the requirements of the brief. It will also contribute to the production as you need to apply your knowledge and understanding of the theoretical framework.

What research should I do?

Research involves gathering information about the type of product you are going to produce and the audience that you need to target. You should use a combination of **primary and secondary research methods** to help you to respond to the set brief.

Textual analysis of similar products

It is very important to apply your knowledge and understanding of the theoretical framework to your production. Analysing similar products to the one you intend to produce will help you to identify the codes and conventions that you should use in your work. It is important to find products in the same genre as the brief and for a similar target audience.

You should focus your analysis on the following areas:

- How does the product use media language to communicate meaning?
- Depending on the type of product, you might analyse visual codes such as colour and mise-en-scène; technical codes such as camera work and editing; layout and design; and narrative and language.
- Identify the codes and conventions of the specific genre and form.

Key Term

Primary and secondary research methods
Primary research means gathering information yourself, for example by analysing a media product to identify genre conventions or creating a questionnaire to find out information about your audience. Secondary research involves using sources that other people have written such as books and websites. This can provide information about the audience for a particular media product, for example.

Top Tip

Look back over your textual analysis notes from your studies in Components 1 and 2 to help you to research your chosen products. This will remind you of the codes and conventions you should analyse.

- How are representations constructed?

- Analyse the way media language is used to construct representations of individuals, social groups, issues and events.

- Consider whether these representations are stereotypical, and why.

- How does the product appeal to its target audience?

- Consider who the target audience is and how the text appeals to them.

- Analyse the ways in which the product engages the audience through its mode of address.

Audience research

You should undertake some **secondary research** to help you to develop your understanding of audiences. This might include:

- Investigating how media organisations categorise and target audiences, for example online research of the media companies whose products you have analysed to find out the target demographic for the text.

- Exploring how a product is marketed, distributed and circulated, for example the scheduling of a television programme or the use of social media to market a film. This will also help you to understand the intended audience.

Quickfire 7.1

Is textual analysis of products primary or secondary research?

Identify Your Target Audience

Once you have completed your textual analysis and secondary research, **primary audience research** will help you to find out about your target audience and the types of product that will appeal to them. This can help you to decide which elements to include in your own production in order to engage and appeal to them. You could also plan some initial ideas for your production and test these out with an audience. Types of primary audience research that you might use include:

- **Questionnaire**: a set of written questions that you ask people to answer. This type of research is useful for finding out some key information about people's interests and preferences. Your questionnaire should include a mixture of the following:

If you compile a questionnaire, make sure you include a mixture of open and closed questions.

- Closed questions, which require a definite answer. This could be 'yes' or 'no', for example 'Do you like watching television crime dramas with a female protagonist?', or you could give a range of options for respondents to select from. Closed questions allow you to quantify your findings by comparing results and drawing conclusions.

- Open questions, which usually begin with words such as 'why' or 'how', for example 'Why do you enjoy reading magazines?'. Open questions can be used on their own or as a follow-up to a closed question. They allow respondents to express opinions in a little more detail, and can help you to understand more about how and why people consume media products.

- **Focus group:** a group discussion involving a small number of people who fit into your target audience. You should prepare some specific questions, similar to the type used in your questionnaire, for them to discuss. You will need to manage the group carefully to make sure that everyone gets a chance to speak. You could, for example, ask each person to give their answer before they discuss the question. You could also show your focus group some media products to find out what appeals to them, or even share your draft designs to make sure they appeal to your target demographic.

  - You will need to decide how to record the responses from your focus group. You could make notes, but you might find it hard to write down all of the ideas quickly. You could record the session, with your participants' permission, on a voice recorder or mobile phone and then make notes afterwards.

  - Make sure that you know the people you ask to take part in your research: do not approach strangers. If you are aiming at an audience of teenagers, you can ask friends and fellow students. If you are targeting an older audience, you could ask your parents, family friends or teachers.

Planning your production

When you have completed your research you should have a clear idea of the codes and conventions of the form and genre of your product and of the target audience. Now it is time to start to plan your own production carefully to ensure that you meet the requirements of the brief and the deadlines set by your teacher.

It is a good idea to put your ideas down on paper at this stage by producing a pitch or **treatment** for your new product. This could include:

- the title of the product
- a short statement summarising your production
- media language, for example genre codes and conventions and features of the design or narrative of the product
- representations of social groups and individuals, considering, for example, gender, ethnicity and age
- the target audience: who they are and how you will appeal to them.

When you have completed your treatment, you will need to develop more detailed plans that will help you as you progress to the production stage.

Top Tip

Your primary research should be aimed at people in the same group as the intended audience in the set brief. So, if you are creating a product for an audience of 16- to 24-year-olds, you should interview or question family and friends in this age group.

Top Tip

When planning your production, think carefully about the mode of address you will use.

Key Term

Treatment
A detailed summary of ideas for a product, considering elements such as genre conventions and narrative.

Time for planning

Beginning the creative process

This will vary depending upon the brief you have chosen, but will include plans and drafts to make sure you have the best chance of success when you create your final production.

If you are going to construct a print or online product you should create draft designs and **mock-ups** of the pages of your production.

Draft designs allow you to experiment with ideas before you decide on your final product. At this stage you do not need to focus on much specific detail. You might wish, for example, to sketch in your images and show where you will place blocks of text. This will help you to visualise your product, and from here you will begin to think about the design elements in more detail.

Creating mock-ups will prompt you to think about the key elements of the layout of your print or online pages, for example the positioning of key elements of the text and images. It is advisable to use the software that you will be using for the actual production. Here, you will 'flesh out' your ideas, such as applying a colour palette, or incorporating passages of text and images, which could be as a result of a visit to your shoot location or practice shots that you have taken.

Audio-visual productions usually have a storyboard and, if you are creating a television sequence, a script is also a standard preparatory task.

A **storyboard** is a visual outline of your production. It will help you to meet the requirements of the brief and include the relevant details. When you create a storyboard you need to think in detail about all the elements – visual, technical and audio codes – and how these will communicate meaning to your audience. You will also focus on the structure of the sequence, for example how the narrative will be pieced together, and how the sequence will be edited. Your storyboard should include:

- images that give a clear idea of what will appear in the frame (you can sketch pictures or take some practice shots to use in your storyboard)
- shot duration – the length of time each shot will last
- type of shot – details of the distance, angle, movement
- editing transitions
- audio notes such as dialogue, sound effects and music
- notes about mise-en-scène.

The storyboard will help you to plan the footage you will need to film. Pay close attention to shot duration and camera angles here, to ensure you have a sufficient range of shots when filming. Your storyboard will also be helpful at the editing stage as it is a plan of how the footage will fit together to construct your sequence.

Top Tip

When creating your draft designs, make sure you include the elements listed in the brief. This will help you to meet the requirements when you construct the finished production.

Top Tip

Remember to include a range of shots in your storyboard; use the findings from your research to help you to plan this.

Key Term

Mock-up
A detailed draft version of designs for a print or online product, showing elements such as the layout and composition of the pages.

Storyboard

Name of Project

Shot duration	Images	Camera details: shot type, angle, movement	Sound: dialogue, effects, music	Notes: mise-en-scène, lighting

Organising the logistics

When you have planned your production you need to consider how you will use the time and resources available to create the product. Ask yourself the following questions.

Where will I need to go to take photographs or film footage?

If you are planning a location shoot you should do a **recce**. This means finding a place to film or take photographs that is appropriate to the brief. Your research into similar products from the same genre should inform this decision: a crime drama is likely to be filmed in a different location from a romantic comedy, for example, and a fashion magazine will not usually feature photographs taken in the same place as a football magazine.

- Visit the location in advance to think about where you will place your models or performers and where you will position your camera.

- Also consider lighting: if you are filming a band in a dark rehearsal room, for example, you might need some additional light.

- Think about weather conditions for outdoor locations: a park might be ideal on a sunny day, but will be less suitable if it is raining heavily.

- You might need to gain permission to film in certain locations, such as a café or a shop, so it is important to check and obtain this in advance if necessary.

A recce allows you to check out a location and think carefully about how you will frame your shots.

Key Term

Recce
A visit to a location where you intend to film to make sure it is suitable for your production. You should have a clear idea of the photographs/footage you want to obtain so that you can position your camera and performers.

Top Tip

Take a camera on your recce to shoot some practice pictures and footage. This will help you to plan your product in detail.

When will you complete all the elements of your production?

Your production work, including research and planning, will need to be completed within a period of 12 weeks. Your teacher will set the deadlines and you will need to plan your time accordingly. Some elements, such as writing the text for a website or article, can be done at any time. However, your shoot (for photographs or footage) will need to be planned carefully to make sure that your cast, crew and possibly your location are available. You might also need to book time in the editing suite at your centre to complete your work.

Who will be involved in your production?

You are likely to need a cast of performers or models. Think about the brief and the target audience when deciding who should feature in your photographs or footage, as you will need to construct appropriate representations. If you want to include an older character, for example, you could ask a fellow student to play the role, dressing them in appropriate clothing and directing them to use suitable gestures. It is important that your cast members are reliable and are able to commit to the times you have planned to film.

It is also likely that you will need additional crew members, especially if you are completing an audio-visual production. These people might help by operating sound or lighting equipment, for example. Remember, you must direct your crew members as it is your production.

What equipment and resources will you need?

Will you need to book equipment out in advance, for example if you are using a camera or props provided by your centre? Make a list of all the technical equipment and props and costumes that you will need to take on your shoot.

It is a good idea to create a shooting schedule, including a list of the photographs or footage you will need and when and where you will take them. Your draft design or storyboard will help you to compile this list.

Example extract of a shooting schedule:

Date and Location	Shots	Equipment	Cast and Crew	Notes
15 June Sam's Café	Storyboard shots 3–8; 15 and 16; 23–27	• Camera and microphone • Props – Ali's big shopping bag, Jude's computer magazine	Cast: Ali and Jude Mic: Ed	• Need to get permission to film in the café. • Book out camera for the weekend.
20 June Playing field	Storyboard shots 9–14	• Camera and mic • Costume: Sal's football kit and ball, Ali's heels and handbag	Cast: Ali and Sal + 'extras' playing football Mic: Ed	• Practise using mic outdoors. • Check football team are free to be extras.

When you have completed this stage you will write a short **Statement of Aims** before you begin your production. See Chapter 8 for further details about the Statement of Aims.

See Chapter 8 for further details about the Statement of Aims.

Top Tip

It is a good idea to draw up a timeline plan for your production to ensure you can complete all elements by the deadlines set.

Quickfire 7.2

Why is it really important that you set up each shot, positioning all cameras at the appropriate distance and angle, and giving your crew clear directions?

Top Tip

Remember to keep a record of all of the people who help with your production. You will need to include their names and roles on your cover sheet.

Top Tip

You might film or take photographs in different locations and on different days, so think about continuity. If the characters/models need to look the same, make sure you always have the correct props and costumes at your shoot.

Briefs in Individual Forms

The following sections cover the research, planning and production process for each of the forms: Television, Magazines, Film Marketing and Music Marketing.

Online options are offered for all of these (except Film Marketing) and they all have similar requirements: a website homepage and another, linked, page. These will be specific to the form and genre in the brief. As well as designing the webpages, you will need to produce original images and written copy, and a short piece of audio or audio-visual content for the site.

You need to create a working website, but you do not need to use computer code and might use web-design software or templates. You must, however, design the webpages yourself and all of the content on the site must be your own original work.

Television

The brief will offer you the option to create an audio-visual sequence **or** a website for a new television programme.

> **Sample brief: Audio-visual:**
> Create an **opening sequence** from a new **television crime drama** aimed at an **audience of 16- to 24-year-olds**. You may choose to produce a sequence from a subgenre of television crime.
> **Length:** 2 minutes – 2 minutes 30 seconds.

The brief will change every year, setting a different genre and target audience, but you will always have some choice about the product you create. There will also be a list of minimum requirements that you must include in your product. The sample brief expects, for example:

> **Opening sequence, including the title of programme:**
> - One or more filming locations
> - At least three characters (including a protagonist and antagonist)
> - Disruption of the narrative
> - Range of camera shots, angles and movement, including establishing shots of the location
> - Diegetic sound (including dialogue) and non-diegetic sound (including soundtrack)
> - Editing of footage, dialogue and soundtrack (continuity editing, may include montage if appropriate).

Responding to the brief

The brief will offer you some choice, so you will need to make some initial decisions about the product you are going to create. The sample brief above allows you to choose a subgenre of crime, from which you might decide to produce a police procedural or psychological crime drama, for example.

You should research products that are similar to the one you will construct: narrowing the focus will help you to select appropriate programmes to inform your own production.

Top Tip

Consider the practical aspects of creating your production at this stage. If you live in a large town, for example, it might be sensible to create an urban drama rather than a sequence set in the country.

Research: product analysis

You should analyse two or three television programmes in the genre (or subgenre) that you intend to produce. Use the brief to structure your research. If you need to create an opening sequence, for example, then you should analyse some opening sequences in detail. Pause the clip and note down details of specific shots: the technical and visual codes that have been used and how these create meaning. The minimum requirements in the brief will also give you areas to focus on and you should consider how the product appeals to the audience.

Example analysis of a television opening sequence: *Thirteen*

The BBC Three crime/psychological drama *Thirteen* was first broadcast in February 2016.

Opening sequence

The opening sequence of a television programme needs to establish the location and setting of the programme, as well as the genre. The sequence will often introduce the main characters and might provide vital clues about the narrative, although there might also be enigmas to be solved as the programme or series develops.

Media language

The establishing shot of a suburban location in *Thirteen* pans from right to left towards the house where the action takes place. This reverse pan hints at narrative disruption, although the location looks 'normal' and the birds are singing.

As the door is framed in mid-shot an eerie non-diegetic sound effect suggests that something is wrong. The mise-en-scène of the peeling paint around a shabby and dark front door connotes that the house is uncared for and hints that a crime might have taken place here.

As the door opens, continuity editing is used to create meaning. A match-on-action edit conceals the identity of the female by cutting to an over-the-shoulder point-of-view shot. Here, the background is out of focus and the lens flare from the bright natural light shows that the character's eyes are adjusting to the outside world, connoting that she has been indoors for a long time.

Close-ups reveal clues to the narrative, for example the shot of Ivy's bare feet and dirty toes connoting that she has been neglected.

As Ivy runs down the street, the audio codes of non-diegetic music and the enhanced diegetic sound of her breathing begin to build tension and suggest that she is trying to escape.

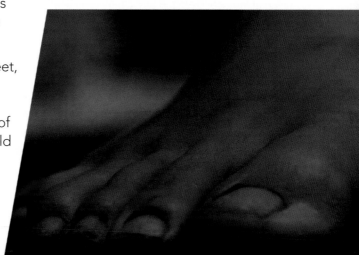

Top Tip

Make sure you analyse television programmes from the genre specified in the brief that you have been set.

So, the opening sequence begins with this narrative enigma that is then partly explained when the young woman calls the police, telling them that she is Ivy Moxon, was taken 13 years ago and has just escaped. The escape itself can be seen as a disruption, but the main disruption of the narrative took place in the past and the programme goes on to explore the backstory of this event, to try to solve this bigger enigma.

After the title sequence, Ivy arrives at the police station and many conventions typical of the police crime drama are then introduced (such as a police car, the interview room, detectives who interview Ivy).

Representation

The shot of Ivy on the steps constructs an image of a young, vulnerable female through:

- the dress code of the white nightdress connoting childhood innocence but its crumpled and dirty state suggesting that her innocence has been destroyed

- visual codes of her messy hair, bare feet, pale skin and fearful facial expression indicating that she is running away and is not prepared for the outside world that she has just entered.

This could be considered to be quite a stereotypical representation of a young woman, implying that she has had a traumatic experience and that she is a victim in need of rescue, reinforced when she calls the police to ask for help.

The male police officer in the car seems to doubt Ivy's story, implying that she might not be reliable, and therefore reinforcing the character type of the cynical male police officer often used in crime dramas.

The female family liaison officer is constructed as a friendly and professional character who will help Ivy, a typically caring older female.

Audience appeal

Thirteen is a psychological drama from BBC Three that reflects contemporary social contexts. It offers some familiar pleasures to genre audiences but also elements of difference by beginning with an escape from captivity and linking to real-life events such as Natascha Kampusch's escape in 2006.

Younger audiences might be drawn to the younger characters in the drama while older audiences might respond to the serious issues being covered in the series and the echoes of real-life stories from the past.

The opening sequence creates many enigmas to hook the audience and make them curious to find out what has happened to Ivy, and even if she is who she says she is.

The representation of a female protagonist might appeal to women who are interested in experiencing the drama from her point of view.

Stretch and Challenge 7.1

Consider how your own production might reflect contemporary contexts.

Stretch and Challenge 7.2

Analyse the trailers for the programmes you study and note how they appeal to the target audience.

Key Term

Press pack
A set of publicity materials about a new product, including information and photographs, released to media organisations to help to promote the product. Most press packs can be found on an organisation's website.

Quickfire 7.3

Why will your planning documents be vital during the filming and editing stages?

Quickfire 7.4

What element of narrative is required in the sample brief?

Top Tip

Think carefully about narrative structure when planning your storyboard. Chapter 1 of this book outlines some of the key elements and theories of narrative.

Top Tip

Remember to include all of the requirements listed in the brief.

Stretch and Challenge 7.3

Consider subverting stereotypes if appropriate.

Secondary research

A television company usually produces a **press pack** for the launch of a new programme, which should give you an idea of the target audience. You can find press packs and other articles about new programmes on, for instance, the BBC and Channel 4 websites. For example, an article about upcoming *Thirteen* from the BBC's Media Centre news feed in 2015 included the following quote from BBC Three Controller, Damian Kavanagh: 'BBC Three is all about nurturing emerging UK talent and the most innovative ideas that appeal to young people.' (bbc.co.uk/mediacentre/latestnews/2015/bbc-three-cast-thirteen?lang=cy)

The marketing of a programme will also give an insight into the target audience. You can usually find trailers for a programme on the programme's website or YouTube channel and you might also be able to read or watch interviews with actors and directors that are released to publicise the programme or latest series.

Researching when and where the programmes were broadcast will also give you information about the audience. For example, the first series of *Thirteen* was released on BBC Three and Episode 1 was made available on Sunday 28 February 2016. BBC Three is an online-only channel that primarily targets 16- to 34-year-olds, suggesting that the programme was aimed at a young adult audience with an interest in serious drama.

Planning your audio-visual production

When you have completed your research, use the findings to help you to plan your own production. At this stage you could outline your main ideas in response to the brief as a pitch or treatment, to provide a starting point for more detailed planning.

You should complete a recce of your locations and plan the logistics of your production, as outlined on page 193.

It is really important to plan your sequence carefully, as detailed below. This will help you to make sure you include all of the required elements in the brief as well as appropriate codes and conventions.

A **storyboard** will allow you to visualise your sequence in detail, planning all elements of the sequence including:

- the shots you will use, for example to establish the location and characters, and to show the action unfolding
- the duration of your shots – remember to vary the length of these according to what is happening
- editing transitions – how you cut between different shots and scenes to make sure the narrative makes sense
- audio codes – dialogue, sound effects and music to communicate meaning and add atmosphere
- how you will signal important information to an audience, giving them clues to the narrative, for example an object that is significant to solving a crime.

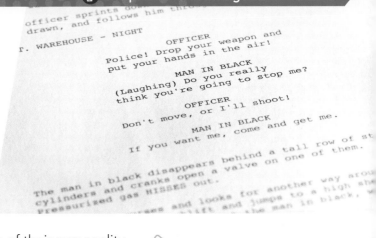

Script

The **script** is a written document that plans the action and dialogue in each sequence of footage. It will help you to direct the action during your shoot and will give your actors clear instructions.

A script should include details of:

- The setting: interior or exterior, where the action happens and details of the time of day.

- The characters in a scene, including some information about each character when they first appear, such as their age, appearance and brief details of their personality. Think carefully here about how you construct the representation of each character.

- How a character enters a scene. Do they march in purposefully suggesting they are confident and in control, or do they creep into a room, hoping not to be noticed?

- The action in a scene, for example a character opening a letter and reacting in shock. Here, you can include clear direction about how the character is behaving, which will help your actors on set.

- The dialogue, or words that the characters speak. You might include brief details of how the actor should say the lines, for example 'nervously'. You can also indicate pauses.

The dialogue is very important, so plan this carefully. It is often the case that 'less is more': an actor can reveal a lot about a character by their facial expressions and gestures as well as how they say the words. Try to give each character an individual voice through the language you use.

Production tips

- Make sure you know how to operate the equipment you are using: practise using the cameras and any sound and lighting equipment before you shoot your footage.

- Take your storyboard and/or script to your shoot and make sure that you film all of the planned footage. It is a good idea to compile a list of shots that you will need and tick these off as you go.

- It could be worth shooting more footage than you think you need in case you want extra shots when you come to edit the sequence. This will prevent you having to go back to shoot more footage at a later stage.

- When filming, always begin recording a few seconds before the action begins and let the camera continue recording for a few seconds after the action is complete. This will allow you to cut the footage appropriately and add transitions such as fades if you want to.

Stretch and Challenge 7.4

Research the scriptwriting section of the BBC Writersroom website, bbc.co.uk/writersroom/, and create your own script using the appropriate format.

Top Tip

Think about the genre when creating your script and storyboard and make sure you include key codes and conventions.

Top Tip

Analyse the dialogue in the products you research.

A young director on location gives instructions to his creative team.

- Give your actors and crew really clear instructions, and reshoot if someone makes a mistake or you are not completely happy with the shot. Your actors might not be experienced in performing to camera and might feel self-conscious to begin with, so try to be patient and let them practise until they feel comfortable.

- Sound is one of the more challenging aspects of television production work. If you are recording dialogue, especially on location, you will need to use a microphone to make sure the voices can be heard clearly. You could consider recording the dialogue separately and adding it when you edit the production.

- You might want to include a voiceover or sound effects in your sequence. You can record these in a studio (or quiet room) and import them into your production.

- You are likely to use some music in your television sequence, for example to create a particular atmosphere. You are able to use existing music here (you do not have to compose your own!) but it must be free of **copyright**. Your teacher can advise you of where you can find copyright-free music that you can use in an educational project. It is worth spending time listening to different pieces of music to find an example suitable for your sequence.

An example of a student television sequence: *Runaway* by Liam Brusby, Heaton Manor School

The example of work shown below is a sequence from a television crime/thriller that was produced for a previous GCSE qualification. It does not demonstrate a response to an Eduqas brief, but shows how the main codes and conventions relevant to all television sequences have been applied.

Technical codes of media language are used to communicate meaning:

- Establishing shots of the urban location and the park help the audience to understand the key settings for the action. Urban landscapes are often used in crime dramas, while the isolated location of the park allows the protagonist to conceal a key object.

- An appropriate range of shots convey information about the narrative and characters.

Familiar genre codes and conventions are used to appeal to audiences of crime and thriller dramas:

- Many enigmas are established and some identities are concealed, for example a character in a bookshop who passes information to the protagonist.
- Some shots show a partial view to withhold information and connote that the characters are trying to hide something, which offers pleasures of trying to solve the narrative.
- Close-ups of an object, a small black case, connote that this is important to the narrative. A further enigma occurs when a concealed character picks up the hidden case.
- The protagonist is a young male who acts independently for the most part, a typical convention of crime drama.

Quickfire 7.5

Identify the range of camera shots used in this sequence. What do they connote?

Quickfire 7.6

What other elements could this example include in order to meet the requirements of the sample brief?

Television: website option

Sample brief: Online:

Create a **working homepage and one other linked page** for a website for a new **television crime drama** aimed at an **audience of 16- to 24-year-olds**. You may choose to produce a website for a programme from a subgenre of television crime.

Length: 2 pages, including 30 seconds of audio or audio-visual material related to the topic.

There will also be a list of minimum requirements to include in your product. For example, in the sample brief:

One working homepage and a second, linked, page:

- Original title of programme
- Menu bar
- Main image plus at least two other images (all original) that establish the locations, characters and narrative of the programme
- One working link to a second page from the website (either 'Episodes' or 'Characters')
- Written text that introduces the characters, narrative and/ or themes of the programme (approx 150 words in total)
- 30 seconds of original audio or audio-visual material related to the topic embedded into one of the pages, for example an interview with the director or 'making of' footage

Analysing an online example: website for Channel 4's *Hollyoaks*

Hollyoaks is a long-running Channel 4 soap opera. It is shown at 6.30pm on weeknights so people can watch when they arrive home from work or college.

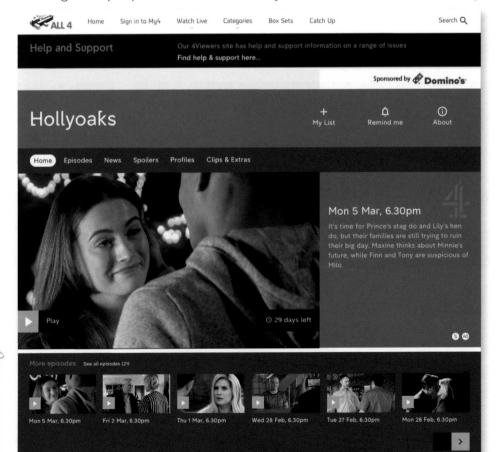

Stretch and Challenge 7.5

Make a list of the uses and gratifications that audiences might gain from a programme's website.

The *Hollyoaks* **homepage** includes links to episodes, clips and interactive features such as 'My List' to engage the target audience and encourage them to become regular viewers.

- The use of language is intended to appeal to the audience. Further down the homepage, 'Access All Areas', for example, suggests that they are gaining exclusive insights into the programme.

- The millennial target audience is likely to include active social media users, so the website engages them through links to the *Hollyoaks* Facebook, Twitter and Snapchat pages, and also includes a Spotify playlist of music used in the programme.

- The menu bar links to typical features of a television programme website, for example Episodes and Profiles, where users can catch up or find out more about the characters and storylines.

- The link to the 'Help and Support' page allows viewers to find more information about some of the issues raised in the programme, which is quite typical of a public service broadcaster's website.

One of the requirements of the sample brief is to write some text about characters, narrative or themes in the programme. The character profiles on the *Hollyoaks* website use an informal mode of address to engage a young adult audience. The written language anchors the image to construct the representation of the character. Cleo, for example, is depicted as an intelligent and independent young woman to appeal to young girls who might identify with her character.

Another requirement is to include some audio or audio-visual footage for the website. The 'Clips and Extras' page features many different videos such as behind the scenes footage, interviews with actors and clips about issues that have been covered in the show.

There are many 'exclusive' video clips that give audiences extra insights, for example the *#HollyGoss* feature. In this video, one of the stars of the programme interviews another actor about her character, Yasmine, who is new to the show. This will help the audience to get to know the new character and the topics they discuss, such as school and female friendship, will be familiar to many of the young viewers. The direct and informal mode of address is likely to engage the target audience.

Quickfire 7.7

Why are public service broadcasters likely to include help and information about personal and social issues on their websites?

One of the character profiles on the Hollyoaks website, appealing directly to a particular target audience.

Home   Episodes   News   Spoilers   Profiles   Clips & Extras

See all profiles

Cleo McQueen (Nadine Mulkerrin)

Just like her namesake, Cleopatra "Cleo" McQueen is leader of the outcasts and celebrates the qualities that make her different from all the other kids at school. She's a child genius and has an IQ higher than the rest of the McQueen girls combined!

We all know the McQueens are tight, but no more so than Cleo and her sisters. Porsche and Celine will do anything to give their sister the best life possible, and they put all their money into sending Cleo to boarding school to give her the education she deserved.

Now Cleo's in Hollyoaks, she's slowly adjusting to life in a house full of alpha females. Cleo has no time for the dramas of a broken nail or fighting over the bathroom mirror, you'll find her hiding away engrossed in a good book. FINALLY, a drama-free McQueen!

Home   Episodes   News   Spoilers   Profiles   Clips & Extras

See all clips & extras

#HollyGoss - There's a New Mean Girl at Hollyoaks High

Brace yourselves, Yasmine is gonna stir up some trouble at Hollyoaks High. Ruby (Peri) tests her new BFF's partner-in-crime potential in this #HollyGoss...

This website-only video, gives *Hollyoaks* fans access to further insights into the characters and their lives.

Stretch and Challenge 7.6

Analyse any themes and issues that programmes' websites reference and consider how these relate to their social context.

Planning the website

Draft designs will help you to plan the website and think about where you will place the different features.

Mock-ups: Think carefully about the layout of the pages and how the user will navigate the site. Consider the colour palette and style of font you will use to create a brand identity for your programme's website and to appeal to the audience.

Images: Plan the photographs that you need to take. Television websites usually include a range of different types of image, so use your research as a guide to the pictures you will create.

Text: Draft the written text for your website, using an appropriate mode of address for your target audience.

Sounds and moving images: Plan your audio or audio-visual footage. You should script the dialogue and create a storyboard if you are filming an audio-visual sequence.

Magazines

The brief will always offer you the option to create a new print magazine **or** a website for a new magazine.

> **Sample brief: Print:**
>
> Create a **front cover** and a **double-page spread article** for a new **music or sport magazine** in a subgenre of your choice, aimed at an **audience of 16- to 24-year-olds**.
> **Length:** 3 pages.

The brief will change every year, setting a different genre and target audience, but you will always have some choice about the product that you create. There will also be a list of minimum requirements to include in your product. For example, in the sample brief:

> **Front cover plus double-page spread article: three pages including at least six original images in total.**
>
> **Front cover:**
> - Original masthead/title for the magazine
> - Strapline
> - Cover price and barcode
> - Main cover image plus at least two smaller/minor images (all original)
> - At least four cover lines
>
> **Double-page spread article:**
> - Headline and standfirst, subheadings
> - One main image and at least two smaller/minor images (all original)
> - Feature article (approx 300 words) relating to one of the cover lines on the front cover
> - **Pull-quotes** and/or **sidebar**

Responding to the brief

The brief will offer you some choice, so you will need to make some initial decisions about the product you are going to create. The sample brief above allows you to choose either a music or sport magazine and to create a product in a subgenre if you wish, such as a magazine about 'indie' music or horse riding.

You should research products that are similar to the one you will construct, so, narrowing the focus will help you to select appropriate magazines to inform your own production.

Product analysis: print magazines

You should analyse two or three magazines, ideally in the subgenre that you intend to produce. Use the brief to structure your research. So, if you need to create a front cover and double-page spread article, you should analyse magazine covers and feature articles in detail. The minimum requirements in the brief will also give you areas to focus on and you should consider how the product appeals to the audience.

You will be familiar with the codes and conventions of magazine front covers from your studies in Component 1. The section below analyses the features of a double-page spread article that you can use as a starting point for researching your own examples.

Example analysis of a double-page spread: Q magazine

The article on the following page is taken from Q, a music magazine, published in March 2018.

The **layout** includes one full-page image and a page that introduces the written article through a headline, standfirst, written copy and smaller images. The red, white and black colour palette is typical of Q's house style and reinforces a sense of brand identity. The article is laid out in columns and is about songwriters in the music business, so is likely to appeal to serious music fans and those with an interest in the industry.

Top Tip

Analyse examples of magazine front covers, using the codes and conventions outlined in Chapter 3 of this book.

Headline: The font looks like the type produced by an old-fashioned typewriter and connotes that this is an article about songwriters. A pun, 'big hitters', is used to signify that songwriters have a lot of power in the industry but also links to the idea of a 'hit' song.

The **main image** depicts the songwriter in his studio. His dress codes and body language suggest that he is relaxed and down-to-earth, and the audience might be comfortable with this persona. The recording equipment adds meaning to the image as this relates to music industry and the subject matter of the article.

The **pull-quote** from Antonoff adds a personal touch to the article, using direct address to engage the audience. Pull-quotes often reflect the key messages in an article and add emphasis.

Subheading: This introduces the first songwriter, using the same font as the headline and standfirst to ensure a consistent style across the feature.

The following is the reproduced magazine article:

SONGWRITERS FOR HIRE

The Secrets Of The Big Hitters

How do today's hit-makers cajole gold from the likes of Taylor Swift, Lorde, Harry Styles and Ed Sheeran? Tom Doyle tracks down four modern masters of their trade to find out.

The role of the modern songwriter-for-hire is a tricky and complex one. They can be part collaborator, part psychiatrist, part confessional priest. Working knee-to-knee with artists, they also serve as magicians of a kind – conjuring something from nothing.

In recent years, a new wave of co-songwriters has emerged, all of them from indie/alternative backgrounds, all of them having been in bands or artists in their own right.

The result has been subtle changes in the job of the professional tunesmith and a greater level of intimacy to the songs which they produce. Here, Q meets four of the premier league co-writers of the moment.

Jack of all trades: Antonoff in his Brooklyn studio.

"Don't be some weird hero version of yourself. Be yourself. Be honest."

1. Jack Antonoff

Hit-maker with Taylor Swift, Lorde, St. Vincent.

The Brooklyn Heights studio of Jack Antonoff doesn't exactly look like the home of the hits. It's a small room at one end of the apartment he shares with his partner Lena Dunham (star/creator of HBO series Girls), the walls of which are decorated with the same tiger-print wallpaper that the slightly nervy, slightly nerdy 33-year-old had in his childhood bedroom growing up in New Jersey. These surroundings are clearly a source of some comfort for Antonoff and a world away from the often clinical atmospheres of professional recording studios.

In this compact and intimate environment, Antonoff has co-written hits with the likes of Taylor Swift, St. Vincent and Lorde, drawing on his own experience as an artist with his alternative pop band fun. and synthy solo project Bleachers.

"When I work with som... ...and when I work alone," he explains. "Go there. ≫

(Above) Antonoff with Taylor Swift; (right) their 2017 co-credit, Look What You Made Me Do, which references Right Said Fred.

48 Q MARCH 2018

Reproduced with the kind permission of Bauer Media UK

Standfirst: This includes a rhetorical question to engage the audience and make them want to read on. The reference to different elite music stars might appeal to a wider range of music fans. There is a clear outline of what the article will contain: insights into four songwriters who have achieved success in the music industry.

The **smaller images** reinforce the message of written copy by showing Jack Antonoff on stage with Taylor Swift and the cover of a single he co-wrote, showing the level of his success. Audiences are likely to recognise Taylor Swift and might read the article even if they are not particularly interested in songwriting.

This article constructs a positive **representation** of a young songwriter who has achieved success in a competitive creative industry. He is shown as an elite persona, onstage with major stars, which creates a sense of an aspiration for the reader, but also as a 'real' person working in his studio, which the audience might identify with.

Secondary research

You can usually find useful information about a magazine's audience from the advertising section of the publisher's website. This will often define the target audience very clearly. The advertisements in the magazine also reveal information about the audience demographics, particularly the socio-economic group, and their possible interests or desires.

Research the circulation of the magazine. Where is it sold, for example? Some popular magazines aimed at a large mainstream audience will be available in every newsagent and supermarket, while publications targeting a narrower audience might only be sold at specialist outlets or via subscription.

Q is published by Bauer, a major publisher, and targets serious music fans of different ages. It is available in most outlets and also on subscription. By contrast, *Women's Running* (see page 209) is published by Wild Bunch Media, an independent organisation specialising in running-related products. The magazine targets females with an interest in running, both new and more experienced. There are many options to subscribe to the print and digital editions on the website.

An example of student magazine production: *Fashionista* by Ahmedy Khatoon, Heaton Manor School

The example of work shown on the next page is a cover of a specialist fashion magazine that was produced for a previous GCSE qualification. It does not demonstrate a response to an Eduqas brief, but shows how the codes and conventions of magazine covers have been applied.

- The title captures the genre and subject of the magazine effectively and the masthead is placed centrally at the top of the cover, adhering to conventions of magazine layout.

- The word 'fashionista' is contemporary and connotes someone who is passionate about clothes and the latest trends, so is likely to engage the target audience of females who have a serious interest in fashion.

A range of music magazines on display at an airport newsagent's.

Top Tip

Make a list of the products that are advertised in each magazine you research. Consider what these adverts reveal about the publication's target audience.

Stretch and Challenge 7.7

Research the websites of the magazines you analyse, identifying the ways in which the audience is targeted and how the organisation is appealing to them.

Many magazines offer digital editions as well as print versions ideal for reading on tablets.

Stretch and Challenge 7.8

When you plan your own magazine, ensure that there is a clear 'house style' evident across all pages of your production.

Quickfire 7.10

What mode of address is the cover model of *Fashionista* adopting, and why?

- The visual and technical codes demonstrated in the main image are appropriate to the genre, for example the black and gold colour palette and embellishment on the cover model's dress.
- The cover creates a clear house style for the magazine through the consistent use of colour and font.
- Cover lines are clearly linked to the content of the magazine and positioned around the model, a convention of magazine covers.
- The cover is likely to engage and appeal to the target audience of sophisticated women who aspire to the images and lifestyle constructed in the magazine.

Magazines: online option

Sample brief: Online:

Create a working **homepage and one other linked page** for a website for a **new music or sport magazine** in a subgenre of your choice aimed at an **audience of 16- to 24-year-olds**.

Length: 2 pages, including 30 seconds of audio or audio-visual material related to the topic.

There will also be a list of minimum requirements that you must include in your product. For example, in the sample brief:

One working homepage and a second, linked, page:

- Original title of magazine
- Menu bar
- Main image plus at least two other images (all original) that relate to the chosen subgenre of magazine
- One working link to a second page from the magazine website (a linked music or sport story/feature)
- Written text relating to the music or sport content of the magazine (approx 150 words in total)
- 30 seconds of original audio or audio-visual material related to the topic embedded into one of the pages, for example an interview with a musician or sportsperson, or footage of the music or sport featured in the magazine

Example analysis of a sport magazine website: *Women's Running*

The **title** of the magazine is informative and clearly identifies the target audience: females with an interest in running. The **masthead** uses a cursive font that slants to the right, connoting forward movement.

The **layout** of the homepage follows conventions for a magazine website: the masthead is positioned top left (similar to a print magazine), the menu bar is clearly shown under the masthead, a main image dominates the page above links to different articles. There is also a **plug** top right, encouraging readers to subscribe to the magazine, and **banner advert** for products that might appeal to runners. Social media links are clearly displayed near the top of the homepage.

The **menu bar** links to different pages relevant to the magazine, such as health and nutrition, and information about racing: topics that are likely to appeal to an audience interested in running. The clear layout allows readers to navigate easily around the website.

The pale **colour palette** is calming and the use of the blue arguably subverts gender stereotypes. Running is more traditionally associated with men, but many women now take part in this sport and the website constructs positive representations for the female audience.

The **main image** is a medium shot of a young woman running towards the camera, which clearly reflects the subgenre of the magazine. The accompanying text anchors the meaning of the image: the woman looks happy, strong and healthy, potentially as a result of running to help her cope with challenges in her life. This communicates a positive message about exercise and also links to social contexts, as issues such as anxiety affect many people.

Key Term

Banner advert
Adverts that appear in rectangular boxes on webpages. They usually relate to the content of the website. Clicking on the banner takes the user to the advertiser's website. This type of advertising can benefit both the magazine and the advertiser, similar to advertising in a print publication.

Quickfire 7.11

How might the main image of the cover model appeal to the audience of female runners?

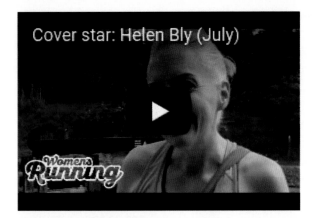
Cover star: Helen Bly (July)

Video clips are embedded into the homepage, for example 'Meet the Cover Star', where the cover model from an earlier edition of the magazine talks directly to camera about running. This enhances the experience of the magazine website, giving the audience additional information and insight into other people's lives. Readers might be touched by the experiences in the videos and be inspired to start running themselves.

Planning the magazine or website

When you have completed your research, you should use the findings to help you to plan your own production. At this stage you could outline your main ideas in response to the brief as a pitch or treatment, to provide a starting point for more detailed planning.

You will need to create pages that are appropriate to the genre specified in the brief.

Mock-ups: Think carefully about the layout of the pages and how the user will read them or navigate around the site. Consider the colour palette and style of font you will use to create a brand identity for your magazine and appeal to the audience.

Images: Plan the photographs that you need to take. You will need main images for your front cover or homepage and feature article, as well as other images to engage the audience and link to the magazine content. Magazines and magazine websites usually include a range of different types of image, so use your research as a guide to the pictures you will create.

Text: Draft the written text for your magazine or website, using an appropriate tone and mode of address for your genre and target audience. Try to include appropriate language, such as specialist terms in relation to the content of the magazine.

Sound and moving images: Plan the audio or audio-visual footage if you are creating a website. You should script the dialogue and create a storyboard if you are filming an audio-visual sequence.

Production tips

- Compile a list of shots you will need and tick these off as you go. It is a good idea to take several photographs for each planned shot as this will give you plenty of choice when you construct your production.
- Give your models very clear direction. Position them carefully and think about the mode of address you want to achieve. Do you want them to look directly to camera, for example? Should they be smiling or more serious?

Quickfire 7.12

Why is it important to create draft designs of your magazine or website pages?

Top Tip

Think carefully about how you will construct representations, paying close attention to the dress codes and body language of the 'models' that you photograph.

Stretch and Challenge 7.9

Experiment with linguistic devices to create engaging headlines and cover lines.

Top Tip

When you are creating your designs, make sure you include all of the requirements listed in the brief.

Take several images on your photoshoot and choose the most appropriate for your magazine.

- Remember that you must create original material, so avoid using 'found' images of celebrities or sports people. You can create your own elite personalities or feature a young 'up and coming' star using appropriate codes and conventions identified in your research.

- When constructing the pages, pay close attention to the house style and be consistent in your use of design features, colour palette and fonts. These should be appropriate to the type of magazine you are creating and the intended audience.

- Try to create engaging cover lines, headlines and standfirsts to engage the audience and encourage them to read on.

- Check that you have included all of the requirements in the brief, making sure you adhere to the conventions of the genre.

Top Tip

If you create a website, remember that you can use a template but you must design the layout yourself, and all of the images, written text and audio-visual material must be your own work.

Film Marketing

The brief is a print marketing campaign for a new film.

Sample brief:

Create a **DVD front and back cover and a main theatrical release poster** for a new film in the **crime genre** aimed at an **audience of 16- to 24-year-olds** (maximum 15 certificate). You may choose to produce marketing material for a film in a subgenre of the crime genre.

Length: 3 pages. (Note: the front and back cover count as one page each.)

The brief will change every year, setting a different genre and target audience, but you will always have some choice about the product you create. There will also be a list of minimum requirements to include in your product. For example, in the sample brief:

DVD cover (front, back and spine) plus one main theatrical release poster to include:

- a minimum of **eight original images** in total
- at least two different locations for photography
- at least three different characters (including a protagonist and antagonist).

DVD front cover:
- Main image
- Original title for the film
- Age rating
- Names of director and actors

DVD back cover:
- Background image and main image
- Four 'thumbnail' images depicting different scenes from the film
- Promotional 'blurb' for the film (approx 150 words), including reference to narrative disruption
- Billing block
- Production company logo, age rating and technical information

Spine:
- Title
- Production company logo
- Age rating

Poster (portrait format):
- Original title for the film
- Tagline
- Main image (different from the images on the DVD cover)
- Release date
- Billing block and production company logo

Responding to the brief

The brief will offer you some choice, so you will need to make some initial decisions about the product you are going to create. The sample brief above allows you to choose a subgenre of crime, for example a police or psychological crime drama.

You should research products that are similar to the one you will construct, so, narrowing the focus will help you to select appropriate film marketing materials to inform your own production.

Research: product analysis

You should analyse print marketing materials for two or three films in the genre (or subgenre) that you intend to produce. Use the brief to structure your research. If you need to create a DVD cover and poster, you should analyse these products for your chosen films. The minimum requirements in the brief will also give you areas to focus on and you should consider how the product appeals to the audience.

Example analysis of film marketing materials: DVD cover of *Brighton Rock*

You will be familiar with the codes and conventions of film posters from your studies in Component 1. The section below analyses the features of a DVD cover, which you can use as a starting point for researching your own examples.

Brighton Rock is a British film released in 2010. It is an adaptation of a novel by Graham Green and stars many well-known British actors. This version of the film is set in the 1960s, and depicts the popular 'mod' culture as well as featuring conventions of the crime genre.

Top Tip

Analyse examples of film posters, using the codes and conventions outlined in Chapter 3.

Cover

A DVD **front cover** needs to appeal to the audience and encourage them to watch the film. It is likely to use media language to convey the genre and elements of narrative, and construct representations:

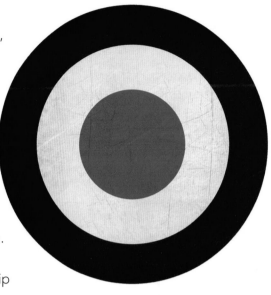

- The **title** is positioned on a diagonal across the cover, possibly connoting narrative disruption, similar to a canted frame. 'Brighton' is established as the setting of the film, while 'Rock' has multiple meanings: the stick of rock sweet that is popular at seaside resorts, but also a potential weapon, connoting the crime genre.

- The red, white and blue **colour palette** communicates the message that this is a British film.

- The circular **motif** in the background was originally the symbol of the Royal Air Force but was also adopted by the 'mods', a popular subculture in the 1960s. The DVD cover references actual events in Brighton, riots between the rival gangs of 'mods' and the 'rockers', which many audience members will recognise and have an interest in.

- The main **image** depicts three main characters. The image creates enigma relating to the identity of the characters and the relationship between them, potentially intriguing the audience.

- The canted-angle shot (see page 113) of Brighton Pier anchors the location, while the dark-blue filter connotes crime and danger, expected features of the genre.

- Further features help to 'sell' the film, such as review comments – four stars and hyperbolic language in support of the film.

Spine

- The front cover image wraps over onto the spine. The mod 'logo' is repeated here.
- The title of the film runs vertically, in the same colour and font as on the front cover.
- The company logo and age certificates are placed on the spine.

Back cover

- **Blurb**:
  - The main characters and narrative situation are introduced, and the first paragraph ends on a question. This creates an enigma to hook the audience into the narrative.
  - The well-known British cast and director are listed, appealing to a range of audiences who might recognise them. This creates a sense of status for the film.
- **Thumbnail images** give a sense of the different scenes in the film and clues to the narrative, without revealing too much information.
- The thumbnails include scenes of violence and gun-pointing to convey the crime and gangster conventions and support the quote from a review that this is a 'gripping thriller'.

Quickfire 7.13

How are the representations of the three characters on the front cover of *Brighton Rock* constructed?

Key Terms

Blurb
A brief outline of a creative product to hook an audience and encourage them to engage.

Thumbnail images
Most DVD back covers have three or four small images of scenes from the film to give an insight into the action and characters to appeal to the audience.

- Other images reinforce the mod iconography, showing characters on scooters, suggesting that the distributor is aiming to appeal to an audience who recognise and are interested in this culture.
- The '**Extras**' box includes the special features that audiences will gain if they purchase the DVD, which suggests that the buyer will gain even more additional content, providing value for money. This is a persuasive technique to appeal to fans of the genre or the film.
- The **billing block**, company logo, age rating and technical information are typically placed at the bottom of the back cover. The production company logos (Optimum, Studio Canal) are also placed on the cover and the spine.

Audience

- The film is based on a novel by Graham Greene, which some audiences might recognise.
- The younger stars Andrea Riseborough and Sam Riley might appeal to younger adult audiences, especially Riley, who featured in the 2007 film *Control* about Joy Division singer Ian Curtis. Actors such as John Hurt and Helen Mirren are more likely to have relevance to an older demographic, suggesting this film suits a wide age range.
- The iconography and cast might attract viewers who tend to enjoy and support British films.
- The reference to the mods offers gratifications to a middle-aged audience who might feel nostalgia for the 1960s if they enjoyed the music associated with this subculture.

Secondary research

A film distributor might produce a **press pack** for a new film, which will give you information about the film, the narrative and genre and the people involved and should also give you an idea of the target audience.

The marketing of a film will give an insight into the target audience. Trailers will be on the film's website or YouTube channel. The film is likely to have social media pages and you might also be able to read or watch interviews with actors and directors made to publicise a film.

Researching when and where the film was released will also give you information about the audience. *Brighton Rock*, for example, was shown at film festivals in London and Toronto before release in cinemas in February 2010. This suggests that it had more of a niche audience and did not gain widespread international exhibition.

Many small-budget films premiere at film festivals before cinema release.

Planning film marketing materials

When you have completed your research, you should use the findings to help you plan your own production. At this stage you could outline your main ideas in response to the brief as a pitch or treatment, to provide a starting point for more detailed planning.

Draft designs will help you to plan the DVD cover and poster and help you to think about where you will place the key features listed in the brief. Remember that these are different products with specific conventions, so make sure that you use the correct features for each product.

Mock-ups: Think carefully about the layout of the pages and how these will promote the film. Consider the colour palette and style of font you will use to create a brand identity for your product and appeal to the audience. Pay close attention to the placing of the different elements, such as company logos, age certificates and the billing block, to adhere to the established conventions of these products.

Images: Plan the photographs that you need to take. You will need the main images for your DVD front cover and poster and some 'stills' of scenes from the film for your thumbnail images. These will need to communicate information about the characters and narrative, so should be planned carefully.

Text: Draft the written 'blurb' for the DVD back cover. You need to engage the target audience and encourage them to watch the film, using appropriate language and mode of address.

Production tips

- Compile a list of shots you will need and tick these off as you go. It is a good idea to take several photographs for each planned shot as this will give you plenty of choice when you construct your production.
- Set up your shots very carefully, thinking about the meanings you are trying to communicate.
- Give your actors clear direction about their body language and facial expression to portray the character representation that you want to construct.
- You might decide to film a short sequence of action and select stills from this footage. This can make the image look more convincing. Again, you will need to give your actors clear instructions about the characters and narrative that you want to convey.
- Pay close attention to the design and layout of the poster and DVD cover. These products have specific codes and conventions, and the back of a DVD cover needs to include several different elements. Use your research to inform your designs and make your production look as professional as possible.
- You will need to include the names of your actors, the director and other key personnel. These should be the names of your own actors, or you could 'invent' names (not the names of famous actors).
- Check that you have included all of the requirements in the brief, making sure that you have used appropriate codes and conventions for the genre.

Top Tip
You must use different images on the poster and DVD cover, so plan to take a good range of shots.

Top Tip
Think carefully about how you will construct representations, paying close attention to the dress codes and body language of the characters that you create.

Top Tip
Draft your 'blurb' carefully to hook the audience without giving away too much detail of the narrative.

An example of a student DVD cover: *DCI Meara* by George Hutchinson, Seaford Head School

The example of work shown below is a cover for an imagined BBC crime drama that was produced for a previous GCSE qualification. It does not demonstrate a response to an Eduqas brief, but shows how the codes and conventions of DVD covers have been applied.

Quickfire 7.15

How has this DVD front cover established the location, genre and protagonist?

- The candidate has constructed an appropriate layout and design that establishes the genre, location and protagonist.
- Visual codes are likely to appeal to an audience of crime genre fans, for example the iconic use of the colour red throughout the cover connoting violence and blood. The use of a dark sky demonstrates an understanding of conventions and the title font suggests the newspaper cuttings sometimes used by kidnappers and relates to the themes of crime, threat and possibly revenge.
- The blurb summarises the backstory and sets up the narrative for the audience. The use of the rhetorical question is an effective device to engage potential viewers.
- Thumbnail images show four different scenes from the drama and offer narrative clues but also enigmas. The use of typical crime conventions such as concealed identity and partial view through the smoke offer clear genre appeals to the audience.
- An appropriate representation of the protagonist is constructed as a serious and troubled detective, quite typical of the crime genre. He is smartly dressed and displays confident body language, connoting that he is professional and will be active in the narrative.
- There is close attention to detail in applying conventions of a DVD/Blu-ray cover through the appropriate positioning of the age certificates, company logo and technical information.

Stretch and Challenge 7.11

When you plan your production, pay attention to all pages to make sure you create a consistent house style.

Music Marketing

The brief will offer you the option to create a music video **or** a website for a new artist or band.

> **Sample brief: Audio-visual:**
> Create an original music video for a new pop band or artist in a subgenre of your choice, aimed at an audience of 16- to 24-year-olds.
> **Length:** 2 minutes – 2 minutes 30 seconds.

The brief will change every year, setting a different genre and target audience, but you will always have some choice about the product that you create. There will also be a list of minimum requirements to include in your product. For example, in the sample brief:

> **Promotional music video in the pop genre, which interprets the music and lyrics of the song:**
> * At least two locations (such as studio, rehearsal or live venue, or other locations)
> * Range of camera shots, angles and movement
> * Shots of the artist or band
> * Performance footage (rehearsal or live)
> * Narrative, including disruption and resolution
> * Editing of original footage to the music track
> * Original name of artist or band, title of the track

Responding to the brief

The brief will offer you some choice, so you will need to make some initial decisions about the product you are going to create. The sample brief above allows you to choose a subgenre of pop music, for example indie pop, folk pop or dance pop.

You should research products that are similar to the one you will construct, so narrowing the focus will help you to select appropriate music videos to inform your own production.

The brief also states that you may use an existing song for your music video, but the song must not have an existing official music video. When you are looking for an appropriate song to use for your video, you could select a track from an artist's album that has not been released as a single. If you have friends who are in a band, and write their own music, you could use one of their original songs – with their permission of course.

Research: product analysis

You should analyse two or three music videos in the genre (or subgenre) that you intend to produce. Use the brief to structure your research. For example, the minimum requirements will give you areas to focus on and you should consider how the product appeals to the audience.

Top Tip

If you use a song by a well-known artist or band, you should not try to recreate that artist's image, but invent an 'original' artist in the same genre. For example, if you choose an album track by Taylor Swift, you could create a new young female pop artist who may sing this song.

Example analysis of a music video: 'Story of My Life' by One Direction

One Direction's 'Story of My Life' is a single taken from their third album *Midnight Memories* and was released in 2013. The music video for this pop song has high production values and mainstream appeal, combining performance footage and narrative sections to engage the audience.

Media language

The video interprets the title of the song through technical and visual codes:

- Images from the band members' family lives contrast the past and present. This creates a sense that we are glimpsing the band members' 'real' lives and offers pleasures of identification for the audience.

- The 'home' settings are recognisable and have mainstream appeal, typical of the pop genre.

- There is limited literal illustration of the lyrics, although some phrases are interpreted visually. For example, 'Written in these walls are the stories that I can't explain' is shown by hundreds of images being displayed in a large wall, connoting that these are the band members' life stories. This supports the personal nature of the video and has universal appeal.

There is a combination of narrative and performance footage, typical of music videos in this genre.

Mini-narratives show how the young men have grown up. The device of the polaroid photograph acts as a recurring motif and allows the director to communicate these stories very clearly and quickly. For example, a shot of Niall and his brother as children cuts to the same shot of them as young adults. This is something that most people can relate to and so has appeal to a range of audiences. The inclusion of parents and grandparents widens the potential reach of this video.

The narratives are conventionally edited between performance footage. This low-angle shot of the band performing directly to camera, for example, connotes status and dominance. The video includes a wide range of shots, including many close-ups of the band to reinforce their individual star personas and appeal to the audience.

Representation

The band members are shown as thoughtful young men who care about their relationships with their parents, siblings and grandparents.

Dress codes construct representations of the young men as individuals although the colour palette of black, white and dark-grey clothing creates a consistent image and reinforces the identity of the band.

Quickfire 7.16

How does the representation of the One Direction band members in 'Story of My Life' reflect contemporary ideas of masculinity?

'Story of My Life' offers a representation of mature young males and contrasts with some of the band's earlier videos that show a more youthful, carefree side to the band.

Audience

The primary audience for this video is young females, who were the core fan base for One Direction:

- The video is quite sentimental and emotional, which might typically appeal to the target demographic.
- The performance footage reinforces the performers' personas as successful pop stars attractive to young fans.

The reference to families and shots of the band as young children might also appeal to older audiences, such as the parents of young fans, who would relate to the themes of children growing up and the passing of time.

Secondary research

A record label will usually produce a press kit for a new release, although nowadays this is usually a digital 'pack' of webpages, such as a biography and the music video. The website will give you information about the band or artist. Elements such as the design and mode of address will also give you an idea of the target audience.

The marketing of a new single or album will also suggest the target audience. As well as the music video, there is likely to be a social media campaign and publicity such as the band appearing on chat shows or in magazines. At the time of the release of 'Story of My Life' One Direction was a hugely successful band who staged '1D Day', a seven-hour live stream in the run up to the album release.

Stretch and Challenge 7.12

Research the websites for the artists whose videos you have analysed and note down how the record label is appealing to the target audience.

One Direction with Simon Cowell as part of their 1D Day publicity.

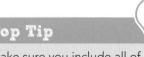
Planning your music video

When you have completed your research, you should use the findings to help you to plan your own production. At this stage you could outline your main ideas in response to the brief as a pitch or treatment, to provide a starting point for more detailed planning.

You will need to construct an identity for the new artist or band that you create. Think about the image of other artists from the same genre of music, using your research as a starting point. From here, you can begin to develop the representations, paying close attention to the dress codes you will use and how you will direct your performers, for example the body language and expressions they should use. If you are creating a band, consider the individual identity of each performer as well as the image of the group.

Think about how you will interpret the song:

- Write down the lyrics and think about their meaning. Consider the visuals that you will use to interpret the lyrics. Remember, music videos could show a literal representation of the lyrics or a more metaphorical interpretation.
- Do the lyrics tell a story? How can you construct a narrative quickly and clearly?

You might also be required to include performance footage of the artist or band, for example live performance or lip-synching to camera.

A storyboard will help you to visualise your ideas for the video:

- Include the lyrics on your storyboard alongside the planned visual images.
- Remember to include a range of shots and vary these to fit with the narrative and performance sections.
- Note the timings of the sections of music and lyrics so you can plan your shots to fit to the music. This will also help you to edit to the beat.
- Pay close attention to the duration of shots. Most music videos are edited much more quickly than a television drama sequence, so plan accordingly.

You should complete a recce of your locations and plan the logistics of your production as outlined on page 193.

Production tips

- Make sure you know how to operate the equipment you are using. Practise using the cameras, lighting and sound equipment before you shoot your footage.
- Take your storyboard when you go filming and make sure that you record all of the planned footage. It is a good idea to compile a list of shots that you will need and tick these off as you go.
- It is a good idea to film more footage than you think you will need in case you want extra shots when you come to edit the video. This will prevent you having to shoot more footage later.
- Give your performers and crew very clear instructions, and reshoot if there is a mistake or you are not completely happy with the shot. Your performers might not be experienced in performing to camera and might feel self-conscious, so try to be patient and let them practise until they feel comfortable.

- Pay close attention to filming the lip-synching sections. This is one of the more challenging aspects of a music video production. You should play the song while you are shooting so that your performer/s can sing in time to the track. This will help you to edit the video accurately.

- If you are going to film performers playing instruments, make sure that they can actually play the instrument and record them playing along to the song. This will ensure that the footage matches the audio track when you edit the video.

- Make sure you plan your schedule to allow plenty of time to edit your music video. This is a crucial stage of the process and it will take time and careful attention to edit your video to a high standard, applying appropriate codes and conventions.

An example of a student music video: '2+2=5 (Radiohead)' by Elliot Rae, Heaton Manor School

The example of work shown below is a video for an alternative rock band that was produced for a previous GCSE qualification. It does not demonstrate a response to an Eduqas brief, but shows how the codes and conventions of the music video form have been applied.

The music video includes a combination of performance footage and narrative, using conventions of the form and genre:

- The setting of the performance footage is a rehearsal room, reflecting the alternative genre of the music. It is not filmed at a live concert or in a studio. The room is quite dark and uses natural light to connote the independent nature of the video, creating a sense of authenticity in contrast to the high production values often seen in the pop genre.

Stretch and Challenge 7.14

Include intertextual references in your music video if appropriate. This is a convention in many examples of this form.

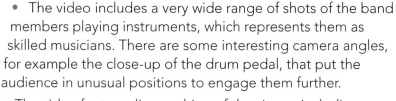

- The video includes a very wide range of shots of the band members playing instruments, which represents them as skilled musicians. There are some interesting camera angles, for example the close-up of the drum pedal, that put the audience in unusual positions to engage them further.

- The video features lip-synching of the singer, including several close-up shots, demonstrating an appropriate use of conventions.

- The narrative interprets the serious messages in the song. Both the song and video intertextually reference George Orwell's novel *1984*, shown in close-up in the opening shot. This communicates meaning to audience members who recognise the book and are likely to gain pleasure from identifying the link to the song.

- Close-up shots of CCTV cameras connote the theme of surveillance in society, which also reflects the lyrics and echoes the novel.

- A wide range of shots is used to convey the isolation of the main character, his anguish and his inability to communicate his anxieties. This constructs a representation of contemporary masculinity, subverting stereotypes of strength and dominance, and showing a young man who is fearful and vulnerable.

- There is no resolution to the narrative, which might appeal to an audience of alternative music fans, who find gratification in less mainstream products, messages and constructs.

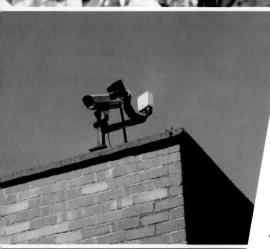

Quickfire 7.18

What different conventions would you expect to see in a music video for the pop genre?

Music marketing: website option

Sample brief: Online:
Create a **working homepage and one other linked page** for a website for a new **pop band or artist** in a subgenre of your choice, aimed at an **audience of 16- to 24-year-olds**.
Length: 2 pages, including 30 seconds of audio or audio-visual material related to the topic.

There will also be a list of minimum requirements that you must include in your product. For example, in the sample brief:

One working homepage and a second, linked, page:
- Menu bar
- Main image plus at least two other images (all original) to promote the artist or band
- One working link to a second page from the website, either 'News' or 'Biography'
- Written text promoting the band or artist and their music (approx 150 words in total)
- 30 seconds of original audio or audio-visual material related to the topic embedded into one of the pages, for example an interview with the artist or band, or live performance/ rehearsal footage

Top Tip

Revisit your analysis of music websites from Component 2. The codes and conventions outlined in Chapter 5 of this book will help you to analyse your own examples.

You will be familiar with the codes and conventions of music websites from your studies in Component 2, but you should also analyse other websites independently. Think carefully about the type of artist or band that you are creating and find similar examples of websites.

Planning the website

First, you will need to construct an identity for your new artist or band. Think about the image of other artists from the same genre of music, using your research as a starting point. From here, you can begin to develop the representations, paying close attention to dress codes, for example, and how you will direct your models/performers in terms of body language and expression. If you are creating a band, consider the individual identities of the performers as well as the image of the group.

Mock-ups: Think carefully about the layout of the pages and how the user will navigate the site. Consider the colour palette and style of font you will use to create a brand identity for your artist or band and appeal to the audience.

Images: Plan the photographs you need to take. Music websites usually include a range of different types of image, so use your research as a guide to the pictures you will create.

Text: Draft the written text for your website, using an appropriate mode of address for the genre and your target audience.

Sound and moving images: Plan your audio or audio-visual footage. You should script the dialogue and create a storyboard if you are filming an audio-visual sequence.

Top Tip

You can use a template for your website but you must design the layout yourself, and all of the images, written text and audio-visual material must be your own work.

Component 3: Completing the Cover Sheet and Statement of Aims

You will need to complete a **cover sheet**, which is provided by Eduqas, and submit this with your production for Component 3. The cover sheet is in three sections:

- **Section A**, which you will complete, giving details about your production work and signing an **authentication statement**.
- **Section B**, which you will complete by writing a **Statement of Aims** for your production.
- **Section C**, which your teacher will complete, commenting on your work and noting the marks that they have awarded.

Section A: Details of Your Production

In Section A you will need to include the following information:

- The brief, form and title of your production, for example:

Brief 1 Television; audio-visual sequence; title 'Baxter'

If you are creating a football magazine, for example, research the interests of your target audience.

- Details of the different stages of your production:
  - **Research**: Note the main products that you analysed, your secondary research and audience research. For example:

I analysed Match and Four Four Two – front covers and articles, looked at the online media packs to find out information about the target audiences, and then ran a focus group with students from my school to find out what features of football magazines would appeal to them.

- **Planning**: Note down the main planning tasks that you undertook. For example:

I produced draft designs for my website for a new band, went on a recce to a local park and took practice footage, and then made a mock-up of my webpages and a storyboard for the video sequence (showing a rehearsal and an interview with the band).

- **Production**: Give details of your finished production, including the length or number of pages. For example:

I produced a music video for a song called 'Change' by a local unsigned band. The video is 2 minutes and 15 seconds long. I cut the song down by editing the last verse to fit the time limit.

You will need to sign the cover sheet as you complete each stage to authenticate your work. Your teacher will also sign to confirm that this is your own work.

You will also need to include details of how the following have been used in your work:

- Music, for example the name of a track or song you have used for a music video, or music that you have used in a television sequence. You should note down where you found the music, such as the url of the website.
- Software packages or web templates and how you have used them, for example the editing software you have used for an audio-visual sequence.
- Credits, listing the names of everyone who has helped with your production, by appearing as models or actors, for example, or assisting as crew members.

You must sign the authentication to confirm that the work is your own.

Section B: Statement of Aims

You will complete a short outline of the main ideas for your production, which will form part of the assessment for Component 3.

Key Points about the Statement of Aims

The Statement of Aims will explain to your teacher and, possibly, an Eduqas moderator how you will apply your knowledge and understanding of media language and representation to your production. Your teachers will refer to your Statement of Aims when they assess your production, so make sure that you stick closely to your aims when you construct your practical work.

- It should be approximately 250 words.
- The statement is about **your aims**, so it must be written after you have completed your research and planning but before you begin your production.
- You should show how you will respond to the set brief and apply your knowledge and understanding of media language and representation.
- The statement itself is worth 10 marks.

The template on the cover sheet will help you to structure your Statement

Top Tip

Complete the cover sheet in detail to inform your teachers and the Eduqas moderator about the work you have undertaken.

Top Tip

Your teacher will monitor the progress of your work at each stage. They will offer general guidance and will also check to make sure that the work is your own.

Software packages you have used, such as this editing software, must be listed on your cover sheet.

Top Tip

Make sure you stick to the word limit; you will need to select key examples to show your ideas.

of Aims. You are advised to use evidence from your research into similar products and your target audience to explain your decisions:

- How and why will you apply knowledge and understanding of **media language** to your media production?
- How and why will you construct **representations** of individuals, groups or issues/events?
- How will you target your **intended audience/users**?

Tips for completing the Statement of Aims

- Make sure you discuss in detail how you will respond to the set brief.
- Include findings from your research to show that you are applying your knowledge and understanding.
- Give specific examples of how you will use media language, for example appropriate conventions, and construct representations.
- Explain the methods you will use to target the audience specified in the brief.
- Make sure you give reasons for your decisions.

Examination Preparation

Component 1: Exploring the Media

In the Component 1 exam you will be expected to:

- analyse and compare how media products construct and communicate meanings and generate responses
- use relevant theories or theoretical perspectives and subject-specific terminology
- show knowledge and understanding of media issues
- construct and develop a sustained line of reasoning in an extended response.

Preparing for Component 1, Section A: Exploring Media Language and Representation

Section A assesses your ability to apply your knowledge and understanding of media language and representation in relation to two of the forms that you have studied in this section:

Top Tip

Check the number of marks available for each question and plan your time accordingly. In Component 1, the timings equate to one mark per minute.

- print advertisements
- film posters
- magazine front covers
- newspaper front pages.

There will be two questions in Section A:

Question 1 will assess media language in relation to one of the set products you have studied.

Question 2 will assess context and representation in relation to a different form from that in Question 1.

- Part a will focus on knowledge and understanding of context in one set product.
- Part b will ask you to compare a set product with an unseen product in the same form, for example one of the set magazine front covers and a cover that you have not studied.

It is important to plan your time in the examination, to ensure you are able to complete all of the questions.

Question 1 and Question 2b focus on Assessment Objective 2: 'Analyse media products using the theoretical framework of media, including in relation to their contexts, to make judgements and draw conclusions.'

Question 2a is based on Assessment Objective 1: 'Demonstrate knowledge and understanding of the contexts of media and their influence on media products and processes.'

You are advised to spend approximately 55 minutes on Section A, including 10 minutes to study the unseen print product.

Preparing for Question 1: Media language: analysis of a set product

- You will be able to look at a clean copy of the set product for this question in the exam.
- Make detailed notes on the products when you study them in class and revise these before the exam.
- You will need to apply the knowledge and understanding gained during the course when you answer the question in the exam. However, you should not write everything you know about the product, but focus on the specific points raised in the question.
- Question 1 will always be worth 15 marks, so you should spend approximately 15 minutes answering it. The question might be broken down into parts, and the marks for these can vary.

Sample question: Media language

Question 1 is based on the 1950s advertisement for Quality Street from the set products. Use the advertisement when answering the question.

1. Explore how the advertisement for Quality Street uses the following elements of media language to create meanings:

   (a) images [5 marks]

   (b) language [5 marks]

   (c) layout and design. [5 marks]

This question asks you to focus on three key elements of media language in your answer. There are some suggestions below of points that could be included for each element. These are possible areas to cover and should be discussed in relation to examples from the product:

Images

- The positioning of people and/or objects within the main image and other images on the page.
- The colour palette / range of colours used.
- The dress codes, hair and make-up.
- The setting or location of the images.

Language

- The selection of words and the meanings that these communicate.
- The use of persuasive language, for example in the slogan.
- Specific language techniques such as alliteration, puns or hyperbole.
- Use of formal and/or informal language, complex or specialist terminology.

Layout and design

- The positioning of images, graphics and text on the page.
- The placing of the title, or name of a product. How does this attract the attention of the audience?
- The placement of key images and the messages suggested.
- The size, style and colour of the fonts and the connotations of these.

Marks in the higher band: Media language

These will be awarded for:

- detailed analysis of media language in the set product and how it has been used
- focus throughout the response on the connotations or intended meanings of elements of media language.

You will be assessed on your ability to analyse the product. This means that you should think about the meanings and messages that are communicated, rather than describing the product.

A difference between describing and analysing is, for example:

Describing ✗	The dark-haired man in the middle of the main image is wearing a white shirt with a red tie and a dark blue suit with thin white stripes. He wears a handkerchief in his jacket pocket and is holding a tin of Quality Street sweets.	This description of the male figure is superficially very detailed, but does not consider the meanings communicated by the use of media language in the image.
Analysing ✓	The man in the main image is placed centrally on the page to <u>connote his importance</u>. This is reinforced by the <u>visual codes</u> of his smart dark suit, which suggests he has a <u>professional job</u> and shows that men had <u>more power than women</u> in society in the 1950s.	This analysis of the image applies knowledge and understanding of the theoretical framework by using terminology and discussing the meanings and messages communicated by the media language.

Preparing for Question 2: Representation: comparison of an unseen product and a set product

Question 2a will assess your knowledge and understanding of contexts. It will always be worth 5 marks, so you should spend approximately 5 minutes answering it.

- Aim to show your knowledge and understanding by making key points in direct response to the question.
- Give a brief example from the set product to support each point.

Question 2b will ask you to compare an unseen product with a set product. It will always be worth 25 marks, so you should spend approximately 25 minutes answering it.

This is an extended-response question, so you will need to make judgements and draw conclusions.

In the exam, you will be given a copy of an unseen resource to analyse. You will also be able to look at a clean copy of the set product for this question.

Top Tip

Always consider the connotations of elements of media language that you write about. This will ensure that you are analysing the product and not simply describing it.

Top Tip

Practise analysing the media language in relation to the other set products you have studied. You will need to be prepared to answer questions about any of the areas of media language you have studied.

Top Tip

Remember to revise the contexts of each set product before the exam.

Quickfire 9.4

Which key words in the sample question would you underline to help you to structure your analysis of the products?

Top Tip

When a question asks you to 'compare', you need to explore the similarities and differences between the products.

Top Tip

When a question or bullet point asks 'how far…', you will need to make judgements and draw conclusions. You might decide, for example, that there are more similarities than differences between products.

Tips for preparing your comparison

- You should spend approximately ten minutes studying the unseen print resource and comparing it with the set product before you begin writing your response.
- The unseen resource will be in the same form as the set product, so you will be familiar with the codes and conventions that you need to analyse.
- Make notes as you notice aspects of the unseen product. You will be able to refer to these as you write your response.
- Use the key words in the question, and any bullet points provided, to focus your analysis and structure your answer.
- Consider the ways in which representations are constructed and meanings communicated.
- When you have written your notes on the unseen resource, compare these with the set product. You will be familiar with the set product, so this should not take too long, but you should consider how these products are similar and different.

Sample question: Representation

2. (b) Compare the representation of women in the *Pride* front cover **and** the *Glamour* front cover. [25 marks]

In your answer, you must consider:
- the choices the producers have made about how to represent women
- how far the representation of women is similar in the two front covers
- how far the representation of women is different in the two front covers.

Steven Pan / Glamour © Condé Nast

Activity 9.1

- Make notes about the representation of women on this *Glamour* front cover, considering:
- Visual codes: dress, hair and make-up; gesture codes; use of colour palettes
- Technical codes: shot type (angle and distance), lighting and shadow
- Mode of address
- Language in the cover lines
- Note examples and then analyse the meanings that are communicated, for example considering the connotations of the floral pattern on the dress.
- Spend no more than ten minutes making your notes!
- Now, compare the representations on the *Glamour* cover with the *Pride* cover. Use the list of points above to help you to identify similarities and differences.
- You can use your class notes on *Pride* for this activity, but remember that you will need to revise these for the examination.
- Now write one paragraph summarising the ways in which the representations are similar and a second paragraph outlining how they are different.

The sample question is asking you to analyse the representation of women in the products. Question 2b, however, could be focused on any of the areas of representation you have studied: gender, age, ethnicity, issues or events.

Marks in the higher band: Representation

These will be awarded for:

- excellent, detailed analysis of the set and unseen media products and detailed and appropriate comparisons between the products
- engaging with complex aspects of the representations
- consistent use of the theoretical framework, appropriate use of subject-specific terminology and possible reference to relevant theoretical perspectives
- well-reasoned judgements and conclusions about how far the representation of women is similar and different.

You can demonstrate **detailed analysis** by:

- making a point, for example 'Glamour represents women in a stereotypically feminine way'
- giving a specific example from the product, such as a cover line or visual code to support your point
- considering the connotations or meanings communicated through the representation.

In this question you should also link your key points together, by comparing the set product with the unseen resource.

Top Tip

PEA is a useful way to remind you how to structure your work: Point, Example, Analysis.

Complex aspects of representations include the ways in which:

- an individual or group might be misrepresented
- representations demonstrate a point of view and communicate messages and values
- representations reflect the context in which they were produced.

How can I demonstrate that I am using the theoretical framework?

- Discuss how representations are constructed, for example by selection and combination of elements of media language.
- Analyse how and why stereotypes may be used, or deliberately subverted.
- Use appropriate subject-specific terminology.
- Refer to theoretical viewpoints, such as mediation or feminist perspectives.

What are well-reasoned judgements and conclusions?

- Points that are supported by appropriate examples.
- Judgements that are logical and show understanding of the theoretical framework. In response to the sample question you might judge, for example, that:
  - Glamour, a mainstream lifestyle magazine targeting a large audience, constructs stereotypical representations of women through the cover lines about fashion and beauty, and the visual codes such as pastels, floral images and high-key lighting.

- *Pride*, a niche lifestyle magazine targeting a specialised audience, represents some stereotypically feminine interests but focuses on more serious issues and communicates a feminist message through the cover lines and dominant stance of the cover model.
- Conclusions that are consistent with points made in the answer. If you have discussed many ways in which the products are similar, it would not make sense if your conclusion then stated that they were very different.

Structuring an extended response

Question 2b requires an extended response, where you need to develop a line of reasoning. This means that your ideas should link together and you should draw logical conclusions. It is important that you should structure your answer carefully. A possible approach would be:

- Write a brief introduction to outline the key points you will cover. Make sure these ideas link to the question.
- Organise the main body of your response around the bullet points in the question.
- Write in paragraphs of continuous prose, using one paragraph to explore each key point or idea. Avoid note form or bullet points.
- Start each paragraph with a 'signpost sentence': refer to the wording of the question and link to the previous paragraph if possible.
- Provide a summary with your conclusions at the end. Consider the 'how far' part of the question.
- Remember to include subject-specific terminology.

Top Tip

Practise writing a plan for responses to sample questions. You could begin by planning an answer to the sample 2b question, above. Include an introduction, an outline of the key paragraphs and the conclusion.

Essay Plan	
Question:	
Introduction	
Paragraph 1	**Key point:** **Example:** **Analysis:**
Paragraph 2	**Key point:** **Example:** **Analysis:**
Paragraph 3	**Key point:** **Example:** **Analysis:**
Conclusion	

Preparing for Component 1, Section B: Exploring Media Industries and Audiences

Section B assesses your knowledge and understanding of media industries and audiences in relation to the following forms:

- newspapers
- radio
- video games
- film (industries only).

There will be two questions in Section B:

- **Question 3** will be a stepped question that will focus on knowledge and understanding of media industries in relation to one of the forms you have studied.
- **Question 4** will be a stepped question assessing your knowledge and understanding of audiences in relation to a different media form from that in Question 3.

Questions in Section B will focus on Assessment Objective 1: 'Demonstrate knowledge and understanding of the theoretical framework of media.'

You are advised to spend approximately 35 minutes on Section B.

The questions will be broken down into several steps, so it is very important that you check the number of marks for each question and manage your time accordingly.

There are no unseen resources in Section B. You will be asked to refer to the set products you have studied, but you do not need to analyse the media language or representations in detail.

Sample questions

Media industries

> 3. (a) Name the organisation that regulates films in Britain.   [1 mark]

Age Ratings You Trust

This question has only one mark and there is one correct answer. You could write this in full: the *British Board of Film Classification*, or use the common abbreviation: the *BBFC*.

Top Tip

Read the question very carefully and make sure you give the correct information or number of examples.

> 3. (b) 12 and 12A are examples of age certificates used in the UK. Give **two other** examples of age certificates used in the UK.   [2 marks]

This question has a number of correct answers and you need to state **two** of the following to achieve two marks: U, PG, 15, 18, R18.

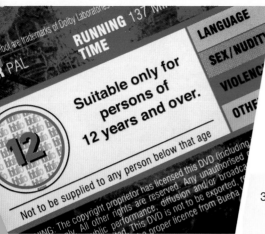

3. (c) Briefly explain the difference between the **12** and **12A** age certificates. [2 marks]

This question has only two marks, which is why you are asked to **briefly** explain.

You must show your understanding of **both** age certificates in order to achieve two marks, for example:

- The 12 certificate is for video works (including films released on DVD/Blu-ray) for home viewing. No one under the age of 12 can rent or buy a 12-certificate film.

- The 12A certificate is for films shown in cinemas. Children under 12 must be accompanied by an adult to watch a 12A certificate film at the cinema.

3. (d) Explain why a film may be given a 12A or 12 certificate.
Refer to *Spectre to* support your points. [12 marks]

This question carries 12 marks, so you need to develop your answer by giving detail and examples.

You will be expected to show knowledge and understanding of film regulation, for example:

- the role of the BBFC as the film regulator in the UK
  - the functions of regulation, for example to protect audiences (especially younger viewers) from harmful or offensive material
  - the difference between the different age certificates, such as 12/12A and 15, and why these might be awarded.

You will also need to give examples from your study of *Spectre* to support the points you make, for example:

- The BBFC considers specific factors to decide on an age rating, including language and violence. The BBFC rated *Spectre* as a 12A as it contains 'moderate violence and threat'.

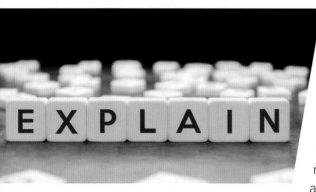

- Film distributors will have a desired age rating in order to attract the target audience. The BBFC will advise about certification if an unfinished version of the film is submitted in advance. This happened with *Spectre*. The BBFC advised that it was likely to be rated as a 15, and producers would need to make cuts to violent scenes for the film to have a 12A certificate.

- Cuts were made to *Spectre* to achieve the 12A, which was important in enabling the film to reach a wide global audience as possible and increase the chances of commercial success.

Audiences

 Quickfire 9.5

Answer sample question 4a: Which radio station broadcasts *The Archers*?

> 4. (a) Which radio station broadcasts *The Archers*? [1 mark]
> 4. (b) Identify **one** audience for *The Archers*. [1 mark]

There are a number of possible answers to 4b, for example:

• older audiences

• people from a high socio-economic group (ABC1s)

• soap opera fans.

You need to give **one** suggestion. There is no need to explain your answer further here.

> 4. (c) Explain **two** ways in which *The Archers* is aimed at **the audience you have identified**. [4 marks]

This time you will need to give more detail about your choice of audience. Possible areas you could include:

• It is a long-running programme dating back to the 1950s, so older audiences might have been listening for a long period of time. The older 'star' characters and rural setting also suggest that it is aimed at older listeners.

• There are many middle-class characters, such as the Aldridges, which suggests audiences from a similar background are being targeted, and issues related to farming, rural affairs and the environment might also appeal to this demographic.

💡 **Top Tip**

Read all of the questions in a section before you begin to respond, as they might relate to each other, as sample question 4c develops from 4b.

• It is aimed at soap opera fans as there are many familiar genre conventions such as multi-stranded narratives based around family and relationships, and familiar character types. The programme is in 'real time' to mirror people's lives, which will also appeal to fans of the soap genre.

> 4. (d) Explain why audiences listen to *The Archers*. Refer to the Uses and Gratifications theory in your response. [12 marks]

🎯 **Quickfire 9.6**

What is the other named theory that could feature in an exam question?

In Question 4d, you will be rewarded for drawing together knowledge and understanding from across your full course of study, including different areas of the theoretical framework and media contexts.

The question asks you to use the Uses and Gratifications theory, so you must refer to this in your response.

Activity 9.2

Apply the Uses and Gratifications theory to *The Archers*. Use this table to organise your ideas. Make sure you support points with examples.

Then write up your notes as a response to sample question 4b.

Uses and gratifications	Example from *The Archers*	How does this explain why audiences listen to the programme?
Information		
Entertainment		
Personal identity		
Social interaction	*Facebook and Twitter comments after Matt's hit-and-run*	*Pleasures of sharing responses with others and the possibility of these being used on the official website make people feel involved with the programme.*

Stretch and Challenge 9.3

Complete a Uses and Gratifications table for the set newspaper and the set video game.

Marks in the higher band: Audiences

These will be awarded for:

- demonstrating detailed and accurate knowledge of audiences in relation to *The Archers*
- showing thorough understanding of audiences and why they use the set product
- making detailed and accurate reference to the Uses and Gratifications theory and using subject-specific terminology.

Drawing together knowledge and understanding

Question 4d also offers you the chance to draw together your knowledge and understanding from different areas of the course. You could do this by referring to different areas of the theoretical framework and media contexts, for example:

- **Contexts**: The historical context of *The Archers* as the world's longest-running radio soap opera and its social and cultural relevance. Audiences might have 'grown up' with the programme and/or might identify with the social issues represented.
- **Media language** such as:
- Narrative: ongoing storylines, multi-stranded narratives and 'real time' narrative construction.
- Genre: There are many familiar conventions of radio soap operas, but the programme has developed over time, introducing aspects of variation such as younger characters and more controversial contemporary social issues including domestic abuse.
- **Media industries**: The BBC as a public service broadcaster; the use of digital technology to reach new listeners and maintain the loyal audience.

Component 2: Understanding Media Forms and Products

In the Component 2 exam you will be expected to:

- analyse and compare how media products construct and communicate meanings and generate responses
- use relevant theoretical perspectives and subject-specific terminology
- show knowledge and understanding of media issues
- construct and develop a sustained line of reasoning in an extended response.

Preparing for Component 2, Section A: Television

You will answer two questions on the topic you have studied, either crime drama or sitcom.

Question 1 will assess either media language or representations based on the extract from the set product that you have studied.

- Part a will require you to analyse media products.
- Part b will assess your ability to analyse, make judgements and draw conclusions.

Question 1 will address Assessment Objective 2: 'Analyse media products using the theoretical framework of media, including in relation to their contexts. Make judgements and draw conclusions.'

Question 2 will focus on knowledge and understanding of media industries, audiences or contexts in relation to the set products. It will focus on Assessment Objective 1: 'Demonstrate knowledge and understanding of:

- the theoretical framework of media
- contexts of media and their influence on media products and processes.'

You are advised to spend approximately 50 minutes on Section A, including viewing the extract from the set product.

Preparing for Question 1: analysis of an extract from a set product

Question 1 will be based on an extract from the set product you have studied, either *Luther* (crime drama) or *The IT Crowd* (sitcom).

- You will be given two minutes to read the questions in Section A.
- The extract will be shown twice.
- First viewing: watch the extract and make notes.
- You will then have six minutes to make further notes.
- Second viewing: watch the extract and make further notes before you answer Question 1.

You will be familiar with the extract, having studied the product in class. In the exam, you will need to focus on the specific areas raised in the question when you analyse the extract.

Making appropriate notes

When you watch the extract, you should make notes that will help you to answer Question 1:

- Use the time at the beginning of the exam to read the question as this will identify the areas you need to focus on when you watch the extract.
- Make detailed notes, as you will only view the extract twice and will need to refer to your notes in the exam.
- Use the question to focus your analysis. Avoid trying to note down everything you see. A grid, such as the one shown below, can structure your notes.
- During the first viewing make sure you also watch and listen carefully so that you do not miss important information.
- You should note down specific examples as you watch, but also consider why these have been used: what meanings or messages are communicated?
- The time between viewings is useful for analysing the examples in more detail. This will help you to avoid simply describing the sequence in your response.
- The second viewing should be used to identify additional examples and detail.

Sample questions: Media language

> 1. (a) View the extract from **either** Luther (crime drama) **or** The IT Crowd (sitcom).
>   Explore the connotations of the costume of two characters in the extract.   [8 marks]
>
> The extracts used in the sample question are: Luther: the scene between Luther and Alice on the bridge (approximate timings: 45.30–48.30); The IT Crowd: the scene between Moss and Prime in the Countdown green room (approximate timings: 05.30–06.55).

This question requires detailed analysis of one element of media language: use of costume.

This grid shows how you could structure your note-making. This will focus your analysis on the specific element of media language – and allow you to explore particular connotations. It includes examples of points that could be made when answering the question.

	Examples of costume: Give detail.	**Analysis: what does costume connote about the character, for example are they:** • Fashionable, style conscious? • Smart, concerned about appearance? • Reflecting a particular occupation or status?
Luther	• Luther's shirt and tie • Top button undone, tie loose	• Connotes status and position as a detective • Also a maverick, who doesn't always follow the rules
	Alice's smart, buttoned-up dark jacket, trousers and boots	• Connotes that she is professional – and perhaps hints at her dark nature and ruthlessness
The IT Crowd	Moss's brown corduroy trousers, checked shirt, patterned tie, neutral colour palette	• Not concerned about appearance or fashion • Connotes occupation – IT stereotypically 'dull' job
	Prime's long black velvet coat, dark sunglasses, buckled biker boots	• Black connotes mystery; long coat and sunglasses conceal his identity • Possible threat/disruptive force, high status

1. (b) How far are the characters in the extract typical of the genre?
   Explore two characters.   [12 marks]

Part b asks you to focus on the characters in the extract and to make judgements and draw conclusions about how they are typical of the genre. It would be sensible to use the same characters for both parts of the question.

You will need to make notes about other elements of character construction when you watch the extract, such as their actions, gestures and expressions and use of language. You will then need to apply your knowledge and understanding of the genre by considering whether each character is typical of crime drama or sitcom.

Marks in the higher band: Characters
These will be awarded for:

- detailed analysis of the chosen characters and the ways in which they are typical of the genre.
- appropriate judgements and conclusions about 'how far' the character is typical of the genre.

You might argue that the characters are very typical of the genre, or that they are not, but the points you make must be accurate and supported by examples.

Some examples points you might make
Luther
At the beginning of the extract Luther is not wearing his wedding ring, but says that he loves his wife and warns Alice to stay away from her. This is typical of the crime genre as the detective is 'flawed', potentially vulnerable and has a complicated private life.

Alice taunts Luther about the crime in the extract, as she has made sure there is no evidence that would convict her. This is less typical of the genre as the she is extremely intelligent and manipulative, which challenges the stereotype of the female victim that is more typical in crime dramas.

The IT Crowd
In the extract, Moss appears to be naïve as he does not seem to understand Prime's jokes, such as 'I like a man with appetite' as Moss eats the biscuit. This is typical of the genre as Moss is quite an 'innocent' character and acts as a foil to Prime.

Prime appears as a disruptive force in this extract. He seems out of place in the setting and changes the direction of the narrative as he gives Moss the business card for the 8+ Club. This is also typical of the genre, as sitcoms do not need to stick to codes of realism.

Top Tip

If you are asked to write about two characters, make sure you divide your time between them as you will be awarded marks for each character.

Top Tip

Remember to focus on the extract shown in the exam in Question 1.

Benedict Wong as Prime in the set episode of *The IT Crowd*.

Top Tip

Remember, Question 2 could assess contexts or media industries or audiences.

Sample question: Contexts

2. How do crime dramas or sitcoms reflect the time in which they are made? Refer to examples you have studied to support your response. [10 marks]

This example is assessing your knowledge and understanding of **contexts** and how these influence the set products.

You will need to discuss both set products here: the older example and the contemporary text. The question does not ask you to compare the set products, but it might be helpful to consider the differences between them as a way of explaining how they are influenced by the contexts in which they were produced.

You should consider how the set products link to their contexts in relation to some of the following aspects:

- **Media language**, for example:
  - technology's impact on media language, in, for example, the special effects that are achievable at a particular time
  - how the genre has developed over time, for example in response to social changes.

- **Representations**: how these reflect society at the time a product is made, for example:
  - gender roles or representations of ethnicity
  - stereotypes that are also influenced by the context.

- **Themes**: the issues and ideas explored in a product often reflect society at the time in which it is made, and specific events (for example, the 9/11 attacks or the EU referendum) might also influence media products.

- **Messages and values**: attitudes in society change over time, and certain values that might have been accepted as the 'norm' in the past can become less acceptable in contemporary life. Many attitudes relating to age, gender and ethnicity, for example, have changed over time.

Top Tip

Remember to refer directly to the set products to support the points you make. This question assesses AO1, so you do not need to analyse media language and representations in detail.

Specific events, such as Russia's conflict with Ukraine, or the 9/11 attacks, might influence media products.

Some example points you might make
Crime drama

- *The Sweeney* reflects 1970s values in relation to gender roles in the workplace. The Flying Squad is male-dominated, patriarchal and characterised by a macho culture of drinking and violence. This reflects gender roles in society at the time, particularly within the police force, where women even had a different rank structure from men.

- *Luther* reflects the diversity of contemporary British society in the representation of Luther as a high-ranking black police officer, communicating a message about racial equality.

Sitcom

- *Friends* reflects 1990s values in relation to gender. For example, the male characters demonstrate traits of the 'new man' through their close male friendships, reflecting a move towards less fixed and traditional ideas of masculinity.

- The narrative of the set episode of *The IT Crowd* reflects contemporary themes linked to identity through the focus on 'reinvention'. Roy's concerns that his apparently more successful college friend looks down on him reflect the competitive nature of society and male insecurities.

 Top Tip

You will not be shown an extract from the set products in Section B, so you will need to revise all areas of the theoretical framework for the exam.

Preparing for Component 2, Section B: Music (Music Videos and Online Media)

You will be required to answer questions on the set products you have studied, as detailed in Chapter 5. There will be no extract or other materials to view in Section B.

Question 3 will assess either media language or representations in the set products you have studied. This question will require an extended response. It addresses Assessment Objective 2: 'Analyse media products using the theoretical framework of media, including in relation to their contexts. Make judgements and draw conclusions.'

Question 4 will focus on knowledge and understanding of media industries, audiences or contexts in the set products. It will focus on Assessment Objective 1: 'Demonstrate knowledge and understanding of:

- the theoretical framework of media
- contexts of media and their influence on media products and processes.'

You are advised to spend approximately 40 minutes on Section B.

Revision tips

You will need to be able to make detailed analysis of media language or representations in Question 3. You will also need to refer to examples from the products to support points about audience, media industries or contexts in Question 4.

Aim to retain thorough knowledge of key examples from the set products that can be used in relation to any area of the framework, for example this still from the end of 'Roar' by Katy Perry:

- **Media language**: Narrative resolution. The crashed plane is now her home and the animals are tamed: all is calm and in balance. The bright colour palette and lighting (sunrise) connote positivity and the idea of a 'fresh start'.

- **Contexts**: There is an intertextual reference to *Tarzan* (cultural context), although Perry is queen of the jungle, reflecting greater gender equality in society (social context).

- **Media industries**: The high production values and use of CGI signify that this is a high-budget video, typical of a successful mainstream pop star signed to a major label.

- **Audiences**: The empowering message and positive resolution will appeal to a wide audience. Younger females in particular might look up to Perry as a role model.

- **Representation**: Katy Perry is central in the frame, stretching her arms. She is constructed as a strong, independent female in control of her own life and not reliant on a male. She wears an animal-print bikini top and a skirt made of leaves, connoting that she has adapted to her surroundings, but these clothes are also quite revealing and arguably objectify her.

Top Tip

Select five or six examples from each set product you have studied (music videos and websites) and make notes on each of the different areas of the theoretical framework.

Sample question: Representations

Use the **two** set music videos you have studied in your answer to Question 3:

'Roar', Katy Perry **or** 'Bad Blood', Taylor Swift **and** 'Freedom', Pharrell Williams **or** 'Uptown Funk', Mark Ronson and Bruno Mars.

3. 'Music videos reinforce stereotypes of ethnicity.' How far is this true of the two music videos you have studied? [20 marks]

In your response, you must:

- **explore** representations of ethnicity in **both** music videos
- refer to relevant **contexts**, such as social or cultural
- consider whether you **agree** or **disagree** with the statement.

The question will always allow you to use set products that you have studied. In this example, you will need to discuss the two contemporary videos.

You will need to focus on representations of ethnicity and apply your knowledge and understanding of stereotyping in your answer.

Focus your response on specific points and address each of these in your answer:

- **Explore**: You must analyse how representations of ethnicity are constructed, for example through the choices made by media producers and elements of media language that are selected and combined. In this question, you need to consider the extent to which the representations reinforce stereotypes of ethnicity.
- **Contexts**: Consider how the representations of ethnicity relate to social, cultural or other contexts.
- **Agree or disagree**: Make judgements and draw conclusions about the statement in the question.

Some example points you could make
'Freedom'
There are representations that relate to historical contexts of slavery, for example multiple shots from different angles of black workers breaking rocks, under the control of an aggressive white man. This reinforces messages about the oppression of ethnic minority groups that are still relevant today.

'Uptown Funk'
There is some subversion of stereotypes, for example the white male as the 'shoeshine' man, a lower-status role stereotypically given to a black male in other media texts. Here, the white male is subservient, which shows that some stereotypes are not reinforced and reflects a more contemporary social context.

'Roar'
The white male who survives the plane crash is constructed to be stereotypically arrogant and lacking the skills to cope in the jungle, reinforced by the vain 'selfie' shot and attack by the tiger.

'Bad Blood'
Taylor Swift and Kendrick Lamar are stereotypically constructed as binary opposites: Swift as a stereotypical blonde, slender white female singer and Lamar as black male rap musician, wearing black clothing, sunglasses and driving a powerful car.

Top Tip
Take a few moments to read the question carefully and plan your response, using these bullet points as a guide.

Stretch and Challenge 9.4
Always consider the way in which representations communicate messages and values.

Quickfire 9.7
What must you do in order to address the 'how far…' part of the question?

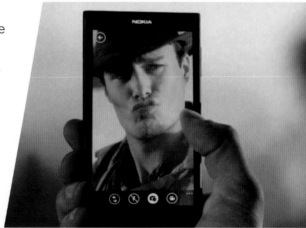

Sample question: Media industries

4. Explain why music websites are important to the music industry. Refer to the official Katy Perry website or the official Taylor Swift website to support your response.

[10 marks]

This example of Question 4 is assessing your knowledge and understanding of **media industries** and the importance of media technologies in the form of websites. You should refer to the set product throughout your answer to support the points you make.

Areas to consider

- Media production in relation to ownership, for example mainstream music labels and conglomerate ownership
- The importance of new digital technologies, for example:
  - Convergence: how websites bring together different types of media product in one place
  - Synergy with other media forms such as film and television
  - Online media platforms that allow organisations to market and distribute products to large, global audiences
  - Website links to social media tools that reach and engage audiences, especially younger audiences
  - Online stores that allow fans to purchase merchandise and digital content
  - Websites that help to establish the brand identity of the artist and can be updated/rebranded to tie in with their latest release. The visual branding can be reinforced across other media products, such as albums, singles and digital artwork on music streaming sites.

WATCH: DELICATE MUSIC VIDEO DANCE REHEARSALS

Mar 13, 2018

Taylor just shared dance rehearsal footage from the 'Delicate' music video! Watch them below.

Read Full Article

Mar 12, 2018

Mar 12, 2018

Mar 11, 2018

MUSICAL.LY CHALLENGE: POST A #TAYLORSWIFTDELICATE VIDEO FOR THE CHANCE TO BE FEATURED ON TAYLOR NATION

Calling all Swifties! Post a funny video in a mirror using

WATCH: OFFICIAL "DELICATE" MUSIC VIDEO OUT NOW

The official music video for 'Delicate' is out now after premiering at the 2018 iHeart Radio Music Awards.

Quick Guide to Theoretical Perspectives

This chapter offers a quick overview of the theoretical perspectives you need to study according to the course specification, including two named theories: Propp's theory of narrative and Blumler and Katz's Uses and Gratifications theory. These are discussed in relation to examples of media products in Chapter 3.

You need to be able to demonstrate knowledge and understanding of these theoretical perspectives. You should do this by applying the ideas to the media products that you study, rather than simply describing a theory or perspective.

The following is a summary of the key areas of each of these theoretical perspectives, but you might study other ideas and theories as well.

Media Language

Genre

Theoretical perspectives on genre

These include principles of repetition and variation; the dynamic nature of genre; and hybridity and intertextuality (these ideas make reference to Steve Neale's theory):

- The idea that products from the same genre will have similarities and differences, offering audiences familiar elements along with new or unexpected elements. This pattern of repetition and variation appeals to audiences and helps to guarantee the success of a product for media producers.
- The idea that genres are not fixed or static:
  - Genres change and develop over time, for example in relation to social and cultural contexts and in response to technological developments.
  - Genres are fluid and do not have clear boundaries: elements of different genres might combine to form hybrids; genres can be divided into subgenres; one product might intertextually reference another to communicate meaning and provide gratification to audiences.

Narrative

You will come across several theories of narrative, including those derived from Vladimir Propp.

Named theory: Propp's theory of narrative

Propp's theory (taken from his book *The Morphology of the Folktale*, 1928) relates to key stages that occur in narratives and key character roles within the narrative. When you consider Propp's theory in relation to the set products, focus on which of the character roles might be applied. Remember that not all of Propp's character types can be applied to every contemporary media product.

Note that, according to Propp:

- There are key stages to narratives, for example the hero being dispatched on a quest.
- Central characters fulfil key roles within the narrative: hero, villain, 'princess', father, donor, helper, dispatcher, false hero.

Most traditional tales follow a linear narrative.

Narrative construction, structures, techniques and conventions

You will study products with different narrative forms:

- Linear narrative: a simple, logical structure with a beginning, middle and end.
- The construction of equilibrium, followed by disruption and then resolution or a new equilibrium. (This is Todorov's theory.)
- Non-linear narrative, for example a structure that moves backwards and forwards in time, or a circular narrative.
- Use of enigma codes to engage and involve the audience. (This is Barthes' theory.)
- Binary oppositions. (This is Lévi-Strauss's theory.)

Representation

Theoretical Perspectives on Representation

These include processes of selection, construction and mediation, with ideas that:

- Representations are constructed by media producers: individuals, social groups, issues and events are re-presented to audiences, not simply presented. (These ideas make reference to David Buckingham's theory.)
- Elements of media language are deliberately selected and combined to construct representations. (Consider what has been included and what has been excluded, and why.)
- All media products are mediated by producers for a specific purpose, conveying viewpoints, messages, values and beliefs.
- Stereotypes might be reinforced or subverted.

Theoretical perspectives on gender and representation, including feminist approaches

- The idea that the media takes part in the discrimination against women in society. This can be linked to the lack of opportunities for women in the media industries.
- Women are under-represented or often absent in the media.
- Women tend to be represented as objects rather than active subjects in the media (this makes reference to Laura Mulvey's Male Gaze theory).

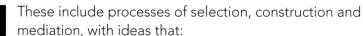

When you analyse a visual media product, consider whose 'gaze' the audience is positioned to have.

Audience

Theoretical Perspectives on Audiences

These include theories on active and passive audiences; audience responses and audience interpretations.

- The passive audience: This argument claims that the audience is a 'mass', rather than individuals, that passively consumes the media and accepts the messages in media products.

- The effects debate: Whether the audience's attitudes and behaviour are affected by the media.

- The active audience: Audiences are made up of individuals who actively select their media products and engage with them, interpreting the media in different ways. This links to interactivity and the opportunities that audiences have to create user-generated media content.

- Audience response: How audiences can interpret the same media products in different ways, and the factors affecting audience interpretations including their own experiences and beliefs, social and individual differences.

- Different kinds of response, for example preferred/negotiated/oppositional readings. (This is Stuart Hall's reception theory.)

Named theory: Blumler and Katz's Uses and Gratifications theory

Blumler and Katz developed this active audience theory in 1974. The theory argues that audiences select media products to consume in order to fulfil particular needs or gratifications, the four main ones being:

- information
- personal identity
- social interaction
- entertainment.

The theory includes ideas that:

- people can use the same media product for different purposes.
- people's individual needs, as well as factors such as their social background, will influence how they engage with and respond to media products.

Glossary

Abstract concept
An idea, such as beauty or happiness, rather than a physical object or something that exists.

Active audience
People who make deliberate choices about the media products they consume, and actively respond by, for example, agreeing or disagreeing with the messages in them.

Active subject
A character who makes things happen and moves the narrative forward.

Advertising campaign
An organised advertising strategy, possibly using a range of different media platforms, to achieve a specific purpose, such as a series of adverts to launch a new perfume or a sequence of adverts for a department store in the lead up to Christmas.

Alliteration
Where several words in a phrase or sentence begin with the same letter or sound to add emphasis.

Analyse
Explore media texts critically, considering the messages that are communicated.

Antagonist
A character who is in opposition to the protagonist; also the villain in many products.

Anti-establishment beliefs
Ideas that challenge authority or go against the accepted 'norms' in society.

Appeal
The element of a product that attracts a particular audience. (There are different ways in which a product can appeal to the audience, for example by using a star persona or familiar genre conventions.)

Aspiration
The desire for a higher level of success or material wealth. Adverts often create aspirational lifestyles, such as a really clean and tidy home or a sophisticated party.

Audio-visual products
Products that have moving images and sound, for example music videos.

Augmented reality
A form of technology that allows pictures of virtual objects to be overlaid onto images of the real world, for example on a mobile phone screen.

Authentication statement
A signed declaration that the Statement of Aims and production are your own, original work. This is a formal requirement that every learner has to complete.

Avid fans
Audiences who are dedicated supporters of a film franchise. They are likely to engage in much social interaction, for example discussing the film, buying merchandise and sharing information on social media.

Baby boomer
A person born just after the Second World War (between 1945 and 1960), when there was a big increase in the population as men returned from the war and couples began to have children.

Banner adverts
Adverts that appear in rectangular boxes on webpages. They usually relate to the content of the website. Clicking on the banner takes the user to the advertiser's website. This type of advertising can benefit both the magazine and the advertiser, similar to advertising in a print publication.

Billing block
The list of the main cast and crew members, such as star actors and director.

Binary oppositions
Pairs of 'opposites' (characters or abstract ideas) that come into conflict within a narrative. The outcome of the conflict can communicate messages, for example that the hero 'should' defeat the villain and restore equilibrium.

Binge-watching
Consuming multiple episodes of a television series at once.

Blockbuster
A major film release, usually a high-budget mainstream Hollywood film that appeals to a wide audience and achieves box office success. The term was used to describe films such as *Jaws* and *Star Wars* in the 1970s, when audiences queued around the block to the cinema.

Blurb
A brief outline of a creative product to hook an audience and encourage them to engage.

BPI
The British Phonographic Institute, a trade organisation that represents the British recorded music industry. The BPI organises the annual BRIT Awards and Mercury Prize.

Brand
The name of a product or the manufacturer of the product, established through a trademark or logo that is recognisable to an audience, such as Heinz, BT, Reebok.

Brand identity
The image of a particular product or company, and the values associated with it. (The Asda brand is associated with good value for money, reinforced by the 'Asda Price Guarantee' that features in
advertising and on displays in store and so on.)

Brief
The production task (set by Eduqas), including details of all the elements you need to include. (All learners following the Eduqas specification will complete one of the set briefs for the year in which they are assessed.)

Broadsheet
A newspaper in large format; also refers to the 'quality' press, the more formal newspapers such as the *Times*.

Categorise
The way media organisations divide an audience so that they can target their products at specific groups.

Cause and effect
Where one event causes another event to happen, such as a robbery causing the victim to have nightmares.

Circulation
The number of copies of a magazine or newspaper issue sold. The readership is the number of people who read each issue, which is usually higher than the circulation.

Cliff-hanger
A structural device where the narrative is paused at a tense or exciting moment, which encourages the audience to watch the next episode.

Climax
A point of high tension or action, for example a confrontation between the hero and villain. A narrative will usually build to a climax over a period of time and the outcome will often provide a resolution, for example the hero defeats the villain.

Codes and conventions
The expected elements that will be included in products from particular media forms and genres.

Column
A regular short article in a newspaper, where a writer – often a celebrity – offers their opinions. Some are specific to a topic, for example a television review column, while others are more general and discuss a range of issues.

Conflict
A clash between two characters or groups of people.

Connote
The way in which a sign communicates underlying meanings. (An image of a rose might connote romance.)

Construct
Put elements together to create a media product.

Consumerist messages
Ideas that it is necessary to buy products and other goods, usually to achieve a particular lifestyle.

Consumer goods
Physical products for purchasing, such as food, cars and cosmetics.

Consumption
The way in which the audience 'takes in' the media product, for example watching television or playing a video game.

Contemporary
Current, of today: products that have been produced in recent years.

Contexts
The background factors that can influence a media product, for example the historical situation. These help us to understand the meanings and messages in a product.

Continuity editing
Putting shots together so that the cutting seems 'invisible' and the sequence looks natural to the viewer.

Convergence
The way in which products or brands are made available to audiences on a number of platforms. (*The Archers* is broadcast on radio, but listeners can also download episodes, and the website offers additional content to engage the audience.)

Copy
The written text in a printed publication.

Copyright
A legal right that protects a piece of creative work from being copied or used by other people.

Cover lines
The short 'headlines' on a magazine cover that give readers a brief insight into the content of the articles.

Cover sheet
A document that must be submitted with your production to provide information to the moderator and confirm that this is your own, original work.

Crane

A camera mount that can move upwards to give a high-angled view of a location. This type of movement might be used at the end of a scene to move the action from one location to another.

Crisis of masculinity

The idea that males suffered uncertainties of identity as women gained more power in society. It can also be linked to a decline in typically masculine jobs in manufacturing.

Current affairs

Programmes, or other media, that explore topical issues or events in detail.

Decode

Audiences interpret encoded messages. They might or might not decode the messages in the way the producers intended.

Demographic

The profile of an audience based on factors such as their age, gender and socioeconomic group.

Dialect

Language specific to a particular part of the country. A dialect will include words and phrases that are not generally used in 'mainstream' English.

Dialogue

The words spoken by characters in a scene, usually a conversation between two or more characters.

Direct mode of address

Where the product seems to speak directly to the audience, for example by using personal pronouns such as 'we' or 'you'.

Discrimination

In this context, discrimination refers to offensive content in a media product, for example about gender, race or religion.

Discursive writing

Writing that develops an argument, makes judgements about a question and draws conclusions.

Disruption

An event or action that interrupts the narrative.

Distribution and circulation

The way in which the product is delivered to different audiences.

Distributor

The company that markets the film and organises the distribution of the film to cinemas and for DVD release.

Dolly

A platform with wheels that usually runs along a track. The camera is mounted onto the platform and can be wheeled smoothly along the track to capture the action.

Editorial process

Newspaper articles are carefully checked before publication to ensure that they conform to the required standards and contain accurate information.

Effects debate

The idea that media products might have a negative influence on an audience's behaviour.

Elite person

A celebrity or person of high status that will appeal to target readers.

Emotive language

Descriptive language that aims to generate an emotional response, such as sympathy for a character or shock at a news item.

Encode

Media producers include messages when creating products. These might be encoded through specific language or images.

Engage

Keep an audience's interest and involvement and, potentially, gain their loyalty. (A television drama series will try to engage the audience in the narrative and ensure that they watch every episode.)

Enigma code

A mystery or puzzle. Media products often don't tell all elements of the narrative at once, but withhold information to keep the audience guessing.

Ensemble cast

A group of actors who have an equal role in the production: there is no main protagonist or star.

Equilibrium

A situation where everything is calm and settled; there is no conflict.

Event television

A 'must-see' programme that attracts a very large audience and generates a lot of discussion in the media. These programmes are usually marketed heavily to generate a 'buzz' before broadcast.

Exclamatives

Words or phrases that 'shout out' to the reader, often using an exclamation mark for emphasis. The intended effect might be to shock or surprise the reader.

Exhibition

The showing of the film in cinemas and on other platforms such as television and online.

Extended response

A longer exam answer where you will need to make judgements and draw conclusions.

Familiar conventions
Elements that we would expect to see in a particular genre. (A convention of a television soap opera is the setting of a pub where characters regularly meet.)

Feminist movement
The move towards women gaining equal rights in society. The 1960s was a particularly significant period when many campaigns and new laws gave women more equal rights and greater freedoms.

Femininity
The attributes that are typically associated with being a female.

Femme fatale
A mysterious and dangerous female character who uses her sexuality to exert power over male characters.

Filler lights
Additional lights placed around a person or object to reduce shadows.

Film noir
A genre that emerged during the 1940s and 50s in which narratives focus on crime and stylish visual conventions include low-key lighting. Character types include the world-weary detective and the femme fatale.

Final girl
A central female character in a horror film who is 'good' – hardworking, responsible, innocent – and survives at the end.

Flashback
A scene where the narrative jumps back in time to show a past event.

Flashforward
A scene where the narrative jumps forwards in time to show a future event.

Foreground and background
The foreground relates the front of an image, the part that appears closest to the audience. This usually has prominence, so what is placed here has greater importance than the background, the part that appears to be further away from the viewer.

Formal language
Using an indirect mode of address and possibly more complex vocabulary. (A broadsheet newspaper is likely to use more formal language than a tabloid.)

Forms
The different types of media, for example television and advertising.

Franchise
A series of films based on an original idea or an adaptation of, for example, a book. Recent examples include the *Star Wars*, Harry Potter and *Lord of the Rings* films.

Gatekeepers
The people who decide which stories to include in the newspaper. Journalists have access to news stories from a variety of sources and newspaper editors need to 'filter' the information and select the stories to feature in the publication.

Generation X
The name given to people born in the 1970s and 1980s, after the 'baby boomers' and before the 'millennials'.

Genre
A category of media product defined by a set of codes and conventions, for example news or comedy.

Gratifications
Pleasures that audiences gain from consuming media products.

Grey pound
A term used to describe the disposable income that older people have to spend on items for themselves, such as holidays.

Handheld camera
A camera not mounted on a tripod or dolly, but held by the camera operator. Handheld camera shots tend to be shakier but can create a sense of realism, immersing the audience in the action. Some documentaries use handheld camera shots.

Hard news
Serious news stories that have national or international importance. Topics such as politics and the economy would be considered hard news.

High-concept
Emphasis on a striking but easily communicable central premise or idea, designed to have wide audience appeal.

Horizontally integrated
The structure of a large media organisation which owns companies that produce the same type of media product.

House style
The consistent use of elements such as colour, design, typeface and language to create a clear brand identity for a product.

Hybrid
A combination of two or more different genres in the same product.

Hyperbole
Exaggerated language to create emphasis.

Hypermasculinity
Exaggerated masculinity, for example extreme strength, aggression or 'macho' behaviour that is sometimes associated with male sports stars.

Image-to-text ratio
The amount of space dedicated to images compared with text. A high image to text ratio means that the images take up much of the space and there is less written copy.

Imperatives
Command words such as 'Read this'. Magazine covers in particular often feature imperatives as a persuasive technique.

In-app purchases
Additional content or facilities to buy from within a mobile phone app. They might enhance the experience or allow gamers to access extra features.

Informal language
Using a more direct mode of address and possibly more colloquial, or slang, terms. (A gossip magazine is likely to use informal language.)

Instant gratification
A pleasure that comes from having everything at once rather than delaying or extending the enjoyment by, for example, waiting for the next instalment.

Interact
The way in which audiences actively engage with media products, mainly as a result of digital technologies (examples include playing a video game and posting comments about a media product on social media).

Intertextuality
Where one media product includes a reference to another media product. (Taylor Swift includes sequences in 'Bad Blood' that are similar to familiar action films. The audience might recognise these references and make connections.)

Key light
The main light that shines directly on the person or object in the frame.

Left-wing
Views that are politically left of centre, for example the belief that wealthy people should pay higher taxes to support people who are poorer. The Labour Party is a left-wing political party.

Licence fee
The charge for everyone in Britain who watches television programmes or accesses them through the iPlayer (on television or other devices). As of April 2018 the annual TV licence is £147.

Lifestyle magazine
A publication that covers a range of topics related to readers' lives, such as fashion, travel, health and money.

Linear narrative
A narrative structure where all of the events happen in logical order, one after the other.

Lip-synching
Mouthing or miming lyrics exactly in time to the recorded song in a music video or other performance.

Logo
A simple design that makes a product recognisable and communicates information about the product or brand identity. (The National Trust logo features oak leaves and acorns which relates to the organisation's work as a conservation charity and promoter of outdoor spaces. The Nike logo is the recognisable 'swoosh' that suggests action and movement, relating to the company's sports products.)

Mainstream media
Products that have mass appeal for a wide range of audiences, such as pop music videos, television soap operas and the dominant newspapers.

Mainstream values
Ideas that the majority of people agree with, such as family values or a desire for material wealth.

Major Hollywood studio
A large film production company such as Warner Bros. These studios have large budgets to spend on films, but also need to ensure that their films are successful and make a profit. The Hollywood film industry consists of a number of 'major' studios as well as several smaller companies.

Male gaze
The person who is looking (usually at a female) is assumed to be male; the audience sees the females through male eyes.

Marketing
Promotion and advertising, including elements such as posters, trailers and online marketing including social media strategies.

Masculinity
The traits that are typically associated with being a male.

Masthead
The name of a newspaper or magazine, usually positioned prominently at the top of the cover or front page.

Matriarch
A strong female who has a lot of power and control, usually within a family.

Media conglomerate
An organisation that owns different types of media company. (Disney, for example, owns film and television companies.)

Mediation
The way in which media producers interpret and represent aspects of reality to audiences.

Metaphor
A comparison between two unrelated objects to communicate a particular meaning. Describing a person as a 'rock', for example, connotes that they are very reliable and supportive.

Millennials
An audience demographic group that describes people who were born from 1980 up to around the year 2000. They are the first group of people to reach adulthood in the new millennium.

Minority ethnic group
People of a different ethnic background from that of the majority of the population.

Mise-en-scène
The manner in which all the visual elements are placed within a frame or product, including the setting or background, props, costume and gestures.

Mockumentary
A fictional, usually comedy, programme or film that is filmed in the style of a serious documentary, which creates satire and a sense of realism.

Mock-up
A detailed draft version of designs for a print or online product, showing elements such as the layout and composition of the pages.

Mode of address
The way in which a text 'speaks' to an audience and positions them through language and other codes.

Montage
A collection of different images edited together in one place. Meaning will be communicated through the selection of the individual pictures as well as the overall effect.

Montage editing
A technique where different types of image are put together. These are usually linked in some way to make the montage meaningful. Images might be linked by a theme or a character.

Multi-stranded narrative
A narrative that contains several different stories or plots running alongside each other.

New man
A phrase that originates from the 1980s to describe a man who does not conform to masculine stereotypes, for example, by being willing to do domestic tasks and look after the children.

Newsstand
A place where magazines and newspapers are displayed for sale; in a shop or at a railway station kiosk for example.

News values
A set of factors that help to determine whether or not an event is considered newsworthy.

Non-linear narrative
A narrative where the events do not happen in chronological order.

Ofcom
The Office of Communications, the regulator for broadcasting, telecommunications and postal services in the UK.

Omnibus
A broadcast of a programme that usually includes all episodes from a particular week. This allows the audience to 'catch up' on a weeks' viewing or listening at once.

Online media products
Products that are available online, via the internet, such as websites.

Online streaming services
Websites and apps that allow users to listen to music (or consume other digital content, such as television or film) via the internet. (Depending on the service and subscription level, listeners might be able to save their music to listen offl ine.)

Opinion leader
A well-known, respected person who has the potential to influence people's opinions about a topic.

Opinion poll
A survey of people's views on a particular topic, such as people's opinions on political parties, carried out by a market research company.

Original material
Work created yourself, such as footage you have filmed, photographs you have taken and text or dialogue that you have written.

Pace
The speed of edit effects: fast-paced editing has many cuts between very short shots (or 'takes'), whereas slow-paced editing features fewer cuts between longer takes.

Partial vision
A technique where the camera frames the scene to show only part of the picture, such as filming the villain from behind so that their face is hidden.

Passive consumers
People who use media products, but do not actively engage with or question them.

Passive object
A character who does not take an active role; events happen around them and they have limited involvement in the narrative.

Pastiche

A work of art or fiction that imitates the original product, possibly in a humorous way. A pastiche is usually a complimentary work, not designed to mock the original.

Patriarchal

A situation or society that is dominated by men.

Paywall

A system where readers pay a subscription fee to access website content. Some newspapers have introduced paywalls as a way of increasing income as print sales have fallen.

Performance capture

A technique where digital motion-capture cameras record the movements of an actor to create a digital character on screen. This makes the character lifelike.

Personification

Giving objects or ideas human qualities, such as Old Father Time. Personification can communicate meaning by helping an audience view an idea or object in a certain way.

Phone-hacking scandal

The revelation that mobile phones belonging to a large number of people, including celebrities, politicians and 'ordinary' people, were hacked and their messages accessed by news journalists, particularly those working for the since-closed News of the World.

Pilot

An initial episode of a television programme that is produced to 'test' whether the idea may be popular with an audience.

Pitch

A summary of the key ideas for a new media product that a writer or producer presents to a media organisation for approval. The pitch is designed to 'sell' the idea to the organisation.

Platforms

Different technological ways in which media products are made available to audiences (a website, for example, is an online platform).

Platinum record

A record that has sold more than one million copies.

Podcast

An audio programme made to be downloaded to a PC, tablet or smartphone, or listened to 'on demand' rather than being broadcast.

Point of view

This relates to whose perspective or ideas are shown in the product. Point of view can be shown in different ways, for example the positioning of the camera or the use of language.

Police procedural

A subgenre that focuses specifically on the way in which the police work to solve crimes.

Political leaning

Supporting a particular political party (such as Conservative or Labour) or set of political ideas.

Polysemic

Communicating different meanings through the use of signs that can be interpreted in different ways.

Position the audience

Using aspects of a media product to put us in a specific place from which we experience the text. (A photograph can position us outside a window looking into a building, so we feel like an 'outsider'.) We can also be positioned in a way to accept an idea or point of view.

Post-production

The stage after filming has been completed. Post-production includes editing images and sound and possibly adding particular effects to shape and 'polish' the product.

Power

Control or dominance. Media products are often constructed by powerful organisations that affect the way social groups are represented.

Practical work

Tasks in which you create your own media products. (It is important to apply your knowledge and understanding of the theoretical framework to your own products.)

Press pack

A set of publicity materials about a new product, including information and photographs, released to media organisations to help to promote the product. Most press packs can be found on an organisation's website.

Press release

A statement about an event or development that a company issues to news organisations in the hope that the story will be included in a newspaper or news broadcast.

Primary and secondary research methods

Primary research means gathering information yourself, for example by analysing a media product to identify genre conventions or creating a questionnaire to find out information about your audience. Secondary research involves using sources that other people have written such as books and websites. This can provide information about the audience for a particular media product, for example.

Primary audience

The main audience group that a media product targets.

Print media products

Media products produced in print form, traditionally on paper, such as magazines, newspapers or film posters.

Production

The stage where a media product is constructed.

Production values
The quality of the technical elements of a product, for example the camerawork, lighting, costumes and sound. Products with a high budget are much more likely to have high production values as the equipment and materials used will be of a very high standard.

Products
Individual examples of media output, such as an advert and a newspaper.

Promotion
Wider activities that draw attention to the film, for example interviews with the stars and director on television or in magazines.

Protagonist
The main character in a narrative; also the hero in many narratives.

Public funding
Money that comes from the government or sources such as the television licence fee.

Public service broadcaster
A TV and/or radio provider that aims to serve the public rather than make a profit. (The BBC is publicly funded by the licence fee. It is required to be impartial and reflect the cultural diversity of the UK.)

Pull-quote
A key quote from an article, usually a quote from an interviewee, 'pulled out' of the main article and placed in the column, usually in a larger font and a different colour to make it stand out. It is usually a significant or interesting idea that captures key points. It breaks up the text and draws attention to key messages.

Purpose
The aim or intention of the product. (An advert's purpose is to persuade; a sitcom's purpose is to amuse.) Purpose also relates to the reasons why media producers select particular elements of media language to communicate their intended meaning.

Quest
A mission that a hero has to undertake or a goal that they need to achieve.

RAJAR
Radio Joint Audience Research Ltd, the organisation that measures radio audiences in the UK.

Recce
A visit to a location where you intend to film to make sure it is suitable for your production. You should have a clear idea of the photographs/footage you want to obtain so that you can position your camera and performers.

Red herring
A misleading piece of information which suggests a particular solution that is actually incorrect.

Repertoire of elements
A set of codes and conventions that are used in products from the same genre.

Resolution
When problems or disruptions are solved, or conflicts have been settled.

Respond
How media audiences receive and react to a media product.

Rhetorical question
A question that does not require an answer as the answer is implied, which is used to create a particular effect and involve the audience as they 'know' the answer.

Right-wing
Views that are politically right of centre, for example the belief that taxes should be kept low to allow the economy to grow. The Conservative Party is a right-wing political party.

Role model
A person in a position of authority or prominence who provides a good example to others.

Royal Charter
A legal document awarded by the King or Queen to create a company or organisation. The BBC's charter outlines the purpose of the organisation and guarantees its independence.

Rule of thirds
A framing technique – if a frame is divided into a 3-by-3 grid, objects along the vertical and horizontal lines or at the intersections have dominance.

Satirise
Newspapers sometimes criticise a public figure such as a politician or celebrity by mocking them or using humour

Secondary audience
Not the main target audience, but another group who might also consume the product.

Second screen
Where a viewer watches a television programme on one screen and uses a second screen, such as a phone, to tweet or text a friend about the programme.

Selecting and combining
Choosing elements to include in a product and putting them together in particular ways to communicate meanings. (Selecting an image and combining it with a caption will communicate a message.)

Self-regulated
An industry that is controlled and monitored by itself, not by the government. The Leveson Inquiry recommended that the newspaper industry should be free from political or government interference and that the new regulatory body should be independent.

Semiotics
A system for analysing products that interprets meanings on two levels: denotation – the literal meaning – and connotation – the deeper or associated meaning.

Services
Non-physical products, such as car insurance, health provision or mobile phone contracts.

Shock tactics
Using elements of media language to shock the audience and create a strong particular reaction. (An image of a war zone in a charity message might make the audience want to help and so donate money to improve the situation.)

Shot-reverse-shot
A filming technique often used for conversations. The first shot shows one character's point of view, looking at the other; then the action is edited to show a shot from the other character's perspective, and so on.

Sidebar
A box placed outside the main columns which might feature key points from the article, linked information, or an opinion from a different source. An article in a music magazine, for example, might feature a sidebar with a brief review of the artist's latest album.

Sign
Any element of a media product that communicates meaning, for example a photograph or logo.

Slapstick
Visual humour created by over-exaggerated actions. Characters in slapstick comedy are often made to look foolish, awkward and clumsy.

Slogan
A short, punchy phrase that communicates key ideas about a product or issue.

Social groups
A way of categorising people, for example by gender (females form a social group).

Soft news
Less serious news that is focused on human interest or celebrity stories. The term 'infotainment' is sometimes used to describe soft news stories.

Specialised audience
A very specific group, sometimes called a 'niche' audience. (Products such as The Railway Magazine target a specialised audience with a keen interest in the subject.)

Specialist lexis
Language relating to a specific topic or subject; the use of specialist lexis assumes that the audience brings a level of subject knowledge.

Sponsorship
Paying to be associated with or have a product featured in, for example, a film. This can benefit both the film and the sponsor.

Star persona
The image or identity associated with a major artist.

Statement of Aims
A short piece of writing you must submit with your production, which should outline how you will apply your knowledge and understanding of the theoretical framework to your media production.

Stepped question
A question that is broken down into a number of 'steps' that require shorter answers.

Subgenre
A more specific genre within a broader genre.

Subject-specific terminology
The specialist vocabulary that applies to Media Studies.

Subvert a stereotype
To go against stereotypical portrayal and present a broader view of a social group.

Surreal
Events or occurrences that are not realistic and do not seem to make sense; they have no logic. (Comedy programmes do not attempt to create fully realistic representations of the world, so surreal humour might be used to communicate a deeper message about society or culture.)

Syndication
Where a company sells the rights to broadcast a television programme to different channels or organisations.

Synergy
Where different parts of the same media conglomerate work together, for example to promote a particular product.

Synth-pop
A genre of music that became popular in the 1980s, where a synthesiser is a main instrument.

Tabloid
A newspaper format that is half the size of a broadsheet; also refers to the 'popular' press or 'red top' newspapers such as the Sun.

Target
Aiming a product at a particular group of people; a target audience.

Target audience
The group of people that a product is intended for. It might be defined by social group (age, gender and so on) or other factors such as lifestyle or interest.

'Teaser'
A poster or web advert that initiates interest in a film, for example, by offering an intriguing detail of the film but with little else. This 'teases' the audience and encourages them to actively look out for more information.

Technological developments
New technologies that enable media producers to create products in different ways, sometimes leading to changes in a genre.

'Tentpole' film
A very high-budget film, usually from a major producer, expecting large audiences.

Terrestrial television
A television signal conveyed by radio waves from a transmitter on Earth and received by the television aerial (in contrast to satellite television where the signal is transmitted by satellites in space). Terrestrial channels in the UK are free to viewers who pay the licence fee.

Theatrical release
The date when the film is first shown in cinemas.

Theoretical framework
The basis for your study of the media, covering media language, representation, media industries and audiences.

Theoretical perspectives
Ideas that have been developed by theorists that will support your study of the media.

Thumbnail images
Most DVD back covers have three or four small images of scenes from the film to give an insight into the action and characters to appeal to the audience.

Transformation
A major change. Characters are often transformed as a result of events that occur in the narrative. (A character might change their lifestyle after a health scare.)

Treatment
A detailed summary of ideas for a product, considering elements such as genre conventions and narrative.

Turnover
A business term for the amount of money a company takes from sales of products.

Unexpected elements
Conventions that we would not necessarily expect to see in a genre to add an element of surprise or develop the genre.

Unique selling point
Something that makes a product stand out from competitors' similar products. Advertisers aim to communicate the 'unique' nature of the product to persuade the audience to buy or use it.

Unseen media product
A media product that you have not studied in class. This will be provided in the exam and you will need to compare it with one of the set products.

Uphold a stereotype
Reinforce a stereotypical image of a social group.

User-generated content
Media content created by audiences not a media organisation. (This is an example of active audience participation as users become creators.)

Version of reality
A particular view or interpretation of actual events. (Different newspapers will report different elements of the same event to denote their version of what happened.)

Vertically integrated
Owning different stages of (the film) process: production, distribution and exhibition.

Video on demand
Audio-visual products such as television programmes and films that are available to stream or download from the internet.

Viral marketing
Advertising that is distributed through non-traditional channels, such as the internet. The term relates to the idea of a virus that can spread very quickly as audiences often pass the information on.

Vlog
A video weblog that can be used to promote a media product. Vlogs might appear on a product's official website, YouTube channel and associated social media pages.

Watercooler topic
A major event or topic that most people have heard about. It is widely discussed in society and in workplaces, where people might gather at break times and chat.

Watershed
The 9pm cut-off after which broadcasters are able to show programmes with more adult content, for example swearing and violence. Before 9pm programmes should be suitable for children.

Wordplay
Using a word that has more than one meaning, or adapting the spelling or meaning of words, often to humorous effect.

Yuppie
'Young urban professional' or 'young upwardly mobile professional', a term used in the 1980s to describe a young middle-class person who had achieved financial success and was enjoying material wealth.

Answers to Quickfire Questions

1 The Media Studies Theoretical Framework

1.1 Crime drama props include visual signifiers that connote crime, such as weapons, and the investigation of crime, for example police crime-scene tape and forensic suits.

1.2 Fashion magazine cover conventions include a main image of an attractive model wearing fashionable clothing and directly addressing the reader. The main cover line will usually reference current trends or styles, with further cover lines relating to image, beauty and lifestyle topics such as travel, careers or health. The uncluttered layout has a consistent use of colour and bright lighting to highlight the model and their clothing.
Conventions of music magazines include a main image of a musician or band, wearing clothing that connotes their genre of music and directly addressing the reader. Cover lines usually relate to music and might use specialist or colloquial language that music fans would understand. The layout is often quite cluttered and the colour palette quite dark, depending on the genre.

1.3 Many television programmes follow Todorov's narrative structure, including fictional programmes such as *Doctor Who*, where each episode usually fits the pattern of equilibrium, disruption and new equilibrium. Documentaries and reality programmes might also feature elements of this structure. *The Great British Bake Off*, for example, includes elements of disruption, when a difficult challenge is set or a baking disaster occurs, before the familiar new equilibrium when one baker is eliminated and another is awarded 'star baker'.

1.4 There are several enigmas in the *Spectre* poster including: who is the person in the skeleton costume? Why is this person lurking in the shadows? Why is the film called *Spectre*? How does the title link to Bond and the skeleton suit? Who is Bond intending to shoot with the gun and why?

1.5 Many media products feature narratives where heroes defeat villains:
- films, for example those based on superheroes such as *Avengers: Age of Ultron*
- television programmes, for example detective dramas such as *Sherlock*.

Other products such as music videos and advertisements might include this element of narrative, and newspapers frequently communicate this narrative in their stories, for example when reporting on a crime or even a sporting event.

1.6 The 'Viola Beach Tragedy' refers to the deaths of the four young members of the band Viola Beach in 2016. They died with their manager in a car crash in Sweden where they were due to perform at a music festival.

1.7 You could choose any event, for example a current story, and consider the different representations. On page 78, the *Sun* and the *Guardian* construct different versions of the royal engagement. The *Sun* focuses on the love story with a medium shot of the couple looking into each other's eyes and a close-up of the ring anchored by the headline 'She's the One'. The *Guardian* selects a long shot of the couple and discusses the issue of attitudes towards race in relation to the engagement.

1.8 Many stereotypes result from historical situations where minority or less-powerful groups in society have been categorised in negative ways in comparison with more dominant or majority groups.

1.9 The Quality Street advertisement depicts a dominant, professional male in a suit and two passive females on either side of him wearing more casual clothing that co-ordinates with the colours of the chocolates. The poster for *The Man with the Golden Gun* shows a powerful, centrally positioned Bond surrounded by bikini-clad women. The males appear to be more active in the narrative than the females.

1.10 The females in the Quality Street advert appear to be 'objects'. They are dressed similarly to the chocolates and the male seems to be making a choice between them.

1.11 The poster for *The Man with the Golden Gun* features an Asian female wearing a karate suit and practising martial arts, which is an example of an ethnic stereotype.

1.12 The producers of media products make decisions about what to include in the text and how to represent groups of people, so it is important to know who has constructed these representations. If a product that features young characters is constructed by older adults, the representations might be more stereotypical than if it had been produced by younger people.

1.13 Many products can provide entertainment, including magazines, radio programmes, video games, television programmes, films and online media.

1.14 Our age, and the period in which we have grown up, will affect the way we view the world. An older person, for example, might not relate to a music video by a young pop star, and could find some of the images shocking, while a young person could identify with the images and messages. A younger person might find historical products old-fashioned and unrealistic as they cannot relate to this period, while an older person might be familiar with this type of product and accept the meanings in the text.

1.15 Encoding is the process whereby media producers construct meanings and messages in the products they create. Decoding is the way in which audiences interpret the meanings in a product.

2 The Media Studies Specification

2.1 The four key areas of the theoretical framework are: media language, representation, media industries and audiences. The GCSE Media Studies Specification is based on this framework.

3 Component 1: Exploring the Media

3.1 These mastheads use a serif font: the *Guardian*, *Daily Express*, *Daily Mail*, *Daily Telegraph*, *Times*. These are broadsheets and mid-market tabloids: the font choice might connote formality, a 'quality' product or traditional values. These mastheads use a sans-serif font: *the Sun*, *Daily Mirror*, *Daily Star*. These are tabloids: the font choice might connote informality, a popular product or modern values.

3.2 The cover uses 'Buy', 'Shop' and 'Refine' in relation to the feature 'How to Dress Now'. These command statements add importance and emphasis to the cover and are grouped as three key pieces of fashion advice to readers. The focus on buying new products is important to many magazines, as they depend on advertising as a source of funding.

3.3 The unique selling point is what will make a product 'stand out' from other products and, ideally, persuade the audience to make a purchase.

3.4 Some charity and public information adverts, such as the UK government's 'Think!' road safety campaigns, have used shocking images and statistics to communicate the very serious messages in, for example, anti-drink-driving and speed-awareness initiatives.

3.5 Many types of advertisement use soft-sell techniques, especially those for luxury products such as perfumes, jewellery and cars.

3.6 The Coke logo is bright and forward slanting, connoting that the brand is youthful, fun and forward looking. The more traditional serif font suggests that the brand is also well established and trustworthy.

3.7 The use of red and white throughout the historical Coke advert reflects the brand image. White connotes purity and the use of white for the background and in the tennis clothing communicates a message that the drink is healthy and wholesome (anchored by the written text). The red in the logo and the slogan is bright and connotes that the brand is fun, youthful and modern.

3.8 Contemporary adverts tend to prioritise visual images as a means of communicating a message more immediately, possibly using 'soft-sell' techniques to construct an ideal lifestyle. Many historical adverts used written copy to explain the specific features of new products that the audience might not be familiar with. The use of lots of words was typical of many text types in the past. Technological advances and marketing trends and developments are also significant.

3.9 Producers of adverts often use rhetorical questions to engage the audience. Asda used 'Spot the difference?' next to a picture of different prices of the same product to emphasise that products are cheaper at this supermarket. McDonald's used 'Gherkin or gherkout?' as a humorous question acknowledging that some people love gherkins in their burgers but others hate them and will take them out. This is an example of turning a potentially negative association into a positive advertising tool.

3.10 The brand identity of the Fiat 500 brand is bright, colourful and informal; suggesting youth, positivity and a modern product.

3.11 There are many intertextual references to fashion magazines in the Fiat adverts, for example 'Spring/ Summer Collection'. There are also broader cultural references to fashion such as 'old skool' and 'retro vibe'.

3.12 The main hard-sell technique in the Fiat adverts is the prominent central positioning of the car, as well as factual information about technical features. Soft-sell techniques include the references to fashion and use of bright colour palettes to suggest that the car is an important accessory in an ideal lifestyle.

3.13 The Fiat adverts use a direct mode of address as the models, particularly the male, look directly towards the audience. Slogans, such as 'Life's too short...' act as imperatives. Language codes are informal and use colloquial phrases likely to be familiar to the target audience.

3.14 The serif font is traditional and suggests formality, to emphasise that this is a serious statement rather than a joke. The logo is clean and modern, connoting the contemporary representations and messages in the campaign.

3.15 The poster constructs an image of an active older female taking part in sport, which subverts stereotypes of age. However, she is holding onto (or pulling against) a young male, connoting perhaps that she is weaker and in need of help, which is more stereotypical.

3.16 *Men on the Ropes* communicates multiple meanings: it connotes the idea of a boxing match, where a boxer might be pinned against the ropes of the ring. The title also connotes a deeper meaning, as the phrase 'on the ropes' is used to describe someone who is having problems in life. *Men on the Ropes* links the boxing metaphor to the serious message of the campaign.

3.17 Red connotes danger and acts as a warning sign to raise awareness of the issues.

3.18 'We're in your corner' continues the boxing metaphor, as, between rounds, boxers sit in opposing corners with their support team. This phrase also connotes that the charity is there to support people who need help, that they are 'on your side' in difficult times.

3.19 Using an 'ordinary' person rather than a famous, elite sportsperson creates realism and believability in the advert, to reinforce the message and enable the male audience to identify with the man.

3.20 Boxing might be stereotypically associated with masculinity, strength, aggression, power, skill, competitiveness. Some of these stereotypes are upheld but the man is not actually fighting, he is leaning on the ropes for support and the language anchors the message that he has demonstrated emotional strength by addressing his problems.

3.21 Some recent examples include the *Transformers* films, the *Divergent* series, *The Hunger Games* and the *Marvel Avengers* films.

3.22 The number connotes Bond's identity as a secret agent, the gun suggests violence and action, which are key narrative features of the films, and the forward-slanting logo reflects the fast-paced nature of the films.

3.23 Enigmas are used as a method of 'hooking' the audience, engaging them by creating mysteries or posing questions that will encourage them to watch the film.

3.24 Lévi-Strauss's theory of Binary Oppositions could be applied to the use of light and dark in the *Star Wars* poster.

3.25 The cover of *National Geographic* features a plain white serif font connoting that it is a traditional, well-established product. The written text does not detract from the main image of the rock formation within the landscape, reflecting the geographical focus of the magazine.

3.26 The main reason is the development of digital technologies and the availability of content online. Much of this content is free to users and so fewer people now buy print magazines.

3.27 Typical women's lifestyle magazine features include:
- the main image of a famous, high status female cover model, directly addressing the reader
- cover lines surrounding the image relating to fashion, beauty, body image and issues (feminism)
- 'standard' layout and design with a consistent use of the colour palette
- linguistic devices such as rhetorical questions, exclamatives and alliteration to appeal to the audience.

3.28 Typical features of a men's lifestyle magazine include:
- the main image of a famous, high status male cover model, directly addressing the reader
- cover lines relating to fashion and style, products such as gadgets and watches, body image and issues (masculinity)
- 'standard' layout and design with a consistent use of the colour palette
- linguistic devices such as exclamatives and hyperbole to appeal to the audience.

3.29 A publication's circulation figure relates to the number of sales of the magazine, but many people might read the same print copy of the product, for example family members, friends or work colleagues. The readership figure is therefore usually much higher than the circulation.

3.30 The use of language on the *Elle* cover appeals to the reader in many ways, such as:
- The rhetorical questions 'Can't sleep?' have answers, suggesting that the magazine will help the reader if they have these problems.
- The use of exclamatives such as 'Fashion!' draws attention to the different cover lines and makes them seem exciting and important.
- Much of the language is empowering for women, for example the use of the personal pronoun 'put *you* in charge of your body' and the descriptive language 'new supercharged woman' to appeal to the contemporary female reader.

3.31 The *Sun* masthead uses a sans-serif font and is forward leaning, connoting a modern, forward-looking publication. The title is white on a red background as the *Sun* is a 'red top' tabloid newspaper. The noun 'Sun' suggests a bright, illuminating product that casts light on events and issues, and is targeting a wide range of people. The *Guardian* uses a serif font and the masthead is upright, connoting the more formal nature of this broadsheet newspaper. However, the masthead is completely lower case, which also suggests that the newspaper is modern and in tune with current trends, and could also reflect the product's liberal values. The noun 'guardian' has connotations of protecting or guarding, suggesting that the newspaper is a guardian of truth and that the reader can have confidence in its journalism.

3.32 The tagline emphasises 'real', which connotes that the newspaper is trustworthy. It also links news and entertainment, both of which are important.

3.33 The plug is the promotion of a 'Free kids book' to entice readers to buy the newspaper and look inside for the tokens. This suggests that the target audience for *The Daily Mirror* includes adults with young children.

3.34 The *Daily Star* headline intertextually references a slogan used in advertisement for breakfast cereal (Kellogg's Rice Crispies: 'Snap, crackle and pop') through the headline which is anchored by the phrase about Brexit. The 'snap' connotes the unexpected election. The *Guardian* headline gives an interpretation of why Theresa May has called the election, using an imperative to connote that she is *demanding* more power. The *Times* headline communicates a clear message, through the use of a definite statement, that May and the Conservative Party will win the election very comfortably.

3.35 The mountainous, snow-covered landscape demonstrates that the filming took place in a beautiful, remote location. The vehicle in the background looks like a high-performance, luxury car. The high-key lighting also connotes high production values.

3.36 A 'tentpole' is a very high-budget film that targets a large global audience. It is a product that film companies rely on to make a large profit. Recent examples include: *Star Wars: The Last Jedi*, *Black Panther* and *Beauty and the Beast*.

3.37 Some of the associated products created to tie in with *Spectre* include: clothing, jewellery, framed prints of the poster, models of the Aston Martin car, keyrings and mugs.

3.38 This is a key period when many high-budget films are released to capture family audiences during half-term holidays and in the run up to Christmas.

3.39 Tabloid newspapers tend to have a high image-to-text ratio, focus on 'softer' news stories (human interest, celebrity etc.) and a more colloquial style. Broadsheets have a high text-to-image ratio, focus on 'harder' news stories (politics, foreign affairs, economics etc.) and a more formal written style.

3.40 The target audience for the *Sun* is middle aged, predominantly male, in middle to lower socio-economic groups (C2-E).

3.41 David Dinsmore's quotation suggests that the *Sun* appeals by being up-to-date with what is happening in the world and by initiating new ideas. It provides gratifications of entertainment as well as information and forms a relationship with its readers, suggesting an element of social interaction.

3.42 Features such as the motoring section and a large proportion of sport, especially football, appeal to working-class males. The 'Fabulous' features, health and money-saving sections appeal to working-class females with children. A focus on celebrity stories might appeal to younger audiences.

3.43 The image of the rising Sun behind the Earth is a clear intertextual reference to *Independence Day*. The link extends to the title of the film, which reflects the newspaper's support for Brexit.

3.44 A conglomerate is the name for a large media organisation that produces different types of media text.

3.45 The BBC reflects the cultural diversity of the UK by having Welsh, Scottish and Northern Irish radio stations, including those that broadcast in the Welsh and Gaelic languages, the Asian Network that reflects British Asian culture and local stations that represent different areas of the UK.

3.46 The BBC's remit is to 'inform, educate and entertain'. The original purpose of *The Archers* was to inform farmers about modern practices to increase food production after the Second World War, which is an educational aim with a social benefit.

3.47 Listeners became actively involved with this story in a variety of ways, for example by discussing the issue on social media, donating money to charity in Helen's name, and predicting the outcome of the trial.

3.48 The weekly votes allow listeners to actively respond to a storyline, for example by suggesting what they think will be the outcome of a situation. Some of these votes relate to farming issues, while others are about other storylines and involve relationships or social issues. This engages a wide range of listeners, who can see the results of the vote on the website.

3.49 Smartphones are portable, so users can play at any time and in any place. Internet connectivity allows users to play and compete with others, while augmented-reality technology allows players to experience the world of the game in their own environment.

3.50 Different audiences might access a media product via different platforms, so making a product available in different ways allows producers to reach a wider range of people than a single platform would. Contemporary audiences may have an expectation that producers will make a product available via different platforms.

3.51 Elements of the earlier Pokémon games such as the Pokémon characters, the premise of finding and catching the Pokémon and the element of competition is familiar. The augmented-reality technology and the ability to play on a smartphone, in 'real time' in the local environment, is new and different.

3.52 The game is based on a very simple concept, so anyone can play. It does not require technical expertise or experience of playing video games. The use of smartphone technology allows most people to access the game easily – a console is not required. The 'buzz' created following the initial release of the game made this game very popular across a range of audiences.

3.53 New updates and special challenges appeal to gaming audiences as they add extra incentives to play and so prevent the game from becoming repetitive or predictable.

3.54 *Pokémon Go* had a variety of age ratings as it was a new concept at the time, so there were no similar games to compare it with. While the game itself does not contain any offensive content or violence, there were concerns about the potential dangers of playing the game, such as the risk of injury and safety issues related to the sharing of personal information, so some organisations awarded a higher age rating.

3.55 New technologies, such as augmented reality, are becoming increasingly popular and many people wish to use them. They do, however, pose challenges in terms of protecting privacy, especially that of young people. This is a wider social issue as society adapts to the digital age and works to protect the safety of young people online.

3.56 The primary target audience for *Pokémon Go* is younger audiences who have grown up with the franchise, who enjoy technology and want to engage with the new augmented-reality game. The game gained a large secondary audience of adults, however, many of whom do not regularly play video games but enjoyed the new experiences of *Pokémon Go*.

3.57 At the time of its release *Pokémon Go* was being talked about most in the USA and parts of Europe, including the UK.

3.58 Audiences might personally identify with *Pokémon Go* through the ability to personalise their own trainer, as well as through the ability to play in their own locality.

3.59 The 'effects debate' is the name given to audience theories that suggest media products such as video games might have a negative influence on people's behaviour.

4 Assessment of Component 1: Exploring the Media

4.1 Using subject-specific terminology accurately will demonstrate your knowledge and understanding of Media Studies. You should use terminology throughout your examination responses.

4.2 You will need to analyse two set products in Section A of the exam. You will analyse one set product in the media language question and then compare a different set product with an unseen resource when you answer the question on representation.

4.3 You will study film in relation to media industries only, to avoid any overlap with Film Studies.

5 Component 2: Understanding Media Forms and Products

5.1
- A heartbeat connotes fear or anxiety and is often used to create tension.
- Thunder can be used to connote a threat or danger, signifying that something bad is going to happen. When weather is used to communicate meaning in a media product, this is called 'pathetic fallacy'.
- A nursery rhyme usually connotes childhood and innocence, but some horror or thriller genre texts use nursery rhymes in an eerie or threatening way.
- A siren or alarm connotes danger, that action needs to be taken.
- A creaking door usually connotes an unexpected or unwanted arrival. It might also connote a ghostly or sinister presence.

5.2 Villains versus victims is an example of a binary opposition, Lévi-Strauss's theory.

5.3 Public service broadcasters have a remit to create programmes for a wide and diverse range of audiences, so their content appeals to many different people. Also, these channels are well established and audiences are familiar with them. They are likely to have built brand loyalty, which is another reason why they account for a large percentage of the television audience.

5.4 The Uses and Gratifications theory states that 'social interaction' is one of the reasons why audiences choose to consume a product. This involves audiences extending their experience of a media product by discussing it with other people, either in person or online.

5.5 The dress codes connote Victorian times, for example the hats, long coats and neck ties worn by the men and the female's high neckline and pinned-up hair. Other visual codes, including the carriage, wicker basket and architecture, also establish the period.

5.6 The 'repertoire of elements' is the set of codes and conventions that audiences would expect to see in a product from a particular genre. Science fiction, for example, might include futuristic props, a setting in space and alien creatures.

5.7 A narrative enigma is a mystery or puzzle included in a product to 'hook' or engage the audience. Roland Barthes' theory outlined enigma codes.

5.8 Propp's theory can often be applied to crime dramas. The hero is the detective or person who solves the crime, the villain commits the crime, the helper is the sidekick, the donors are the experts and witnesses who provide information about the crime, the victim might be a 'princess' in need of rescue.

5.9 The use of the static camera for some parts of the chase sequences allows the audience time to follow the action and understand the narrative as characters move towards the camera or across the frame. This can also have the effect of building tension as the action is drawn out and additional excitement is then created when camera movement is introduced.

5.10 The ending communicates a message that crime does not pay: the criminals have been caught (the main criminal is dead and the two boys have been arrested) and are no longer a threat to society. Regan, the 'hero', relaxes with his girlfriend as a reward for his efforts. This upholds a dominant message that criminality is wrong.

5.11 Urban settings are often used in crime dramas as cities are often the location of many different types of crime. Urban landscapes include many areas where criminals can operate and avoid discovery.

5.12 Jenny can be viewed as a Proppian 'princess' as she becomes a victim of threatened violence by Kemble's men and needs to be rescued. She is Regan's girlfriend and he is rewarded with an evening at home with her after the case is solved.

5.13 Vertical integration describes a media organisation that produces, distributes and exhibits products.

5.14 The poster for the 2012 feature film features the familiar Regan/hero and Carter/sidekick pairing of the original and the gesture codes connote that Regan is a similarly strong, tough and maverick character. The London skyline is visible, but contemporary skyscrapers are evident, which, coupled with the modern dress codes and darker colour palette, connote that this is a modern remake with clear differences from the original.

5.15 The images from *Life on Mars* intertextually reference *The Sweeney* through:
- dress codes, especially Gene Hunt's camel coat which is similar to Regan's
- gesture codes of the 1970s male police detectives: strong, dominant body language connoting patriarchy
- visual codes such as the Ford car.

5.16 There are many familiar elements of the crime drama repertoire evident in *Luther*, including: the crime, the police procedural, the investigation of the crime scene (forensic suits, police tape, evidence markers, blood), interviews of the suspect, the weapon (or lack of it), the flawed detective.

5.17 The ending of the set episode conveys a message that criminals are not always caught and punished – even though Luther knows that Alice committed the murders, he does not have sufficient evidence to convict her. This subverts expectations (that good will overcome evil and the law will be upheld as criminals are punished) and demonstrates that, as in real life, stories do not always end with a clear and satisfactory resolution. This also shows a clear development in the genre from *The Sweeney*.

5.18 Alice demonstrates many traits of the femme fatale. Visual codes of her red hair and bright red lipstick reflect this character type while her flirtation with Luther suggests she is trying to seduce or trap him. She is clearly dangerous. Her intelligence allows her to avoid conviction for the crime.

5.19 Audiences are likely to have talked about the characters and the interesting representations of Luther and Alice in particular, as well as the narrative surrounding Henry Madsen and the Morgan murders, the lack of a typical resolution and the continuing narrative arcs.

5.20 The BBC is able to sell programmes to other countries, which adds to the income that the organisation receives in addition to the licence fee. If a programme is successful globally, this strengthens the reputation of the BBC and British programmes, which is positive for the industry.

5.21 Television is a competitive environment – audiences have a vast range of products to choose from, so media organisations adopt many marketing techniques to attract viewers. Trailers, for example, might be shown on television but also online to 'hook' audiences through elements such as stars, genre conventions and narrative enigmas, similar to film trailers.

5.22 There are many factors that might affect how a viewer responds to *Luther*, including their age, gender and ethnicity. More specifically, if a viewer is a police officer, for example, they will have specific knowledge of policing which will affect their response to the narrative and representations. Fans of crime dramas might have certain expectations about the programme that might be fulfilled – or challenged.

5.23 Channel 4 does not produce media products in house: it commissions some productions and buys others, including many from America. Channel 4 is known for broadcasting new and 'alternative' comedies, many of which are from the USA, and these clearly appeal to the Channel 4 audience.

5.24 Todorov's narrative theory includes the concept of equilibrium, which is important in sitcom.

5.25 Other sitcom types that could be applied to characters in *Friends* include: Rachel as the 'naïve' who has a limited grasp on the realities of life in the city without the financial support of her father, and Phoebe who shows elements of the 'innocent' although she is much more independent than Rachel.

5.26 Wella hair products, for example, reflect the young, predominantly female, audience who might aspire to a hairstyle like the 'Rachel', which became hugely popular as a result of the show. Coffee links to the iconic coffee shop setting in *Friends* and wine is a product targeting an adult audience, suggesting that the audience was 'growing up' with characters from the sitcom.

5.27 It is now many years since the final series was produced and, while the show is still popular, it does not have the mass appeal that it once did.

5.28 Tagliamonte's point about language suggests that *Friends* had a direct impact on real life, as people adopted the style of speech used in the show. This might support the argument in the 'effects debate' that claims media has an impact on people's behaviour, although this is not necessarily a negative impact.

5.29 The appearance of Prime and all of the scenes in the 8+ Club are surreal as they subvert expectations about the 'reality' of the world of the *IT Crowd* characters. The aerobics class that Jen attends at the end of the episode is also surreal as it is unexpected and unusual for an office situation.

5.30 The mise-en-scène of the IT office communicates that the department is untidy and disorganised through the clutter and mismatched furniture. There are many toys and posters that reference popular culture, which is stereotypical of IT workers and connotes that the characters are quite immature. The messy and uncared for nature of the office suggests that the department is not valued in the organisation.

5.31 'Street' connotes urban youth culture, which is referenced in the 'Street Countdown' sequence. This is ironic in relation to *Countdown* as it challenges our expectations of a traditional quiz programme targeting a middle-class audience for comedic effect.

5.32 Roy is a victim of a misunderstanding and could be seen to fill elements of Propp's 'princess' role, as could Jen who is left out of the Heads of Departments meetings – both characters are quite passive in the narrative. Roy is also Moss's sidekick at the 8+ Club, although he does not really fulfil the 'helper' role.

5.33 Moss's personality is constructed through his costume: brown cord trousers, checked shirt and patterned tie connote that he is old-fashioned and 'geeky', also quite smart and formal. Props are also important: his glasses, for example, connote intelligence and his neat backpack and anorak connote a child-like quality.

5.34 Roy displays many traits of the 'joker' character type and also of the 'nerd' in relation to his interest in more 'geeky' elements of popular culture.

5.35 Media organisations such as Fremantle benefit from owning different types of television company because each can specialise in a different type of programme, increasing the likelihood of the organisation reaching different audiences and achieving commercial success.

5.36 The 'surreal' elements of the programme could be seen as 'edgy' or 'risk-taking' as these subvert our expectations of a traditional sitcom. Similarly, the inclusion of references to *Countdown* could be seen as more 'edgy' as they challenge many assumptions about this programme.

5.37 *The IT Crowd's* cultural references, such as *Countdown*, might not be widely known in other countries, limiting the extent to which some audiences might be able to understand or engage with the programme.

5.38 This release suggests that *The IT Crowd* has a loyal audience of fans who want to own all of the episodes and additional material.

5.39 The title sequence for *The IT Crowd* is an animated sequence constructed to look like a video game, which will be recognisable to gaming fans, who might then identify additional intertextual references.

5.40 Fans of *The IT Crowd* might be likely to also be keen video gamers and enjoy the opportunity to extend their experience of the programme by engaging with the game.

5.41 Record companies that own subsidiary labels are able to target many different audiences through labels that specialise in different genres of music. This increases opportunities to make profits.

5.42 A record company might develop synergies with other organisations in the same conglomerate. For example, an artist or band could create the theme song or soundtrack album for a new film or television programme produced by the same organisation. This allows for cross-promotion of the different products and potentially expands the target audience for both.

5.43 There are many similarities between the 'Parental Advisory' guidelines and the BBFC categories for classifying film relating to, for example, discrimination, violence and language. This demonstrates that similar standards apply across different cultural products and shows that contemporary society views these issues as the most significant in terms of regulation. It also helps audiences, especially parents, to decide if a product is suitable if similar regulatory systems apply to a range of forms.

5.44 The Parental Advisory scheme is a voluntary system whereby record companies assess songs and videos using BPI guidelines and place a 'Parental Advisory' logo on a product if necessary, whereas online videos that would fall into the '12' age category need to be classified by law by the BBFC, using their age-ratings system.

5.45 The dress codes of the studded jacket, body piercings and 'Mohican' hair all connote rebellion in the image of the punk. The closed body language indicated by the folded arms and indirect mode of address potentially connote an antisocial attitude also associated with youthful rebellion.

5.46 Fandom might offer pleasures of personal identity. For example, a fan could identify with the artist and the messages and narratives in their music; they might extend this sense of identification by perhaps dressing in a similar way to the artist. Fans might enjoy social interaction with others, for example by discussing their favourite artist in person or online, sharing posts on social media or attending a music festival or concert.

5.47 Additional products released alongside an album increase the publicity for the album and raise audience awareness. These additional products might also make money in their own right and so help to generate profits and contribute to the commercial success of the artist.

5.48 The video for 'Take On Me' depicts a young female becoming part of the world of the band and interacting with the lead singer, which explores the fantasy that many fans might have about meeting and becoming close to the artists they admire.

5.49 In 'Material Girl', Madonna wears a pink satin dress that intertextually references Marilyn Monroe's dress in *Gentlemen Prefer Blondes*. Her hairstyle, make-up and jewellery also resemble Monroe's. The mise-en-scène and Madonna's pose in the music video still are very similar to those in the film. The song that Monroe sings in the film scene is 'Diamonds are a Girl's Best Friend', which also links to Madonna's song and the message about material wealth.

5.50 Shot-reverse-shot is the element of continuity editing evident as the characters run towards each other and the video cuts between each point of view.

5.51 Taylor Swift's star persona has developed from a relatable image of youthful innocence in 'Love Story' to a more mature image of strength in 'Bad Blood'. She is now older, takes a more active role in the narrative and assumes more sexualised and powerful personas than the more passive romantic heroine in 'Love Story'.

5.52 The editing effects in 'Hungry Like the Wolf' link the different 'worlds' of the narrative as Simon Le Bon's character moves from the city to the untamed jungle. The first effect, a page turn, connotes civilisation, while the second effect of a page being ripped suggests the more savage environment of the jungle.

5.53 Charity advertisements often construct representations of poorer people in developing countries that aim to provoke sympathy and encourage an audience to donate money.

5.54 The image views the female from a male's point of view, as he is actually looking at her through binoculars, which clearly demonstrates the 'male gaze'. She is wearing a bikini and the frame within the shot draws attention to parts of her body, which suggests that she is on display as a passive object of desire.

5.55 The image connotes that everyone is equal and communicates a message that babies do not discriminate according to skin colour.

5.56 Kendrick Lamar's representation as a stereotypical rapper will potentially appeal to fans of rap music, more likely to be male and perhaps slightly older than Taylor Swift's audience demographic. Swift is represented as a confident and sexualised action heroine. This is likely to appeal to her core demographic of young females, but possibly also to males and slightly older age groups.

5.57 The low-angle shot of the males in 'Uptown Funk' connotes high status and dominance, typical of a promotional music video that showcases the star. This is enhanced by the use of high-key lighting. The dress codes of brightly coloured smart jackets, gold jewellery and sunglasses communicate a message that these males are rich, powerful and successful.

5.58 The image of the men breaking rocks connotes a lack of freedom, as these people are enslaved. This links to historical contexts of slavery but also suggests that many people in contemporary society, especially those from minority ethnic groups, do not have full freedom. The central image of Pharrell Williams connotes a more empowering meaning as his status as a pop star gives him a powerful 'voice' in society to communicate a positive message.

5.59 When artists collaborate with their audience, this creates a positive response as audiences can feel empowered and closer to the artist. The industry also benefits as the collaboration might be widely publicised, and the artist could ultimately reach a wider audience.

5.60 A song featured on a film soundtrack gives additional publicity to the music and the artist and raises awareness with audiences. This might result in much higher record sales, especially if the film is successful.

5.61 All elements of the Uses and Gratifications theory can apply to social media in relation to the music industry, but perhaps the most significant point is social interaction as audiences can engage in sharing and discussing their favourite artists with other fans from around the world.

5.62 A fan of Katy Perry might respond with a preferred reading of the posts, enjoying the familiar clips from past videos and feeling excited about the tour for example. Someone who is not familiar with the music might have a negotiated reading, not necessarily accepting the exciting message about the music but perhaps responding positively to the post about her charity work.

5.63 Taylor Swift's old Twitter page featured an image of her with long, curly blonde hair, looking in direct address to the audience. This reinforces her youthful, 'girl next door' persona. The descriptors connote youthful carefreeness coupled with 'confused' and 'lonely', which constructs an identity that her young fans may relate to. The new Twitter page constructs a much more mature image of Swift as her hair is slicked back and tousled, and she directly addresses the audience with a confident pout. The phrase 'The old Taylor can't come to the phone right now' reinforces this development and connotes a deliberate change of image.

5.64 Music artists include personal posts on social media to appeal to their audience and allow their fans a glimpse of their 'real' life. This might help fans to feel that they know an artist and increase their loyalty to them.

5.65 Pharrell Williams' involvement with the United Nations International Day of Happiness aimed to raise awareness of climate change through the use of his highly successful song 'Happy'. This shows the significance of social contexts and how music can potentially play a part in bringing about change.

5.66 A range of audiences might be attracted to different aspects of Pharrell Williams' work and might respond differently to the website. Younger people who enjoy his mainstream music and are familiar with traditional pop artists' websites might find the navigation unusual and struggle to engage with some aspects of the site. People who enjoy new experiences and more alternative styles of website might respond very positively to the style. Audiences who are interested in Williams' other ventures, outside his music, might find gratification in the pages on art or social good.

6 Assessment of Component 2: Understanding Media Forms and Products

6.1 Using relevant theories and theoretical perspectives in the examination demonstrates that you are applying your knowledge and understanding of the theoretical framework, so it is important to use these where relevant. You might refer to the Uses and Gratifications theory in a question about audience, for example.

6.2 In order to demonstrate your analytical skills, you should explore media products in detail, giving examples and identifying how meanings are communicated.

6.3 You could you be asked about the contemporary artists' websites in Section B, Questions 3 and 4.

6.4 An extended response is a question that carries a high number of marks and requires you to make judgements and draw conclusions about the question.

7 Component 3: Creating Media Products

7.1 Textual analysis of products is an example of primary research, as this is first-hand research that you conduct yourself.

7.2 It is important that you set up each shot, position cameras at the appropriate distance and angle, and give your crew clear directions as you need to demonstrate that you can use media language to communicate meaning and construct representations. You must show that your production is your own work and anyone who helps you must work under your direction.

7.3 Your planning documents will be a guide when you are filming and editing your work. They will help you to focus and make effective use of your time. They will also ensure that you gain all of the required shots and fulfil the intentions in your Statement of Aims.

7.4 The sample brief requires narrative disruption to be included in the sequence. Considering of the requirements at the planning stage will be helpful when you create the final production.

7.5 The range of shots used in the sequence include: establishing shot of street (urban, isolated); long shot of character; high-angle shot of character running away (is he trying to escape?); medium close-up of character on the phone (might engage the audience and offer clues); close-ups of the book and case.

7.6 This example could establish a clearer sense of who the antagonist is, in order to meet the requirements of the brief.

7.7 Public service broadcasters have a remit to serve the public by, for example, reflecting the diversity of contemporary society and addressing important issues. The BBC has a remit to educate and inform, as well as to entertain. Including information and links to support services that relate to themes and issues featured in a programme is one way in which public service broadcasters can fulfil their remit.

7.8 The standfirst includes use of metaphor to appeal to the audience, discussing how songwriters 'cajole gold', in other words they make a lot of money from hit songs. This phrase also uses rhyme for emphasis. The standfirst includes a rhetorical question to hook the reader, and the phrase 'modern masters' is an example of alliteration and hyperbole to stress the elite status of the songwriters.

7.9 The pull-quote emphasises the importance of being honest and true to yourself, which is a dominant idea in contemporary society and conveys a positive message to aspiring musicians and songwriters.

7.10 The cover model on *Fashionista* adopts a direct mode of address to appeal to the audience.

7.11 The main image of a 'real' female runner will appeal to females with similar interests who might personally identify with this woman. She is active and healthy, which creates a positive representation and could be aspirational to females who are taking up running. The medium close-up shows her smiling and directly addressing the audience, which might engage them and help them to feel involved with the website.

7.12 It is important to draft your designs carefully to make sure you address all of the requirements in the brief and creating an appropriate product. Your drafts will act as a plan for the final production, helping you to complete your work to a high standard within the time limit.

7.13 Male character: visual codes of the smart dark clothing and gun coupled with the serious facial expression and use of shadow connote that he is possibly a gangster and suggest that he will be the villain according to Propp's theory. The females are stereotypically positioned behind the man, a younger woman in a cream coat whose body language suggests a passive role and an older woman in a red coat whose gesture codes connote that she is concerned and might challenge the male.

7.14 An age rating of 15 indicates that a film is suitable for an audience of 15 and over, appealing to an older-teen and adult audience. People in the 16–24 age group visit the cinema more frequently than any other group, so many films target this demographic and the 15 certificate is likely to appeal to them.

7.15 The *DCI Meara* DVD cover features an establishing shot of the seaside location that fills the background and wraps around the spine and back cover, a convention of some DVD covers. The crime genre is established through the image of the red hand print connoting forensic investigation. The protagonist, DCI Meara, adopts a direct and serious mode of address appropriate to his rank and the subject matter.

7.16 The representation of the band members as caring young men with strong links to their families constructs a positive image of males that subverts stereotypes of male independence and shows a more sensitive, contemporary view of masculinity.

7.17 Your storyboard will be an essential document when planning your shot list to take on your film shoot. It will help you to stick to your plan and gain all of your intended footage. When editing your project, your storyboard will help you to construct the product and structure your shots in order to communicate meanings and narratives.

7.18 A music video in the pop genre is likely to include more performance footage and lip-synching; possibly in a 'live' concert rather than in a rehearsal room. The editing would cut to the beat, usually quite fast paced. The image of the band or artist would normally be shown clearly throughout. The narrative would probably be based on an idea that most people can relate to, such as a story about love or friendship.

9 Examination Preparation

9.1 Purple is traditionally associated with royalty. In the Quality Street advert it connotes the high status of the female character. The use of purple for the brand name connotes a sense of luxury and a high-quality product.

9.2 The slogan 'What a delicious dilemma!' uses alliteration and word play: the 'dilemma' relates to the man choosing between the females as well as the chocolates. The exclamation mark adds emphasis and humour.

9.3 We read from top left to bottom-right of the page, so these two positions are dominant places where important information is displayed to capture the audience's attention.

9.4 Compare the representation of women in the *Pride* front cover and the *Glamour* front cover.
In the bulleted list, the important words and phrases are: *choices producers have made; similar; different.*

9.5 BBC Radio 4 broadcasts *The Archers*.

9.6 Propp's theory of narrative is the other named theory that could feature in an examination question, in addition to the Uses and Gratifications theory, which appears in this question.

9.7 To address 'how far', you must consider the ways in which you agree or disagree with the statement 'Music videos reinforce stereotypes of ethnicity.' You should then decide to what extent the statement is true.

Index

Acknowledgements

Image Credits

pp**17** (top), **139** (bottom), **148**, **185** (right), **239** (bottom) and **241** (bottom) FremantleMedia / Channel 4; p**17** (centre) 20th Century Fox; pp**17** (bottom), **53** and **228** Neil Baylis / Alamy Stock Photo; p**21** (*Spectre*) Mim Friday / Alamy Stock Photo; pp**23**, **33** (right), **123** (bottom right), **128**, **141** (top) and **165** (Monroe) AF archive / Alamy Stock Photo; p**24** Gavin Bond / *GQ*: The Condé Nast Publications Ltd; pp**26** (left), **99** (top), **100**, **123** (*Sherlock*), **124**, **129**, **130** (bottom left), **131** (top), **133**, **134** (bottom), **135**, **141** (bottom), **142** (top), **185** (left), **196**, **197**, **235** (top) and **239** (top) BBC; p**28** Nestlé; p**29** (bottom) Tom Munro / Glamour: Condé Nast; p**33** (left) Jeffrey Blackler / Alamy Stock Photo; p**35** Kathy deWitt / Alamy Stock Photo; p**51** (top) National Trust Images; p**51** (right) New York Department of Economic Development; pp**52**, **126** (top) and **153** (top) Pictorial Press Ltd / Alamy Stock Photo; p**55** Fiat; p**57** Nike; p**60** Samaritans; p**63** Moviestore collection Ltd / Alamy Stock Photo; p**64** Eddie Gerald / Alamy Stock Photo; p**69** (top) Pride Media Group; p**70** Dan Martensen / Elle US / Hearst Magazines; p**71** David Harrison / Square Up Media; p**76** World History Archive / Alamy Stock Photo; p**77** Lenscap / Alamy Stock Photo; p**78** (left) Guardian News & Media Ltd 2018; pp**78** (right), **89** and **92** (top) The Sun / News Licensing; pp**80** (top) and **169** (top) Entertainment Pictures / Alamy Stock Photo; p**81** (Gollum) Photo 12 / Alamy Stock Photo; pp**82** (bottom) and **233** (bottom) bbfc; pp**85** (bottom), **94** (bottom), **130** (bottom right), **134** (top), **140**, **147**, **171** (top) Everett Collection Inc / Alamy Stock Photo; p**90** (top) Dinendra Haria / Alamy Stock Photo; p**94** (top) CBW / Alamy Stock Photo; p**99** (bottom) Ian Dagnall / Alamy Stock Photo; p**101** Archers Addicts/Facebook/BBC; p**102** (infographic) Newzoo; p**107** Brandwatch; pp**113** (top), **115**, **202** and **203** Channel 4; p**114** Kudos/Channel 4; pp**118** (top), **142** (bottom), **143**, **144** (top) and **146** NBC; pp**123** (top) and **131** (bottom) Granada Television/ ITV; pp**126** (bottom), **127** and **241** (top) Thames Television/ITV; p**130** (top) Trinity Mirror / Mirrorpix / Alamy Stock Photo; p**137** Raymond Tang / Alamy Stock Photo; p**145** Sam Barnes /Alamy Stock Photo; p**158** (top) Mark Ronson / Sony Music Entertainment / YouTube; pp**164** (Queen), **168** (bottom), **169** (centre and bottom), **170** (top) and **173** (top) EMI; p**164** (A-ha) Warner Bros; pp**164** (bottom), **171** (bottom), **172**, **173** (bottom), **175** (bottom), **176**, **179** and **218** Sony Music Entertainment; p**165** (The Killers) Island Records, (Madonna) Splash News / Alamy Stock Photo; pp**166**, **167**, **174** (left), **175** (top), **178** (top), **243** (bottom) and **244** Big Machine Records; p**168** (top) MediaPunch Inc / Alamy Stock Photo; p**170** (bottom) Universal Pictures; pp**174** (right), **177** (bottom), **181** (bottom), **182** (bottom), **242** and **243** (top) Capitol Records; p**181** (top) Atlantic Records; p**182** (top) and **184** Pharrell Williams; p**183** PjrStudio / Alamy Stock Photo; pp**200** (bottom) and **201** Liam Brusby, Heaton Manor School; p**205** Alan Wilson / Alamy Stock Photo; p**206** Bauer Media UK; p**208** Ahmedy Khatoon, Heaton Manor School; pp**209** and **210** (top) Wild Bunch Media; p**212** STUDIOCANAL Films Ltd; p**216** George Hutchinson, Seaford Head School; p**219** YouTube/Sony Music Entertainment; pp**221** (bottom) and **222** Elliot Rae, Heaton Manor School; p**224** Maria Galan / Alamy Stock Photo; p**230** Steven Pan / Glamour: Condé Nast.

All other images:
Shutterstock:

p**8** PR Image Factory; p**9** Lenka Horavova, oliveromg; p**10** ImageFlow; p**13** Chinnapong; pp**14**, **16** (bottom), **29** (top), **111**, **192**, **204** and **226** Rawpixel.com; p**15** kosam, John-Kelly, Artishock, Stuart G Porter, ESB Professional; p**16** (top) Bruno Passigatti; p**18** Uber Images, Neil Balderson /

Shutterstock.com, Aleksandr Markin, LouLouPhotos, sirtravelalot; pp**19** and **47** emka74/Shutterstock.com; p**21** (top) twobears_art; p**22** 360b/ Shutterstock.com; p**26** (right) Boris15; p**27** tynyuk; p**28** (bottom) Radharani; p**29** (centre) Barry Barnes / Shutterstock.com; p**30** eldar nurkovic; p**31** (top) solomon7/Shutterstock.com; pp**31** (bottom) and **80** (logos) Rose Carson / Shutterstock.com; p**32** Africa Studio; p**34** iko; p**36** (top) Everett Historical; pp**36** (bottom), **72**, **75** and **88** Lenscap Photography / Shutterstock.com; p**37** AsiaTravel/Shutterstock.com; p**38** ALPA PROD; p**39** dizain; pp**40**, **103** (logo) and **104** (bottom) COO7/Shutterstock.com; pp**41**, **50** (NT), **83**, **86**, **90** (bottom), **95** (Radio 1), **121** (top) and **234** (top) chrisdorney/ Shutterstock.com; p**42** Press Line Photos / Shutterstock.com; p**43** Ivelin Radkov; pp**45** (left), **62** (top), **81** (*Star Wars*) and **82** (top) Kathy Hutchins / Shutterstock.com; pp**45** (right) and **74** (top) Hadrian/Shutterstock. com; p**46** Marco Rullkoetter; p**48** design36; p**49** garagestock; p**50** (Nike) August_0802 / Shutterstock.com, (egg) Orange Vectors, (car) Stokkete; p**51** (bottom) lukeruk; p**62** (007) Anton_Ivanov / Shutterstock.com; pp**65** and **68** Lawrey/Shutterstock.com; p**66** (left) Serdar Tibet / Shutterstock. com; pp**66** (right) and **67** Elnur/Shutterstock.com; pp**69** (*GQ*), **81** (Oscars), **136**, **147** (top), **149**, **158** (Spice Girls) and **160** (Katy Perry) Featureflash Photo Agency / Shutterstock.com; p**73** urbanbuzz/Shutterstock.com; pp**74** (bottom) and **97** Claudio Divizia / Shutterstock.com; p**79** gyn9037, Tero Vesalainen; p**84** Kobby Dagan / Shutterstock.com; p**85** (top) Thampapon/ Shutterstock.com; pp**92** (bottom) and **191** (top) GaudiLab; p**95** (top) Forest Run; p**96** Peter Horrox; p**98** TungCheung, Terence Mendoza; p**102** (Pokémon) kamui29/Shutterstock.com; p**103** (store) MADSOLAR/Shutterstock.com; p**104** (top) Matthew Corley / Shutterstock.com; p**105** Wachiwit/Shutterstock.com, dennizn/Shutterstock. com; pp**106** (top) and **207** (bottom) Kaspars Grinvalds / Shutterstock. com; p**106** (bottom) MichaelJayBerlin/Shutterstock.com; pp**108** and **210** (bottom) wavebreakmedia; p**109** KeongDaGreat/Shutterstock.com; p**113** (pylons) Five Buck Photos, (camera) Pitroviz; p**116** Lario Tus, Pete Niesen; p**117** wirakorn deelert, DaymosHR; p**118** (bottom) Twocoms/Shutterstock. com; p**119** (Sky) r.classen/Shutterstock.com; p**120** seeshooteatrepeat/ Shutterstock.com; p**121** (bottom) Piotr Wawrzyniuk; p**122** Olga Popova / Shutterstock.com; p**125** Fer Gregory, PRESSLAB; p**138** Zoltan Gabor; p**139** (top) rattiya lamrod; p**144** Steve Cukrov / Shutterstock.com; pp**151** and **161** Tinseltown/Shutterstock.com; p**153** (bottom) 4 Girls 1 Boy; p**154** Pavel L Photo and Video; p**155** A. Aleksandravicius / Shutterstock.com, kondrukhov/ Shutterstock.com, Natalia Deriabina; p**156** 360b/Shutterstock. com; p**157** Thomas Pajot; p**159** Anton_Ivanov / Shutterstock.com, Marcel Jancovic; p**160** (top left) WAYHOME studio, (top right) Matlinski; p**162** DFree/Shutterstock.com; p**163** (Bruno Mars and Pharrell Williams) s_bukley / Shutterstock.com, (Taylor Swift) Jaguar PS / Shutterstock.com; p**177** (top) John Gomez / Shutterstock.com; p**178** (bottom) Christian Bertrand / Shutterstock.com; p**180** Alexey Boldin / Shutterstock.com; p**186** James R. Martin / Shutterstock.com; p**188** lapandr; p**189** Mikhail Gnatkovskiy; p**190** Niloo / Shutterstock.com, Reservoir Dots, Dmitry Naumov; p**191** (bottom) Roobcio; p**193** sondem, alphaspirit; p**194** xtock; p**199** Mark Poprocki, Khaiwhan Pao; p**200** (top) and **215** guruXOX; p**207** (top) Ned Snowman / Shutterstock.com; p**213** Atlaspix; p**214** Ron Ellis / Shutterstock. com; p**217** donotas1205; pp**221** (top) and **247** Dragon Images; p**225** recklessstudios; p**227** Aysezgicmeli, Alex Staroseltsev; p**229** 3D_creation; p**232** phoelixDE; p**233** (top) ymgerman/Shutterstock.com; p**234** (bottom) Sinart Creative; p**235** (bottom) Budimir Jevtic; p**237** Monkey Business Images; p**238** Kritsada Namborisut; p**240** Gonzalo Aragon, AlexandCo Studio / Shutterstock.com, Ken Tannenbaum / Shutterstock.com; p**246** nito, Duplass.